The Gift of Spiritual Intimacy

The Gift of Spiritual Intimacy

Following the Spiritual Exercises of St. Ignatius

Monty Williams SJ

NOVALIS

Cover design and layout: Dominique Pelland
Cover artwork: "Cruciform," by Michael Hayes

Published by Novalis

Publishing Office
1 Eglinton Avenue East, Suite 800
Toronto, Ontario, Canada
M4P 3A1

Head Office
4475 Frontenac Street
Montréal, Québec, Canada
H2H 2S2

www.novalis.ca

Library and Archives Canada Cataloguing in Publication

Williams, Monty
The gift of spiritual intimacy : following the Spiritual exercises of St. Ignatius / Monty Williams.

ISBN 978-2-89646-033-5

1. Ignatius, of Loyola, Saint, 1491-1556. Exercitia spiritualia. 2. Spiritual exercises. 3. Mysticism--Catholic Church. I. Title.
BX2179.L8W45 2009 248.3 C2009-900595-6

Scriptural quotations are from the Revised Standard Version (The New Oxford Annotated Bible).

Printed in Canada.

We acknowledge the financial support of the Government of Canada through the Canada Book Fund for business development activities.

8 7 6 5 4 26 25 24 23 22

Dedication

for Diane Ayer, whose insistence made this book possible;

for Ron Mercier and Clare Walsh, for inviting me to share a moment in the work of the Jesuit Collaborative;

for Noah Craig and Robert Williams, my grandnephews;

for John Pungente, in gratitude for many things;

for Jack and Nicholas Swerhone, my godsons;

for Brian Cummings, Provincial Marist Fathers, New Zealand, and the Marist communities there;

for the L'Arche communities at Daybreak and downtown Toronto;

for all those involved with Maranatha Retreat House in Malaysia, and for those with the Centres of Ignatian Spirituality in Australia;

in gratitude for the leadership of Peter Hans Kolvenbach;

for all those others, also remembered with gratitude and affection, who have been, and continue to be, companions on the journey.

in memory of Dan Byrne, Jesuit brother and friend
(1923–2006)

"at no moment is love silent
every act is sacrament"

Contents

Preface

We Are All Mystics

We are all mystics. It is our nature. Our truest sense of our selves is inseparably rooted in God, and our identity stems from our lived awareness of that union. Often we live unaware of who we are; the depths of ourselves are forgotten in the round of daily life. We forget God as our constant living source. Then our connection with God withers. But God is the Passionate One who desires us, and for whom every fibre of our being reaches out. Though we may live and die cut off from God, God never withdraws the divine love from us.

The path to intimacy brings us into the awareness that we are created as desire for God, and that nothing or no one satisfies us totally but the One who desires us. When we discover ourselves as desire, drawn in desire by Desire, we discover a passionate God who not only wants to bring us to fullness of life but shares with us the desire to bring everyone to that delight in life.

The Gift of Intimacy

The gift of such radical intimacy is offered to all. It is a gift we are free to accept or to refuse. Should we accept, we are further invited to open, use, share, and finally celebrate that gift. God offers us a passionate relationship, but we may refuse it, fearing that it will require us to give up something. Such was the case with the rich young man of the gospels.

> And as he was setting out on his journey, a man ran up and knelt before him, and asked him, "Good Teacher, what must I do to inherit eternal life?" And Jesus said to him, "Why do you call me good? No one is good but God alone. You know the commandments: 'Do not kill, Do not commit adultery, Do not steal, Do not bear false witness, Do not defraud, Honor your father and mother.'" And he said to him, "Teacher, all these I have observed from my youth." And Jesus looking

> upon him loved him, and said to him, "You lack one thing; go, sell what you have, and give to the poor, and you will have treasure in heaven; and come, follow me." At that saying his countenance fell, and he went away sorrowful; for he had great possessions. (Mark 10:17-22)

We may accept a gift, but not open it. Such is the case of the person who is given one talent and buries it (Matthew 25:14-30).

We may open the gift, but not use it. Think of those cultures where the living room is used only for funerals or for the formal visits of important people.

We may use the gift but never share it. Here, the joy of belonging is exclusive. Like in a gated community, one has to be a member to enjoy the privileges. There is no salvation outside the institution. We forget that Jesus ate and drank with the socially and morally unacceptable.

And, finally, we may open, use, and share the gift, but not celebrate it. Many people are committed to social equality. They identify with the poor and the dispossessed. With amazing courage and witness, they have entered the dark places of the world, giving no thought to self and sacrificing themselves to bring life to the voiceless and the oppressed by creatively living in solidarity with them. To these, the path of intimacy offers a further gift: celebrating life, not only as it is found in places of pain and deprivation, but as it is offered by God present as inexpressible joy arising out of emptiness. The resurrection is present in this world, celebrated as a life the world cannot understand or give in this life.

Jesus talks about the woman who anoints him with a jar of costly perfume instead of selling it and giving the money to the poor. Poets and artists create masterpieces from what is rejected by the world; Picasso's head of a bull (*Tête de Toro*, 1943) is made of a set of handlebars and a saddle from a bicycle found in a junkyard. Yet the most complete form of creation is community. The fullest celebration of intimacy is found in community. Thus, for example, the communities of Jean Vanier's L'Arche, comprised of the small ones of this world, point in their joy to the fullness of life offered to all. Everyone and everything will be celebrated as the beloved of God. All of us, however and whoever we are, are invited to this celebration. Every form of community, from the gathering together of our divided hearts to reaching out finally in harmony with all that is created (cf. Colossians 1:15-17) – leans towards the fullness of life. There the weaving of all, past, present, and to come, is being established. The path of intimacy carries us to this gathering place. This is not pious Romanticism or apocalyptic fantasy. That we are all interconnected is a fact of life. The fullness of life is possible only when all live in such a way that satisfies their desire for life. The path of intimacy invites us to journey towards that state of grace.

The Spiritual Exercises of St. Ignatius give us a guide to that path. They dispose us to be open, to accept, and to participate in the Divine Love that labours to bring all to this fulfillment of their desire.

The Stories We Live By

To understand how God brings us to fullness of life, we must first start by looking at the ways in which we understand our life. What we have experienced has shaped the way we live. Of course, how we live is determined by more than our personal experience. It is shaped by our families, our society, the times we live in. Our experience is more than the histories we make of it. That larger experience makes us. In our attempt to understand ourselves, we create the stories that both reflect our experience and turn our eyes away from it. The stories we live by do not necessarily emerge from the truth of our lives. This truth is that we are loved by God and are capable of loving as God loves, and of accepting love as God's beloved. Often, the stories we hold to be real are distortions of that basic truth.

Held in God's Love

God does not desire that we live out of those misleading representations of ourselves. The path to intimacy starts when we allow God to enter our stories. When this happens we discover that that same God is willing to accept us as we are, but the love we are shown in that acceptance lets us want to reject the lies that prevent us from being fully ourselves. We discover the courage to risk abandoning the false myths that have established our identity, because we know we are always held in God's love. It is only when we realize this that we give ourselves over to that love. It reveals to us how the stories we live in trap us. Ignatius was aware of this point. The First Week of his Exercises offers us ways of being released from those stories that deny us life and the joy of living. Those exercises place us in the larger story of God's constant and abiding love for us. In that first week of the Exercises, we experience the liberating power of the Incarnation coming into our personal lives in an intimate way. That power transforms the false story we lived out of and invites us to live another story: the story that allows us to accept ourselves as truly loved, in all our flaws and disorders.

Ignatius realized that the worlds we live in and operate out of are creations of our imagination. He understood that, for us to be changed, and for the worlds we live in to be changed, the way we imagine those worlds needs to change. He saw, two-and-a-half centuries earlier, the truth of William Blake's (1750–1820) profound awareness that the imagination creates the real or, as Wallace Stevens, in the twentieth century, would assert in his later poems, the imagined is the real. Ignatius, Blake, and Stevens all saw the importance of narrative in questions of subjectivity. Narrative determines what we see. Blake says that we see *through* our eyes, not *with* our eyes. He writes in his "Auguries of Innocence," "We are led to believe a lie / When we see not thro' the eye." What we see and believe is constructed by the imagination. The stories we live out of determine what we see and how we live.

We live in our imagined worlds as if they were real. This is not to say that there is no such thing as reality, but to suggest that we appropriate and construct reality through the imagination, and imagination incarnates itself through stories. We read reality through those stories. We may help in the construction of those stories but, by and large, we live in those stories and those stories construct us. For example, we live out of the stories of our families, and the stories of our cultures, our ethnicities, our spiritualities. We can even say that we live out of the stories of our biologies, and that we are shaped by the narratives that are the forms of our DNA. These stories do not present us with closed myths that fix our identities, though certain ideologies would have us read ourselves in that way.

The Closed Myth

Sin traps us in forms of closure that offer us the illusion of security and allow us to justify ourselves and to demonize what is not ourselves as "other." The closed myth claims to be the most true form of reading reality. As such, it sets and maintains standards, integrity, values, and tradition. It offers security, clarity, and stability. But in effect it benefits only a select few, and controls the media by appeals to orthodoxy. It maintains itself by violence that coerces or destroys what is different from it. The stranger, the alien, the outsider are all forms of the "other." At times even God – however that mystery is enstoried – is given the qualities of the other, and treated with fear, dread, and suspicion. There is a move to domesticate such a God in theologies, displacing spirituality with rituals and institutionalized religion. Then there is the struggle to control orthodoxy; its politics are maintained by the quality control of systematics, canonicity, and the authority of professionalism. The closed myth manifests itself in fundamentalism of any sort and in the displacement of truth by ideologies. They become the breeding ground of revolution, where one narrative displaces another.

All of this is to say that we live in stories. Stories are never closed, but interpretations of stories can be. When we try to impose closure on the stories we live out of – in the form of closed myths – we destroy parts of ourselves and others. We eliminate or distort relationships. We consign ourselves to death. The long process of moving out of closed myths is called conversion. Through conversion, we move from one story to another. It is not an easy process, like changing clothes or brand names. We become disillusioned by the closed myth; we move out of it by facing our fears; we abandon the illusions of clarity and the myths of transparency, simplicity, ease and comfort. We question. We even question the basis of our questioning. We realize just how trapped we are in patterns of perception that have been sanctioned by personal habits, society's laws, cultural norms, and the many levels of tradition that inform us about who we are.

The Broken Myth

At this stage we come to the realization that we live not out of a closed myth, but within broken myths. Broken myths claim to be countercultural, but they define and maintain themselves only in relationship to the closed myth they profess to reject. In effect, broken myths are smaller and less stable versions of the closed myth. Like the closed myth, they use violence to replace what they seek to overthrow. The ethos behind the broken myth is either a nostalgia for a fabled past or a fantasy of a utopian future. Broken myths do not offer us a viable way forward.

The Open Myth

This does not mean that we are trapped by our past, however. We can look forward if we live in the context of an open myth. The open myth sees the limitation of the closed and broken myth, but it also is attentive to, and seeks, the possibilities of life trapped in these. It faces the unknown without trying to control it. Those committed to the open myth risk even their very lives to incarnate their intimacy with God. They give up security, clarity, at times even their liberty, and the exclusivity obtained by affiliation to one particular myth, to witness to their call of spiritual intimacy. The God they embrace calls them beyond themselves. Their authenticity lies in walking in the darkness, in which they seek God and in which God seeks for them. That incarnate intimacy is prophetic. We are all invited to live out of that relationship with God, which alone leads to the fullness of life.

Here it might be helpful to think of ourselves as lovers defined by how the past has interpreted us. That interpretation includes closed, broken, and open myths. But we are also defined by our relationship to the beloved. That beloved holding us in love offers us, here and now, the invitation to step away from closed myths, to abandon our self-image as victims caught in broken myths, and to journey into deeper intimacy that ushers us into life. We discover ourselves constantly being transformed by the Creator. We journey, as lovers, into a love that has no end. We live the open myth.

The open myth is not constrained by a pragmatic existentialism that says, "well, this is what we have; we might as well make the best of it." The open myth, though beset by insecurities and the reversals of fortune, human bias, and cultural chaos, faces the darkness, which is the face of the future, as the context of emerging possibilities based precisely on relationship. Those relationships invite, call, entice, seduce, beckon, and impel us forward. We continually leap into the furnaces of affliction, bearing with us the materials of closed and broken myths to create new worlds. These, in their turn, are subject to the vicissitudes of time: decay, closure, entombment. We are constantly called to be who we truly are by continually moving beyond them when they cease to offer us new life.

The dynamics of the closed, broken, and open myth have been present throughout human history. They have made us who we are today. Our work as we desire a closer intimacy in the Trinity – the community we call God – is first to ask how these myths operate in our world. Our contemporary world is driven by four basic narratives: security, meaning, liberty, and belonging.

The Stories of Our Times

Security

The chaos of our times has challenged us to our core. We have become destabilized by the rapid changes in our world. Ways of communicating have changed; borders have been redrawn and are in flux; our neighbours speak languages we did not grow up with; we have become suspicious of those in authority, whether secular or ecclesial. One can even regard the officials of law enforcement as just another gang. These are just a few obvious manifestations of our unstable world. In the midst of this, we are driven by our basic and deep desire for security. Closed myths offer us security in these times. They claim that their political, or social, or ecclesial ways of reading reality are the true and divinely approved ones. In our vulnerable state, we are often tempted and seduced into accepting their claims. But we need to be aware of how these closed myths operate. They exclude and demonize those who do not go along with them. They maintain their authority by fear. Their orthodoxy and law are established by a centralized government that uses the politics of coercion to intimidate and suppress. The path of intimacy offers those who reject the security of the closed myth a rootedness in God. Intimacy is found not in belonging to socially approved groups, maintained by shame and guilt, but in the shameless and liberating embrace of God.

Meaning

Our postmodern age has often been defined by its lack of meaning. Many conflicting points of view present themselves, each supported by a valid rationale. Our search for an understanding of what is going on, for clarity and direction, to overcome the confusion we feel and see around us is urgent. We find ourselves attracted to leaders who promise us such meaning. They offer an authority that will deal with the crises in our religious, social, and political worlds. Often they claim their authority is from God. Yet their behaviour and their policies do not accord with our own awareness of how God operates. The path of intimacy that allows us to witness to God's compassionate mercy leads us not to clarity and systems of meaning, but rather to mystery. Intimacy creates real relationships. We are asked to live those relationships in the mystery we call God, rather than in the clarity of systems. We are asked to place our first trust in God, rather than in leaders. What such leaders want from us is orthodoxy, not intimacy with God.

To live in mystery does not mean we abandon meaning, institutions, and those socialized forms of interaction that give us access to ourselves and each other. To live in mystery means that we appreciate these ways of being as like fingers pointing to the moon. The fingers are not the moon. In fact, the moon illuminates the pointing fingers. Mystery gives institutions life, but it is wrong to equate institution with mystery. Institutions give us socially approved ways of living, yet they avoid the deeper question of whether those ways of living are spiritually healthy.

Liberty

Too often in we confuse license, liberty, and freedom. *License* is the social permission to behave in particular ways that can be ethical or unethical. *Liberty* defines license. Institutions can grant us liberty, but our understanding of liberty is dependent on that institution we adhere to. The quest for liberty is often seen as the overthrow of oppression and victimization. But what is not understood is that the secular longing for liberty – personal, social, or cultural – creates oppression for some other. The price of the liberty we desire may be the enslavement of some other. We must distinguish very carefully between liberty and freedom. Christ in the Garden of Gethsemane gives up his liberty to maintain his freedom. *Freedom* is how spiritual intimacy manifests itself in the world. That intimacy declares that the right relationship with God is more human than the social constructions of liberty. It declares that sometimes, to be human, we give up our liberty to be free. When we abandon our freedom and seek liberty, on the other hand, we inflict violence on our world. This is not to say that we do not desire liberty, or that it is not a good thing. But the liberty we desire flows from freedom, not from enslaving others.

Belonging

Often we define our freedom by myths of belonging. We demand to be free to worship, to live out social and cultural identities of race, gender, or creed. These identities create boundaries. The other becomes the alien and is held as secondary to our primary values of self-determination. But before we are defined as racial, or gendered, or members of a religious tradition, we are first human; everyone, a creature of God. We are all called to spiritual intimacy. Each call is unique but of equal value. To abandon that call divides us into camps, ghettos, and forms of exclusivity. By accepting our identity so defined, we deny or ignore a simple fact. As creatures, we do not define ourselves. God defines us. We are unfinished business. We are open myths; exclusivity of any sort traps us into accepting ourselves as closed myths. When we live this way, we use violence to assert who we are by destroying the other.

Security, meaning, liberty, and exclusivity are the plots of the stories by which we live today. These are not bad things in themselves. But they become harmful when they replace a relationship with God. Then socially defined forms of orthodoxy replace spiritual intimacy. The temptation for social acceptance betrays the deeper human desires for a rootedness in God, for a life lived in mystery, for freedom, and for the drive to community where no one and nothing is excluded.

God Enters Our Closed and Broken Myths

Closed or broken myths freeze our growth into humanity. The gift of God's love for us enters into those myths. It seeks to liberate us into seeing, knowing, and loving ourselves as the Father sees, knows, and loves us. We need to experience the power of that love in our own lives before we can become aware of its presence in the world, not just some 2,000 years ago, but today, here and now. What happened in the Incarnation happens to us when God's love enters into our personal lives, and liberates us, and we live in such a way that others become liberated. We experience the entry of God into our own brokenness as a spiritual intimacy. Our journey with God as those freed into love is a deepening of that intimacy. That path of intimacy carries us to the fullness of being human. It calls us beyond how we imagine ourselves. It brings us to a creativity that builds up the community of love in which we are all intimately connected. That spiritual intimacy begins with the Incarnation.

The Incarnation Contemplation of St. Ignatius

The Incarnation describes the act of God becoming a human being. St. Ignatius, in the Spiritual Exercises, asks us to contemplate the Trinity's viewing the destructive state of a humanity that has separated itself from God, and deciding to save it. The Second Person of the Trinity will take on human nature to show us the human path that, through intimacy, leads from destruction to the fullness of life. Someone must be found who is suitable and willing to bear God-made-man as a human child. Mary, a young virgin, accepts the risk of mothering Jesus. He is born in Bethlehem.

The Ignatian contemplation itself begins with the usual preparatory prayer:

> I will beg God our Lord for the grace that all my intentions, actions, and operations may be directed purely to the praise and service of His Divine Majesty. (#46)

The prayer brings our attention to our desire. The prayer asks us to look not at God, but at how we relate to the world. What gives praise and service is Incarnational. We are directed in the prayer to contribute to the work of the Trinity engaged in creation. As we pray, we continue the work of the Incarnation.

Spiritual Intimacy

That work in this context is an act of contemplation on the Incarnation. We become what we contemplate. In contemplations we look at what holds our attention; we become engaged. Thus engaged, we become involved. That involvement draws us outside the boundaries of the myths through which we construct ourselves. In prayer, the intimacy we experience with the divine at the very roots of our being cannot be constrained by our closed and broken myths. That intimacy, which is freely offered to us, enters those myths and exposes them for what they are. It liberates them into the open myth, which desires only God. St. Ignatius tells us that, before we contemplate the Incarnation, we should pray "for an intimate knowledge of our Lord, who has become man for me, that I may love Him more and follow Him more closely" (#104). Out of that intimacy comes love, and out of that love comes service. It is important to note that the intimacy is the foundation of the love, and not vice versa. That intimacy engages all the levels of being human, and manifests itself in contemplation-in-action as a creativity that works to transform the worlds we inhabit into communities of love.

The particular grace for which we pray in this contemplation acts as the underlying dynamic of the entire Exercises and is the root of Ignatian spirituality. We pray for our desire to be united to the Desire who desires us.

The grace we pray for here replicates what occurs in the first stage of the path of spiritual intimacy, where we are the world that the Trinity contemplates and transforms. In that stage, we discover how we are conscripted by sin. We pray to be liberated. We pray to be open to be liberated. Then God graciously comes into our closed and broken worlds.

Liberated, we desire to love in the same way we have discovered we are loved. This carries us to the second stage of spiritual intimacy. There we learn – with an intimately personal knowledge – how to be present to the world as the Trinity is present to the world. As intimates of Christ, we share in a deeply personal way the mission entrusted to him by the Father: the mission of loving the world back to life.

Through our intimacy with the Father, similar to the bond Christ has with the Father, we find ourselves moving beyond the purely social dimensions of the open myth into the narrative of the Trinity. At this stage we journey with Christ through his sufferings and death. He remains faithful to the intimacy with his Beloved even in trials that tempt him, and us, to turn away from our chosen paths. St. Ignatius notes that, at Christ's death, "he sets free the souls of the just" (#219) who are trapped. Even in death, the work of the Trinity continues. We discover, in our path of intimacy, a fidelity with the Father that remains even though we are stripped of all human comfort.

Waiting in that emptiness is a form of intimacy. It is a feeling of nothingness because that level of connection goes beyond the senses. We may have experiences of this when someone close to us dies. Our emotions are exhausted. We feel nothing. But if we wait and endure that nothingness, resurrection comes to us.

In the fourth stage of intimacy with the divine, we experience the resurrected humanity of Christ at work in the world. He shares with us the joy of his resurrection, finally sending us the fulfillment of the deeply personal love He and the Father share, so that we, filled with the Spirit "created in the likeness and image of the Divine Majesty," labour in the world as "God works and labours for me in all creatures upon the face of the earth" (#236). This is the intimacy of a community, extending through space and time, called the Body of Christ. It is made up of those throughout the ages who continue the acts of the apostles. They bring the salvation of God to the world. They do this because they are woven in relationship with all those who, in often simple and unnoticed ways, create communities that are inclusive, life-giving, and rooted in that mystery who is the source of all life.

The Incarnation contemplation initiates us, quite self-consciously, into that ever-deepening journey into love, so that we become one with the Beloved, and not only share the Beloved's life and mission, but, in doing so, become the continuing manifestation of the Word-Made-Flesh in the world today.

Longing and Desire

We live in a disordered world. Even our perspectives on this world are disordered. We cannot save ourselves. We know that something is very wrong, but we are suspicious that even our intuitions about what is wrong might be incorrect. Rather than being trapped by the despair this might engender, we can turn, as best we can, to a God who desires to save us. The first stage in spiritual intimacy arises from such a longing, which we need to acknowledge. That longing seeks to satisfy itself in any way possible. Sometimes what satisfies us causes more disorder and confusion. But sometimes that longing gets glimpses of something that, deeply and intimately, it knows is right. This connection converts longing into desire. Our desire might be for a perfect world, a perfect self, a perfect God. When we follow the path of desire, we encounter the intimacy that answers all our needs, gives us a sense of identity and meaning, and offers us a path that brings us, and all whom we encounter, to life. Such intimacy is not constrained by age, gender, nationality, ethnic characteristics, or religious tradition. It is available to all.

Ignatius and Desire

In this book, the language we use in this exploration of the path of intimacy is Christian. It emerges from a religious tradition in Catholic spiritual life articulated by St. Ignatius of Loyola. Ignatius was a venal, ambitious member of the Spanish minor nobility in the sixteenth century, who, by reflecting on his life, discovered his path to God. It transformed him, and he transformed the known world. He founded the Jesuits, whose charism is to offer, to whoever desires it, a way of discerning that leads to a lived intimacy with God in the world. Such intimacy does not make life easier, or more successful. But it gives meaning, joy, community, and direction that allows anyone to say, truthfully, "the kingdom of God is with us."

That journey begins when we realize that we are trapped in a creation – cosmic, human, and personal – that is disordered. The first stage of intimacy carries us to the realization that even here we are loved, protected, and held in God's love. We realize we do not have to contribute to the violence that seeks to maintain our narcissisms against all others. To know that we are loved even when we are closed in on ourselves, and that that love is better than our self-care, opens for us the liberated perspective to see creation as a work in progress to which we can contribute positively.

Models of Desire

In the story of the Incarnation given in the Scriptures, we are shown models of that incarnate activity. For example, the angel Gabriel – whose name means "the power of God" – comes into a human world to make a request of a very human person. The power of God does not demand or force. It asks and respects whom it addresses.

The humility of the Incarnation also manifests itself in Mary, who allows her personal story to be rewritten by God. Mary's emptying herself of her self-will allows the work of the Trinity to be done. The Second Person of the Trinity empties himself – as stated in Philippians 2:1-11 – in the service of the redemptive work of the Trinity: "Though he was in the form of God, he did not count equality with God a thing to be grasped, but made himself nothing, taking the form of a servant, being born in the likeness of men. And being found in human form, he humbled himself by becoming obedient to the point of death, even death on a cross." St. Ignatius, in his Incarnation contemplation, puts it like this. He is to be "born in extreme poverty and ... after many labours, after hunger, thirst, heat, and cold, after insults and outrages, He might die on the cross" (#116). We are invited to place ourselves in that same stance of humility. The second exercise asks us, in the circumstances of the Nativity, to "make myself a poor little unworthy slave" and from that perspective to place ourselves in the scene "as though present," and in that place to "look ... contemplate ... serve ... with all possible homage and reverence" (#114).

In this stance of humility, we are asked to live out of an open myth. We accept that we do not have an identity in ourselves. (The alternative is narcissism, that prime sin of pride that opposes relationships in the kingdom of God.) Instead, we effect our truest sense of self as creatures in relationship to God. This view realizes that we are still being formed, and are subject to change as relationships change, or as our understanding of those relationships changes. The Incarnation occurs within a set of relationships. They change because of the entry of God into their world. Jesus, Mary, and Joseph are no longer their own people. They are now defined by their intimate relationship with God. That intimacy takes away from them their security. The bonds of their religious betrothal to each other are broken for a deeper trust. They cannot even find hospitality in any family home in Bethlehem, since Joseph had brought shame on the clan by maintaining his relationship with a woman who became pregnant (and not by him) during that betrothal. They are excluded from the clan. They give up the established paths to meaning in their lives in order to live out of the mystery of God's call. They lose their liberty and their rights in their flight and long residence in Egypt, the place of Jewish captivity.

They give up security, freedom, meaning, and acceptance along their path of spiritual intimacy. Yet they gain a personal rootedness in God, a liberty that goes beyond cultic ways of behaving, a trust in Divine Providence, and an openness to a way of life that shaped the early life of the Christ and that manifested itself in his years of public ministry. There he discovered himself as the "Beloved" of the Father; he shocked the scribes and Pharisees by valuing love over the law; his miracles proclaimed his existential trust in the Father; and his compassion for the sinner, the possessed, and the outcast scandalized the exclusive Jewish cult.

The Gift of Intimacy

Incarnation enters broken and closed myths of security, civic and personal freedom, institutional acceptance, and established ways of behaving, and allows us to see in those broken and closed myths the possibilities of redemption. Broken and closed myths, and even open myths, do not offer the possibilities of redemption. It is a gift. It is the offering of a God who desires our intimacy. However we live, that gift is always there, whether we acknowledge it or not. Within the explicit myths in which we discover ourselves is always the implicit myth, the narrative of the Trinity. As we contemplate the Incarnation, we allow that implicit myth of God's mercy to be expressed in the explicit myths of our lives. When that happens, the work of the Trinity continues through us. It offers us the grace we ask for in Ignatius's Nativity contemplation: "to follow and imitate more closely our Lord, who has just become man for me" (#109). We note the word "just." That Incarnation has not occurred in some distant past in some foreign land. It occurs when we contemplate the Incarnation. It happens here and now.

Introduction

Who Is Ignatius?

To understand the Exercises, it helps to know something about the man who created them, and about the spirituality of the Jesuit tradition that has kept those Exercises alive for the past 450 years. In Ignatius's own life, we see the dynamics of the Incarnation operating. We discover a man walking the path of intimacy that led from a life of narcissistic self-interest to one of service to the suffering Body of Christ present in the peoples of his world.

Ignatius of Loyola was born of minor Basque aristocracy in about 1492. Like the nobility of his time, he was interested in maintaining his position in the world by promoting himself through honour and glory. He was vain, venal, and charismatically aggressive, obsessed with the secular ideals of courtly love and chivalry. The world he sought to promote came crashing down at Pampalona, Spain (now famous for the running of the bulls), in 1521, when he was badly wounded and had to return to Loyola for a long period of enforced recuperation. There he distracted himself by reading both the lives of the saints and the worldly romances of chivalric exploits and love. He discovered that both stirred his heart to perform deeds of dramatic action. But he also noticed that the excitement he felt while reflecting on the lives of the saints remained with him, while the pleasure he felt reading the romances soon went away, leaving him desolate. He decided to follow the path of the saints rather than seek earthly glory.

There began a long period of the purification of his desires. In 1522, he found himself in a cave at Manresa, where he spent the next several months in a regime of extreme asceticism, alternating between severe depression, scruples, thoughts of suicide, and amazing mystical experiences. He decided to use his religious experience there – upon which the Spiritual Exercises as we know them today are based – to help others. Indeed, Ignatius used these Exercises to direct others, and, in 1540, with some of these people formed the Society of Jesus, or Jesuits. The Jesuits have their charism from that direct encounter with God that Ignatius discovered is possible for all. For St. Ignatius, and in Jesuit spirituality, God is in constant and intimate dialogue with us. We experience this in our daily lives as feelings of union with or disconnection from God. It is only when we reflect on these movements within ourselves that we discover that language of love.

The Exercises

The Spiritual Exercises that you now hold in your hands has been tested for over 400 years. It offers a way to discover God's unique love for each of us and to learn that language of love with which God speaks to us. We learn this language by looking at our own lives and at the forces that shape them. This gives us an inner compass that shows each of us the path of intimacy with God.

The stages of that intimacy are divided into what has traditionally been called the Four Weeks of the Exercises. But Ignatius did not expect the person making the Exercises to complete them in one calendar month. They are meant to be adapted, to accommodate individual situations. Ignatius writes, "It is not meant that each week should necessarily consist of seven or eight days ... It may be necessary ... at times to shorten the Week, and at others to lengthen it" (#4). It is not crucial to fit them into a specific time frame, but rather to have enough time to get "the fruit that is proper to the matter assigned" (#4). Each stage is the basis for the next stage; to abbreviate a stage before its dynamics are fully established in a person's life distorts the relationship that a person may be developing with God.

The first part invites us to discover God's love by looking at those areas of our lives where we have not experienced love. This week ends when we experience a personal liberation from the forces that make us see ourselves as unlovable and unloving. The second part channels those liberated energies into a personal relationship with Christ, who manifests the compassionate mercy of God. The third part invites us to accompany that love in the face of suffering and death. The fourth part celebrates the triumph of God's love over the forces of destruction in the world, and invites us to share in that triumph by working together to transform the world through acts of love.

Underlying each section is the constant mercy of God. The weeks elaborate on this basic attitude of God towards us. The First Week emphasizes the theme that we are God's beloved who have been distorted by sin. The Exercises here help us get in touch with the fact that God loves us even as we sin, and desires to free us from the entrapment and illusions of sin. The theme in the Second Week is one of growing intimacy with Christ as the embodiment of the Father's mercy. The Third Week deals with the passion Christ has for his God, which allows Christ, and us, to endure the passion and destruction common to all humankind without falling into despair. The depth of our spiritual intimacy with God allows this to happen. In the Fourth Week, we experience the joy of Christ's resurrection and our entry into it. Then we become manifestations of God's mercy to all.

Our Imagined Worlds

St. Ignatius insightfully proposed that we all live in imagined worlds, and that our imagination constructs these worlds using our experiences, our lived contexts, our hopes, our pains, and our joys. In effect, we live in a highly selective world, which defines what is possible for us. It also defines how we see ourselves, how we interact with others, and the contexts in which we find ourselves.

In Ignatian prayer, our imagination is the meeting place where our stories encounter the presence of God. In this personal and sacred space of encounter, the energies of our lives are integrated with the divine energies of God. This imaginative prayer is not personal fantasy. Nor is it divine hypnosis. It is the result of an intimate union between ourselves and God. It is a form of Incarnation. This intimacy so transforms us that we become the living word of God in our world. For Ignatius, this is "contemplation in action." Through this path of intimacy we enter into the process of incarnating God in the world. We become changed, and, as a result, become agents of change.

Consolation and Desolation

In this path of intimacy we experience consolation and desolation. How these are understood depends on whether our basic orientation is towards intimacy with God or away from that intimacy. If we desire that intimacy, we experience consolation when the energies of our life are in harmony with the energies of God. We experience desolation when the energies of our life are occupied in works that do not contribute to building up a community of love. The opposite occurs if our orientation is away from intimacy. Those who delight in selfishness experience consolation when they get the opportunity to live selfishly. But those who are trying to be free from their selfishness experience desolation as they struggle against those habits that give pleasure but are not liberating.

Consolation and desolation are not feelings. They are indicators of the direction in which we are pointed based on our underlying attitude. If we are basically selfish, looking at the greater good causes desolation; if we are basically caring, then looking at the greater good causes consolation. In spiritual direction, a good director will first allow us to find out who we are, then help us see which direction we are going in, then help us figure out the next step to take on the path. This is not a path to or from God. We are always in God. This is a path towards a lived intimacy with God.

Discernment

Discernment is not that simple, however. When we are turned away from God, we might get feelings of pleasure from doing what is wrong. That is not consolation. Moreover, even if we are on the right path and are doing what is pleasing to God, we can still be given a false consolation: what we think and feel may be good, but it leads us away from the true good. We only know that it is a false consolation when we see the effects and discover that entering into that "good" feeling leads us to disturbed and ego-centred states. We note our consolations and desolations, but we also need to note where they lead us.

Consolations and desolations reveal to us "like bearings on a compass" where to go and how to behave if we truly are seeking to know God. If, on our path to God, we experience desolations, we know that we are encountering forces that seek to block our progress. It helps to examine what might be causing that disturbance. Does it come from an inappropriate attitude or understanding of our relationship to ourselves, to others, or to God? Bringing that blockage to consciousness allows us to bring it to prayer. Then God's mercy can deal with whatever is hindering us from loving freely and joyfully. It might be a hurt in our past or an undeveloped aspect of ourselves that has become so much a part of our personality that we are unconscious of it, yet it influences the way we see and feel and behave.

Consolations also help carry us closer to God. Ignatius defines consolation as our being so inflamed with the love of God that we love in an ordered manner and so "can love no creature on the face of the earth for its own sake, but only in the Creator of them all" (#316). That love can move us to tears for our sins, and sorrow for the sufferings of any member of the Body of Christ. It is present when we relish things properly, when we grow in faith, hope, and love, when we are attracted to all that leads to God, filling our souls with peace and quiet. Consolation is not just feeling good. Sorrow and pain can also be signs of consolation. What is significant, for our spiritual awareness, is what the feelings mean and whether they orient us to seeking God.

So the first step in discernment is being able to identify the feeling. The second step is to become aware of what those feelings mean. As we gain more experience, we find it easier to catch ourselves more quickly. The third step is to see in which direction tends the state that manifests itself in a particular feeling. This discernment is extremely personal. These are our feelings and no one else's. They indicate our particular dialogue with God. We might think of our feelings in prayer as the language lovers use with each other.

Journalling these states of consolation and desolation, together with what aroused them, allows us to come to a better understanding of ourselves and of how we operate in the world. God's communication with us is always about how to live in a way that is more focused and more rooted in love. Journalling also allows us to see the patterns in our life. Consolations, like desolations, are interconnected. They reveal to us our redeemed history and God's care for us, even in those times when we might have felt far from God, or not even particularly concerned with spiritual things. Bringing this to our awareness enables us to appropriate more deeply God's constant mercy for us and communication with us.

Imagination

For Ignatius, God is not separate from us. A constant dialogue with God happens continually through our lives and all through creation and human history. For God, and for us, creation is not a fixed, self-enclosed entity. What we experience as creation is the ongoing process of God creating. Creation is not complete. For the Christian, creation is open and incomplete. It finds its integrity beyond itself in God. Sin, in whatever form it takes, is alienation from God. Sin seeks to find its integrity without God. It tries to put closure to creation. The path of intimacy carries us beyond the self-enclosure of closed or broken myths. We move not into nothingness, but into deeper and deeper relationship with God. Within human history, that path is symbolized in the holy people of the times, then through the Christ, then through the gift of his Spirit in each of our lives and in our world.

But just as there is within each of us that basic desire to be one with God, and within God to be one with us, we harbour a selfishness that does not desire that intimacy. Each of us, without exception, is trapped in encompassing forms of destruction that distort human freedom and seek to frustrate the human desire to love and be creative and to create community. Often, knowingly or unknowingly, we participate in them. Sometimes, our institutions – religious, cultural, or juridical – destroy the innocent, the marginalized, or those without power or voice.

In those contexts, we are asked to align ourselves with the good, to overcome our selfishness, and to be creative in transforming the world. But before we can do that, we need to understand who we are and what is possible for us. Otherwise, we contribute to patterns of destruction out of ignorance or a self-will that deludes itself that it is working for the good.

Seeing Ourselves

We cannot step out of ourselves or out of the creation to make some sort of objective judgment about the situations in which we find ourselves. What we can do is enter into the dialogue with the One who makes creation. That dialogue occurs in the contemplative mode.

Here it might be helpful to look at one reason that St. Ignatius says we experience desolation. He holds that "God wishes to give us a true knowledge and understanding of ourselves so that we may have an intimate perception of the fact that it is not within our power to acquire or attain great devotion, intense love ... or any other spiritual consolation" (#322).

The risk that God takes with us is to allow us to experience starkly the destructive consequences of the disorder of creation. We may respond with despair if we lose our sense of that larger context in which we live. God is merciful. God knows and loves us better than we know or love ourselves. God knows that our basic nature desires intimacy with God, and that such intimacy gives us life. When we contemplate the alienating presence of evil in our lives and in our world, we discover a God who, in and through creation, maintains and supports our basic sense of life without denying us our freedom to destroy ourselves if we choose. If we can enter into our unredeemed history and face the disorder in our personal lives and our family history, in our societies and cultures, we discover the abiding presence of a divine Mystery. Its creativity is to maintain our life and to invite us to help transform the disorder of history into a new creation.

Participating in Creation

There are levels to this participation. Although we are part of creation, we can live as if we were separate from creation, or we can dominate creation, or we can live our lives as a purely unspiritual manifestation in creation. But we can go beyond these three levels. We can acknowledge the conflicting forces of good and evil in creation, enter into the critical task of discerning good from evil, and creatively transform evil into good. To perform these last three works, we must discover how we are individually structured: that is, how God communicates with us and the ways we personally need God's help to become truly creative. We also need to know what traps reinforce our narcissism, and how to get the help we need to avoid them.

Prayer gives us such an entry into God's love. That love seeks out the damaged in creation – including us – to repair, console, and transform. Inasmuch as we participate in that love, we too are carried into the world's pain and past the illusions of ourselves that contribute to it. We become present to the source of creativity. By allowing our creativity to be a manifestation of God's, we co-operate with God in showing compassionate mercy to the people and situations in our lives.

That engagement manifests itself in the act of contemplation – contemplation in action. That dynamic contemplation gives life to the sacred texts of our human family. In our culture, the Scriptures of the Old and New Testament are venerated as classic documents that have helped shape our institutions. But as texts, they no longer give access to our spiritual myths and identity in the simple and naive way they once did. It is not just the secularism of the times that has devalued them, or the ways they have been used to justify destructive religious perspectives that have rendered their import suspect. Rather, the easy and present accessibility of multicultural spiritual traditions has relativized their importance. The rediscovery of their vital significance to the spiritual intimacy we all so deeply desire lies in our contemplation of them through Ignatian prayer. Then they cease to be closed or broken myths that harken back to an inaccessible past.

Those texts and stories – the imaginative world of God's ongoing creativity with the productions of human longing and effort – are not closed myths that we quarry to justify present ideological needs. Neither are they the broken myths of master narratives we pillage for pragmatic ends. Rather, scripture presents us with an open dynamic that holds the repositories of the creative effort, both positive and negative, to be one with a God who has existed since even before the birth of time. When we contemplate scripture, we access texts of God that are not exhausted by human limitation, because they allow us the presence of the Spirit of God, restless and unquenchable until it transforms all into the creative image of God.

Contemplation and Spirituality

Such contemplation is a spiritual exercise. Ignatian contemplation is structured to a particular result. It disposes us to receive the grace that we ask for in the given prayer period. That grace is a particular response to our deepest desire, an ever-growing intimacy with God. At one time it may be a profound awareness of God's mercy holding us even when we, blinded by our disorders, sinned to find what we thought was love. At another time, it may be such a personal bonding with Christ, the human manifestation of God, that we desire fully to be with him as he reveals to the world God's unceasing and compassionate mercy for all. At still another time, it may be to follow the path of that divine love through the misery and destructiveness of this world. At the end of the Ignatian Exercises, we pray for the grace to be a part of that joyful labour that transforms creation into a loving home for all.

With shameless intimacy, we ask for these graces with the full expectation that we will receive them in our prayer. At the end of each prayer, we look back over what we have experienced to see where and how we have received them. Our understanding is that God desires to communicate with us and that by disposing ourselves to receive that communication, we signal to God our desire to accept this free and loving gift.

There are, as we saw earlier, levels of gift. A gift can be offered but not received; received but not accepted; accepted but not opened; opened but not used; used but not shared; shared but not celebrated. The gift of intimacy is offered, received, opened, used, shared, and celebrated in the Spiritual Exercises of St. Ignatius. As we journey through these Exercises, we come to a celebration of life that desires to include everyone and everything in the intimate embrace of the mystery Jesus calls "Abba."

The First Week: The Mercy of God

Ignatius's missionary thrust – in imitation of Christ's – is to make all become aware that God loves us, and that God always and at every moment communicates lovingly with us. The way Ignatius devised for us to become aware of this truth is to look at our moments of consolation and desolation. These two states reveal to us how God is present in our lives. When we are bad, bad things console us; when we are good, good things console us. When we are bad, good things bring us to desolation. When we are good, bad things bring us desolation. This happens not only in our daily lives, but in our personal history, our family history, and our social history. It happens in human history and in the history of creation. We are all involved in these histories. Ignatius asks us to be grateful for moments of consolation and to reflect on moments of to desolation to see why they happened and how we can prevent their occurrence. God wants us to be happy. God works in the world to bring us to our true selves and to our true happiness.

This first stage of intimacy has us reflect on ourselves as we are held in God's love. In that embrace we can celebrate what is good in our lives. We also become aware of what prevents us from being happy. We can offer those things to God to be transformed. When we do this, we become more and more aware of being held in God's love, and we discover that God's love holds us even when we sin. We realize that, while sin diminishes our ability to be happy, we have not been destroyed by what we have done, or by the destructive forces in our world.

God loves us even when we are sinners. That love, and not anything we have done or can do, stops us from being totally destroyed. It calls us beyond what traps us and invites us to accept the gift of spiritual intimacy. We are invited to open and live that gift, bringing us to joy and gratitude that nothing else can give.

To achieve that happiness, we must sometimes make important decisions. The Exercises prepare us to make correct discernments. These are not techniques for discovering God's will. Rather, they dispose us to a true relationship with God and offer us a language by which God communicates with us. We can love someone and talk meaningfully with them, but still make bad decisions. This is an existential truth. But that love and communication limit the possibility of making bad decisions. The Exercises predispose us to making positive, life-giving decisions through the personal language of consolation and desolation. The First Week of the Ignatian Exercises prepares us to walk the path to spiritual intimacy by turning us in the right direction. There we desire to live the love that roots us and floods our being.

The Second Week: Walking with God

Ignatius places decision-making in the Second Week of the Exercises, because people first need to experience radically that God loves them even though they have been, and remain, sinners. The First Week establishes a foundational openness to God. Unless that happens, our decisions will be skewered by blindness to our true identity and to our true relationships with others and with God. By the end of the First Week, we will have come to an overwhelming sense of God's mercy in all aspects of our life – personal, communal, social, and cultural – as well as a deep sense of how disorder on all levels of our existence corrupts our true awareness of life. The liberation experienced in the First Week is a liberation to love: to be loving and to accept love. It is felt as a deep desire to live that love out in the world.

But how are we to do this? The Second Week of the Exercises introduces us to God's way of operating in the world as manifest in the presence and actions of Jesus Christ.

In that Second Week, we are invited to journey with Christ and to pray for the grace of such an intimate knowledge of him that we desire only to love and to follow him. In that journey, he shares with us his own relationship with the Father. His mission as the Father's mercy in the world becomes our mission also. That mission may require a concrete plan of action. We can bring the decision we wish to make to our prayer and discussions with God following the prayer. We check to see if, in those moments of dialogue, we are filled with consolation or desolation as we ponder our decision. Consolation means that we have made the right decision; desolation tells us that we are on the wrong track. But even in the contemplations themselves we can learn something useful. If we find God distant or uninvolved with us in those contemplations, we know something is wrong. Or, if in those contemplations we find that we are acting in ways not consonant with Jesus' own activity, then we know we are on the wrong path. The liberated energies of our life are embodied in the decision we are trying to make. These shape the way we relate to the Christ as he journeys through his own earthly life. If those energies are consonant with the energies of the Christ, then we experience consolation and the felt assurance that we are one with the Christ on mission. If there is dissonance, we experience desolation and the signs of a bad decision. Intimacy becomes the criterion for action.

The Third Week: A Passionate Lover

In the decision-making process, consonance and dissonance continue throughout the remainder of the Weeks of the Exercises. If we are making the right decision, we find that we can journey in union with Christ through his passion, death, and resurrection. We suffer and are sad with Christ suffering. Indeed, at times we might even feel nothing, that same nothing we feel during the last days of someone we love, when the predominant emotion is too deep even for feeling. It is our intimacy with the Father that allows us to be companions with Christ in this stage of his human journey through death. With the wrong decision, we find ourselves distant from that suffering, or we want to stop the suffering, or we are distracted from the main event by our own preoccupations. Then we impose our own attitudes and perspectives on what is happening in the drama we contemplate.

We are not sadistic or masochistic here. We do not delight in suffering for its own sake, nor do we take on that suffering to show just how good and holy we are. Christ did not choose his suffering. He chooses, as always, the Father and his path to the Father. The disorders of the world and of evil seek to destroy his true identity. His life reveals the Father as compassionate mercy. Evil imposes a suffering designed to break his relationship with the Father or to eliminate him altogether. Similarly, the suffering we experience in the Third Week is one of identification with someone we love and follow, and with whom we now share the same path, the same spirit, the same passion.

The Fourth Week: A Transforming Life

That passion for the Father leads us to the Fourth Week. In this week we experience Christ's resurrection from the dead. Christ does not raise himself from the dead. The Father manifests his love for his beloved. He reaches into the ultimate power of sin – death – and brings Christ not back to life, but to a new level of creation, uncorrupted by evil. This is resurrection. Ignatius asks us, at this point in our spiritual journey, "to ask for the grace to be glad and rejoice intensely because of the great joy and the glory of Christ our Lord" (#221). We are not asked to experience joy because of what we have done, but rather to share Christ's joy and glory in his return to the Father. This is crucial for our discernment process, because here we can see if our decision has united us with the Christ. If it has, then we can experience the pure gift of Christ's joy. If it hasn't, then we will not. The path of intimacy leads us to a union with the risen Christ and those who share his Spirit to labour in joy to redeem the world. The path of intimacy does not make us divine. It makes us more and more human. The goal of full humanity is to celebrate ourselves as intimately connected to all of creation in the risen Christ. The path of intimacy creates that community.

The awareness of our consolations and desolations can attune us more closely to the creative presence of God in our world and give us a personal language for listening to God. God is never speechless in the world. Everything and everyone is a sign of God's presence. The Buddhists say the pointing finger is not the moon. We do not confuse God with the signs that point to God. We realize that it is the moon that illuminates the pointing finger. We realize that God gives us the grace to see the divine presence through everything.

Ignatius, in the manual called the Spiritual Exercises, introduces the Exercises themselves in the context of a daily examination of consciousness. In this examination he asks us at the end of each day to look at it prayerfully. Where were we consoled? Where did we experience desolation? Even in the ordinariness of our day, God speaks. Ignatius suggests that we give praise for where, in the ordinary, we were consoled, and that we examine the moments of desolation to see what God is telling us.

In this we have a compass for the journey. Each journey, and each step of the journey, takes us away from something and brings us closer to something. To be a pilgrim people is to be always in transition and to live with a sense of impermanence. We can delight in what is given even as it passes. We can celebrate it as gift. It reveals what is abiding. What has been there from before all time is everywhere present now, and exists as the ground for all that is to come, rooting us in the depths of our being. Our identity lies in that rootedness. The path of intimacy carries us to that identity. In this we are all mystics.

An Outline to Follow in Using This Book

1. Make sure you have enough time for the Exercise.
2. Find a quiet space and ask for the Spirit to help you make a good prayer.
3. Ask for the specific grace that is suggested in the introductory reflection.
4. Read the reflection slowly and carefully. Dwell on those sections, one at a time, that have moved you the most, either to a sense of well-being or to a sense of discomfort.
5. Invite God to enter into your prayerful journey through those sections.
6. Discuss with God what emerges in that journey and in those deliberations.
7. Use the questions provided at the end of the reflection to appropriate your experience or to enter further into prayer.
8. Journal the significant moments of this prayer experience.

Note: At the end of every Week of the Exercises, reread carefully the journal entries for that Week. Try to summarize the overall movement of that Week. At the end of the Four Weeks, take time to reread all the journal entries. Summarize what has been given in the experience of journeying through the Exercises of St. Ignatius in this way.

Part I

The First Week: The Mercy of God

Theme: We are God's Beloved Trapped by Sin

Scripture verse

But now thus says the Lord,
He who created you, O Jacob,
He who formed you, O Israel:
Fear not, for I have redeemed you;
I have called you by name, you are mine.
When you pass through the waters I will be with you;
And through rivers, they will not overwhelm you;
When you walk through fire you shall not be burned,
And the flame shall not consume you.
For I am the Lord your God,
The Holy One of Israel, your Saviour. (Isaiah 43:1-3)

From the Spiritual Exercises

I shall also thank God for this, that up to this very moment He has shown himself so loving and merciful to me. (Sp. Ex. #71)

Grace to be prayed for

Lord, teach me to be generous
teach me to serve you as you deserve
to give and not to count the cost
to fight and not to heed the wounds
to toil and not to seek for rest
to labour and not to seek reward
save that of knowing I do your most Holy Will.

(prayer of St. Ignatius of Loyola, founder of the Jesuits)

The Journal

In the journal it is helpful to write

- the questions that were the most significant in each exercise and your response to them,
- what took place in prayer (the significant consolations and desolations), and
- the grace asked for; how it was received and how it was given.

Most of us live in the world unreflectively. We read our lives with a set of preconditioned stories that define who we are and what we should want. Those stories come from our upbringing and the culture we live in. We are even conditioned how to think. At best, we are concerned only with our own interests and projects. These reveal to us and to others the sense we have of ourselves. Indeed, the only times we question that sense of self is when something happens to disturb our carefully controlled universe: the death of someone significant, an accident, the loss of a job, bad news from the routine visit to our doctor ... even misplacing our car keys, being stood up for an appointment, or losing a night's sleep. When those things happen, we struggle to return to our previous state of comfort. But when that cocoon of comfort is no longer available, we are driven to forms of accommodation and adjustment. Sometimes those substitutes work; sometimes they do not.

A spiritual journey often begins when we can find no substitute for what we have lost. The Buddha's journey to enlightenment began when he encountered old age, sickness, and death. These realities led Prince Siddhartha to abandon a life of luxury and comfort in order to come to terms with the issue of human suffering. Significantly, it was the illness that confined Ignatius to his sickbed that prompted his journey to a spiritual life. Two centuries before Ignatius, in 1204, a serious illness was the beginning of another saint's journey to becoming Francis of Assisi. Illness, pain, loss, poverty, lack of social success, and deprivations are things the secular world does not value. But their presence – and they are present in each of our lives – reveals to us that neither we nor the world is in control. This leads us to ask the simple question that starts every spiritual journey: Given this very human situation, how can I be happy? Often we try what the world offers. For many, the pursuit of those things is distracting enough to keep us engaged for some time. But their achievement is no substitute for what we truly desire, because at the root of our being we *are* desire. Nothing less than the fullness of life can satisfy that desire. Even when good things happen to us, affirming our sense of self-entitlement, we need to accept them as gift rather than as privilege. The blindness of illusion lets us confuse the two. This illusion prompts the observation that "Those whom the gods wish to destroy they give gifts to." We tend to equate ourselves with those gifts, living as if we were our gifts. We lose our integrity as creatures radically dependent on others and on God. When bad things happen to us, we discover what beggars we truly are. We cry out for help. And whatever is given to us then is given as gift. Bad things force us to question ourselves – who we are, what we can do, what we must do. Most of us react against such self-examination in the normal circumstances of our lives. Yet only when we do so do we discover the path to spiritual intimacy and move towards the fullness of life.

Ignatius, in the First Week of his Spiritual Exercises, sets up a program that allows us to conduct that radical self-examination. Its aim is not to destroy us, but rather to help us abandon the false self-images we have of ourselves and the false stories we maintain about ourselves. At the same time, it permits us to see, understand, and experience the deeper truth of ourselves: that we are always and everywhere loved by God, who seeks us out as a lover searches for a lost beloved. That lover will not rest until the beloved knows at a profound level the personal and intimate love that constantly creates, supports, and transforms him or her.

The encounter between the beloved and the lover, between ourselves and God, occurs in the context of examining not only our personal history, but also our social and cultural history – indeed, all human history – within the cosmic history of creation. Considering ourselves in this vast context helps diminish the value we place upon our ego, which is a tiny, fragile thing in the vast tides of human and cosmic history.

Creation of the earth began fifteen billion years ago in a burst of creativity that produced galaxies, stars, solar systems, and the blue planet we call Earth. The forces and energies that shape this ongoing process of creation also feature significantly in our own moments of self-consciousness. The divine love that expresses itself in creativity from the beginning of time also expresses itself in every act of human creativity. The stories we live by, the imagined worlds we live in, have their source in that divine creativity. Unfortunately, some choose to live out of those stories as ends in themselves rather than as continuing expressions of the beloved's relationship to the lover. They value the story more than the relationship. They commit the basic act of idolatry by constraining the creativity of divine love to a particular expression of it. Stories never encompass the fullness of reality. At best, they point beyond themselves to aspects of that reality. They are doors through which we encounter God and God encounters us.

This is not to belittle story. We cannot live without story. It is within stories that we find ourselves and find a sense of ourselves.

If we think about it, we did not create our sense of self. My story goes beyond me. In fact, most of the elements of what makes up my story existed even before I was born. For example, one of the stories we live out of is our heritage. We are shaped not only by our parents' genes, and they by those of their parents, back to the dawning of humanity, but also by the historical forces surrounding us and them. Those forces are in turn subject to the environmental and ecological dimensions that mitigate against, or promote, our well-being. All of those forces are themselves caught up in the cosmic tides of a creation that has not yet reached its fulfillment. That fulfillment is to be found only in the mystery we call God. In brief, we come from God and we return to God, and the path we walk in spiritual intimacy is a gift of God. But we are not God.

So who are we? This is not a question we can answer for ourselves; the answer lies before and beyond ourselves. Maybe it is even the wrong question to ask. Maybe a better question to ask is this: What do we think or believe or understand of ourselves? Closely tied into that question are three others: What makes us think of ourselves this way? How does this perception shape the way we see and relate to ourselves, to others, and to that mystery we call God? And how does that perception change?

St. Ignatius knew from personal experience that when we admit that God desires us passionately, and when we open ourselves to that passionate desire as the desire we truly desire, we change. We fall in love. The world changes, unimagined possibilities open, and we become focused and creative in our daily lives.

The First Week of the Spiritual Exercises of St. Ignatius of Loyola invites us to walk this path of love.

Questions for Reflection to Prepare for the First Week

1. Who are you?
2. Why do you say you are this person?
3. Where does this self-understanding come from?
4. Are you content with this self-understanding?
5. What do you think is missing?
6. How do you experience that missing self?
7. How did your family shape that self-understanding? Your relationships with your parents? With your siblings? With the other members of your family? With your spouse or partner?
8. How is your self-image shaped by the culture(s) you grew up in and the one(s) you live in now? List the ways in which you are shaped by your social background, your class, your ethnicity, your economic status, your gender, your sexuality, the part of the world you come from or now live in.
9. How does the environment shape your self-awareness? Which season resonates most with you? Are you a day person or a night person? Why do you say this?
10. What is your image of God? Of religion? Of spirituality? How do your relationships reveal to you who you are?
11. What are the questions that haunt your life? How do you deal with them? How do they deal with you?
12. In what ways is your life in your control?
13. In what ways is your life beyond your control?
14. What do you really desire?
15. How does that desire manifest itself in your life?
16. What happens when you sit in prayer with your desire?

1st Exercise

(1) Cosmic Disorder: This contemplation asks us to consider how we find ourselves surrounded by the forces of destruction that have been there even before human history began, but it is not God's desire that we remain so trapped.

Scripture verse

> Then I saw a new heaven and a new earth; for the first heaven and the first earth passed away, and the sea was no more. And I saw the holy city, a new Jerusalem, coming down out of heaven from God, prepared as a bride adorned for her husband; and I heard a loud voice from the throne saying, "Behold, the dwelling of God is with mortals. He will dwell with them and they shall be his people, and God himself will be with them; he will wipe away every tear from their eyes, and death shall be no more, neither shall there be mourning nor crying nor pain no more, for the former things have passed away. (Revelation 21:1-4)

From the Spiritual Exercises

> We should apply memory to the sin of the angels, that is recalling they were created in the state of grace, that they did not want to make use of the freedom God gave them to reverence and obey their Creator and God, and so falling into pride, were changed from grace to hatred of God, and cast out of heaven into hell (Sp. Ex. #50)

Grace to be prayed for

> To ask for a sense of how I, and all humanity, am implicated in a disorder larger than ourselves and how I, consciously, or unconsciously, participate in and contribute to that disorder.

St. Irenaeus affirms that creation is not sinful by nature but rather is distorted by sin. Everything God creates is good. That goodness comes because it is connected to God. Only in that relationship with God does creation find itself fulfilled. Evil tries to separate creation from God. It suggests that creation can find its meaning within itself, or within the relationships it tries to establish within itself away from God. At times it may suggest that even God is just another aspect of creation. Evil is whatever denies the mutual intimacy and desire God and creation have for each other. This mutual desire does not make one of these desires absorb the other, so that all becomes God or all becomes creation. Rather, such love lets God be God and lets creation be creation. That mutual love allows the integrity of God and of creation to be maintained.

Mutual love is not possessive. It does not seek to control. Mutual love gives the other the freedom to be, in all of the mysteriousness of what that might mean. In the freedom of loving it, God gives creation the choice of a free response in love. Creation is not compelled to love God in return for being created and loved. That would be servitude.

Creation can discover that, in loving God freely, passionately, and intimately, it comes to a fulfillment that it can never find within itself. Within that freedom, which is God's gift to creation, lies creation's freedom not to love or respond to God. It can choose instead to love the goodness it finds in itself. It may be seduced by that lesser love because of the power of self-determination this offers. When this happens, creation separates itself from God. The passionate and intimate relationship of love is broken on one side. Creation becomes sick and distorted. It experiences itself as fragmented, because it is incomplete within itself. In its separated desire for completeness, it closes in on itself. God is no longer an intimate, the lover to delight in and to delight. God becomes the alien Other. Creation becomes fearful of the Other's approaches, because in creation's present state of selfishness, such overtures of love by God wooing back the lost beloved are seen as threatening and disempowering. Creation becomes frightened by the feelings of vulnerability the invitation to love creates.

That is why it is often only in times of vulnerability – such as sickness, the death of a loved one, the loss of a job, or the change from familiar surroundings – that we experience our creaturehood and the awareness of how much of our life is out of our control. Then we go seeking God – often, at the beginning, with the wrong motives of wanting a return to the familiar. Instead, that search carries us past the illusions of a secure and self-sustained life into the mystery of a passionate relationship with God.

The Spiritual Exercises of St. Ignatius carry us on that path to such spiritual intimacy.

Ignatius sees all of creation intrinsically finding its meaning and fulfillment in responding lovingly and freely to God, who creates in love, with love, and by love. This love makes all free, and in that freedom all have the choice of how to find meaning and fulfillment. The mystery of evil is that we can choose not to love, or not to respond to love. We can set ourselves up as knowing better than God how to be or how to manifest our identity.

In Ignatius's mythology, certain cosmic powers, called angels, were the most radical level of created spirituality to misuse free choice. It is hard to imagine that extremely spiritual beings could opt to be evil, yet even in the human realm we know of very spiritually gifted people who become cult leaders or religious fanatics, or who abuse their gifts for selfish or misconceived ends. The truth is that the closer we are to God spiritually, the greater the freedom we have, and the more available are opportunities of turning away from God. That is why the saints who are closest to God often describe themselves as the greatest sinners. Their sensitivity to freedom is so great that they see how they can turn away from God even in the smallest things. Some angels, in their freedom, behaved in such a way. Their disorder contaminated all of creation, all of our human history, and even our very selves. As we pray for an understanding of this cosmic disorder, we pray to begin to recognize how we are complicit, knowingly and unknowingly, in it. We pray for the grace to experience how we are trapped by sin and evil, and how they affect our relationship with God, and even how we understand God.

Ignatius does not try to understand the mystery of evil and sin. For him, these are existential realities. He knows that it is possible to turn away from love. It is possible to become destructive because of that turning away. Sin entered creation because of that one act, and it is unimaginable to hold in one's awareness the damage that that one act has created. When we are asked to meditate on that one single act and on its consequences, we find ourselves in a state of confusion and horror. This state of confusion is the grace Ignatius asks us to pray for as we allow ourselves to become aware of the depths of that absurdity of the angels and of the implications for every single created being.

Ignatius does not ask us to enter into this meditation to depress us, or to titillate us with some Gothic darkness that excites our fantasies and casts us in the role of victims. Indeed, we are warned against those ways of maintaining our egos. Rather, Ignatius asks us to enter into a dimension of the reality of our lives so we will realize, in spite of our own vulnerability, we have not been overwhelmed, subjugated, and destroyed by such powers. How is this possible? It's simple: God chooses in a loving freedom to protect and maintain us without taking away from us whatever freedom we still have under these circumstances.

Second, Ignatius wants us to realize, just as that single act of the dark angels created a world of destruction, any one of our many destructive acts also creates and contributes to an unleashing of chaos and suffering. He asks us to enter into that profound feeling of shame for our own rejection of love, for those times when our acts that lack mercy or compassion create a domino effect of pain, hurt, and alienation beyond our control. Each selfish act opens a Pandora's box of evils. And yet, we discover we are still loved by God and by those who align themselves to goodness.

(Hope)

We become aware of God's love that sustains and forgives and re-creates us. We can do so only when we realize how strong is the opposition to our living good and creative lives.

What usually happens at the beginning of our spiritual journey is denial of the dreadful and profound facts of evil and sin and of the ways each of us is contaminated and implicated. We are not unaware of evil, destruction, or loss. This awareness is, usually, what starts our journey. But we are unaware of just how contaminated we are by what we seek to remove ourselves from. This can be as simple as a refusal to believe what Ignatius proposes we examine prayerfully – the reality of cosmic disorder – is true. Or, our awareness can be a little more nuanced and we can consider this reality from a detached point of view. We can say to ourselves, Yes, I suppose it is true – if you believe in that sort of thing – but it really has nothing to do with me. We can even go further and think about the mystery of evil as an intellectual problem, considering why the angels did what they did, why God permits evil, and how evil and God can co-exist. Then we substitute theological inquiry for prayer. We may also enter into these meditations emotionally and feel overwhelmed by what is presented. Often at this level, incidents from our own past – whether we were the aggressor or the victim – emerge. Then we are trapped once again in sin.

In all of these responses, the ego struggles to maintain itself as the centre of its universe. But Ignatius wants us to realize that in the midst of being dreadfully implicated in cosmic spiritual disorder, we are held by a compassionate God who cherishes us even as we act out of our blindness and disorder. Here the prayer is, as always, an encounter with God, who holds us intimately and compassionately as we struggle to come to terms with our place in an ancient and ever-present realm of cosmic disorder operating even today in all the dimensions of our lives, from the sub-atomic to the galactic. Every aspect of creation is involved and implicated. In that prayer, as we start to face the awful reality of our situation, we see that this evil has not destroyed the cosmos, and has not annihilated us. We are still here. And we are here at this moment held in prayer. Held by a God who passionately enters through the corridors of time and history, through all the dimensions of space, to come to us in this moment holding us, as the lover holding a wounded and bewildered beloved. The wonder of it! Our prayer is to stay in this moment and to accept what unfolds.

Questions for Prayer and Reflection

1. How do you feel when you watch the daily news? How does that feeling contribute to the disorder you see around you? How are you made to feel that what you see is all of reality, or the most significant parts of it?
2. As you contemplate the above reflection, what aspects move you the most? Why? What do they trigger in you?
3. In what ways do you see yourself as a victim of the larger forces around you? How do you respond to that sense of victimhood and entrapment?
4. Within that larger context of disorder, in what ways do you feel truly empowered? Where does that sense of empowerment come from? How does it sustain you?
5. What questions about the nature of God as good or compassionate does the reality of evil raise in your life?

6. In your spiritual life, how do you reconcile a good God with the suffering of the powerless and the innocent?
7. How do you think evil operates? How does it operate in you and on you? What are your areas of vulnerability where you are most susceptible to evil?
8. How are you protected and defended from having that evil destroy you?
9. In your daily life and your life as a whole, how are the forces of life and creativity at work in you and around you?
10. How are you conscious of these forces? What response do you offer to them?

(2) The Disorder of Adam and Eve/The Sin of Humanity: This contemplation asks us to see in our own lives the human history which has produced us riddled with disorder yet we are not destroyed.

Scripture verses

> God said, "Let us make mortals in our image, after our likeness ...." So God created mortals in his own image, in the image of God he created them; male and female he created them. And God blessed them .... (Genesis 1:26-31)

> Now the serpent was more subtle than any other wild creature that the Lord God had made. (Genesis 3:1)

From the the Spiritual Exercises

> Recall to memory how on account of [the sin of Adam and Eve] they did penance for so long a time, and the great corruption which came upon the human race that caused so many to be lost in hell. (Sp. Ex. #51)

Grace to be prayed for

> To experience how I am trapped in the fallen human condition and how I contribute to it and from this to experience shame and confusion.

There was a time when the concept of original sin did not need any explanation. It proposes that we are born in destructive contexts and that patterns, habits, tendencies, and dispositions to destructiveness are inbred in us. We know about inherited traits. In our biologies, we have dispositions to certain diseases. We find in ourselves behaviour patterns, such as anger or melancholy, that are part of our family line; or we discover that, like everyone else, we were born into a dysfunctional family. We can reflect on how our family's way of behaving has shaped how we behave. We might even consider the patterns of disorder in our culture that we accept as part of our national character. For example, in certain cultures, the exaltation of individualism at the expense of the common good is destructive to healthy community. Yet we simultaneously pride ourselves on that rugged individualism. These are all manifestations of original sin.

Original sin is not an abstract theological concept. It describes an existential reality that touches everyone. We are implicated in sin even before we are born. The families we are born into, our parents, the very genes we inherit – all are tainted with a disorder that, in different ways and forms, work against our original goodness. Original sin indicates the very human fact that, because we are all interconnected, the destructiveness of one person affects the lives of all. The destructiveness in the cosmic powers affects the rest of creation. The effects of the destructiveness in historical events generations ago, even centuries ago, are felt even today. Current international and cultural conflicts have their beginnings centuries in the past. We are born into those destructive situations. They affect us. They threaten our vulnerability and we can withdraw into self-protective modes of behaviour that stop us from living fully. This, too, is a manifestation of original sin.

The term "original sin" came from St. Augustine, who used it to counter the Pelagian heresy that free will alone was sufficient to live a full Christian life and obtain full salvation. This heresy suggests that we do not need the constant help of God to achieve fullness of life. But we know that even having a free will cannot make us free, because the context in which we exercise our freedom is dynamically corrupted and distorting. This reality is as old as humankind. The Genesis story exposes that truth. In the Genesis story, Adam and Eve were tempted and fell when God was absent. Even in Paradise, Adam's and Eve's freedom could not sustain the way of their continual relationship with God.

Ignatius asks us to pray the Genesis myth of our first parents to allow us to see that we are situated in a corrupted universe in which human history is further corrupted. That prayer shows us how we are implicated in the web of evil.

In the protected context of the mythical garden of Eden, humans are created by God. But because of the malice of the sin of the fallen angels, that context is already threatened; it is insecure and unstable. Nevertheless, it is the place where humans still communicate intimately and unself-consciously with God. Against the simplicity of that relationship comes the temptation of the evil one. It raises doubts in us about God's love for us. It queries the limitations of our creaturehood by suggesting the possibility of an unlimited liberty and creativity. It does not point out the costs and implications of trying to live out of that suggested possibility. It leaves unsaid its rationale – malice – for broaching the subject. Instead, it stirs up the desire for an impossible good to be attained by human effort alone, the performance of one sinful act.

That one sinful act has harmful consequences for the sinners themselves: it damages their relationships with each other and forces them self-consciously to isolate themselves from God. When their broken trust is brought to their attention, they defend themselves by rationalizing it and by blaming others, but they still suffer the consequences of their actions. While the sinners hide from God, God seeks them out and confronts them with the reality of their choices.

Once again Ignatius asks us to reflect prayerfully on this. He asks us to consider how temptation causes mistrust of God, offers an illusory way for immediate gratification, and incites the ego to seek an equality with God. Sin offers the illusion that creatures may take on the role of Creator. We no longer allow God to be God, because we desire to be more than just human. We desire to be like what we imagine God to be – not loving and creative, but omniscient and omnipotent. We desire to displace God and become the centre of the universe. Through this sin of pride, we separate from God and are thrust into a heightened and alienating self-consciousness, now burdened with the humanly impossible task of redeeming ourselves. Out of this presumption comes our restless striving and our despair.

The object of this meditation is to become vividly aware of the human cost of choice, especially such choice made without taking into account its implications and consequences. Every human act is significant for all of creation. The enormity of this notion is overwhelming. What are we to do? What is the right thing to do? How do we judge what is right? We feel confused in the face of such implacable questions. The ego is stretched beyond its boundaries and defenses, which normally prevent it from thinking of such things. This meditation works against the ego's illusion of believing that it knows best how to behave, and so does not need God, or that it knows better than God how things should operate.The ego's self-maintained superiority collapses, because it realizes that it does not know all that is going on. When the ego's defenses are broached in this way, there arises in the self a sense of confusion and shame.

Confusion occurs when the tidy systems we live by are discovered to be inadequate; shame arises when we are compelled to enter into the taboo areas of our psyche to discover that we operate very much as Adam and Eve did.

Of importance in this meditation is our growing discovery of the constructions of our ego. We see that we are shaped by our parents – by their genetic makeup, their attitudes and values, their experiences, and their own parents' struggles in raising them. In an almost infinite regress, we discover that our identity has been shaped by the prison of DNA, of family histories, of social and economic class, of cultural and ethnic background, of an intricate weave of multi-layered histories in which we find that our self-identity is not as unfettered as we thought. We discover that our way of relating to ourselves, to others, and even to God has been determined in ways that are closed and broken. As Ignatius puts it, it is "to see in imagination ... my whole composite being as an exile here on earth" (#47). If these reflections produce a growing sense of entrapment, we are bringing to light the real situation of our lives, devoid of the illusions that seduce us. This may be painful. We can endure that pain only when we realize that we are held by God even as we break out of the cocooned comfort of our deceptions. While we might think and feel we are far from God, God is not at all far from us. Indeed, that loving God is closer than we are to ourselves. That God has been holding us, and saving us from destruction, even when we were blind, even as we sinned.

Questions for Prayer and Reflection

1. How do you see yourself as trapped?
2. What do you do to escape these traps?
3. In what ways can you not escape these traps?
4. How does that make you feel?
5. How can you live with the notion of "no escape"?
6. In what ways do those traps define who you are?
7. In what ways do those traps define how you relate to others?
8. In what ways do your image of religion and of God entrap you?
9. How do you feel when someone says to you in your traps, "God loves you"? Does it feel real? Does the true knowledge of God's love not only come from a real sense of being freed? Have you ever experienced that sense of being freed? That sense of constantly being freed?
10. What does being free feel like for you? How do you experience being free? How does it manifest in your daily life?

(3) The Sin of One

Scripture verse

> Have mercy on me, O God,
> According to your steadfast love;
> According to your abundant mercy
> Blot out my transgressions.
> Wash me thoroughly from my iniquity,
> And cleanse me from my sin!
> For I know my transgressions,
> And my sin is ever before me.
> Against you, you only have I sinned,
> And done what is evil in your sight. (Psalm 51:1-4)

From the Spiritual Exercises

> Imagine Christ Our Lord present before you upon the cross and begin to speak with him asking how it is that though he is the Creator, He has stooped to become human, and to pass from eternal life to death here in time, that thus he might die for my sins. (Sp. Ex. #53)

> This conversation is made by speaking exactly as one friend speaks to another, or as a servant speaks to a master, now asking for a favour, now blaming himself for some misdeed, now making known his affairs to him, and seeking advice in them. (Sp. Ex. #54)

Grace to be prayed for

> To be open to what Christ offers me.

Here Ignatius asks us to consider the personal destructiveness of one deadly sin. In the Scriptures, the most common understandings of sin are 1) the intentional rejection of the known will of God, 2) rebellion against God and God's love, and 3) guilt, as the way sin twists and distorts a person's integrity. The example of David's manipulations for Bathsheba (2 Samuel 11:2-28) reveals these three aspects. In committing adultery, he rebelled against God's commandment, placed greater value in his lust than in God's love, and sacrificed his conscience by his abuse of power in taking what he desired. In none of this is God essentially harmed. Those harmed are the sinner, those connected to the sinner, and, ultimately, humanity and all of creation.

The New Testament deepens and transforms those themes because it depicts a more intimate relationship between us and God, who becomes human to be with us. He becomes mortally vulnerable to the ravages of sin. The blind malice of evil as manifested by Judas's betrayal, by the conspiracy of the Jewish priesthood in Jerusalem to silence Jesus, and by the Roman bureaucracy in maintaining a status quo result in the death of Jesus – whose sole mission was to reveal the depth of his Father's love for a creation turned against God.

Ignatius asks us to consider how one radical sin can destroy a person spiritually, just as a single foolish or impassioned or negligent act can destroy a person physically. A tainted needle, a moment of blind anger, an unbuckled seatbelt, and a life is lost. Ignatius asks us further to consider just how many such acts have actually killed real people, and how many times we have committed such acts or worse without having been destroyed.

The point is not to drive us to a position of hyper-attention, as if we can be in total control of all aspects of every situation all the time. That would just submit us further to the tyranny of the ego trying to maintain control. Rather, the point is to admit and feel and experience what it is *not* to be in control – the sense of confusion, of vertigo almost, that results when we see the illusions we build our lives on are without substance. We experience that profound sense of shame as we realize the many times and the many ways we have tried to maintain control at the cost of losing our integrity and our soul. As Jesus asks, "What does it profit us to gain the whole world and to suffer the loss of our own soul?"

The goal of the prayer is our experiencing the amazing and unacknowledged mercy of God as we realize that we have not destroyed ourselves, but have been rescued time and again from self-destruction or from the destruction of others. Often we are not even aware we are so protected and helped. This does not deny we have been wounded or have wounded others. But we have not been destroyed, and we have been given the time and the opportunity to return to God. This holds true not only for those who have wounded us, but also for those whom we have wounded. At this place in the Exercises, we can simply rest in the wonder of such a love and allow that love to encounter our intransigence. Our unredeemed selves experience this encounter as shame and confusion; our redeemed selves know a growing sense of wonder and gratitude. Let us abandon ourselves to that all-encompassing embrace of God. Let us allow ourselves to be loved shamelessly and passionately. What we might feel as shame and confusion is simply transformation into love at those levels of our being that are beyond our control. What we experience as awe and wonder is our coming home to a right relationship with God.

Questions for Prayer and Reflection

1. Do you experience God as forgiving?
2. Do you experience God as creatively building new life out of the ruins of your life?
3. And out of the ruins of those whose lives you have ruined?
4. Can you bring to mind the situations and moments when you have been destructive? Self-destructive?
5. Why were you not destroyed?
6. How did your destructiveness affect you? How did it affect others? What were the consequences?
7. How do you live with those consequences?
8. Can you allow God to enter into those areas? How does it feel when you let that happen?

2nd Exercise: Repetition

Scripture verse

> Create a clean heart in me, O God,
> And put a new and right spirit within me.
> Cast me not away from your presence,
> And take not your holy Spirit from me.
> Restore to me the joy of your salvation,
> And uphold me with a willing spirit. (Psalm 51:10-12)

From the Spiritual Exercises

> I shall reflect upon my self and ask:
> "What have I done for Christ?"
> "What am I doing for Christ?"
> "What ought I to do for Christ?" (Sp. Ex. #53)

Grace to be prayed for

> To experience my whole being as an exile here on earth (Sp. Ex. #47) and being offered the path home to the fullness of life.

Carrying Our Past

Most of us live our lives focused on our immediate needs and problems. If we think beyond these, it is usually in terms of our immediate relationships. We figure, pragmatically, that the past is the past and cannot be changed, and so much of the future is beyond our control that it is no use worrying about it. We see ourselves as tiny, insignificant people caught in a world too large and complex and powerful for us. We consider such a perspective mature; it certainly helps us avoid lots of anxiety and insecurity.

But such an approach to life is not real, not true. It carries with it the barely hidden burdens of repression, blindness, and despair. During moments of quiet reflection, or during a sudden interruption of our daily habits, we are forced to reconsider who we are and what we are doing. These are the cracks that let in the light.

Our lives are shaped by our past. Often we carry that past around with us, as if we were houses haunted by ghosts that refuse to leave. These are the traumatic moments that have stunted our healthy growth and made us cautious, closed off, insecure, pained, and wounded. Unless those moments are brought to light and transformed by love, they fester and pervert us. They can even kill us spiritually. They are the sorts of things that make us think we must look after ourselves. No one else will.

This brokenness renders us immobile in the larger sphere of world action. It is also the nature of the world to create passive citizens who maintain the status quo. We do this by denying our responsibility towards creation. That responsibility goes beyond social justice and ecological wholeness. It goes beyond understanding our evolving creation on a purely natural level. We are not asked to be involved in the social and political and cultural dimensions of our world, we *are* involved. We must become aware of our involvement: that each of us matters, and that any one of us can be an instrument for change – for good or for evil. If we understand that, then we can examine how we, personally, have been involved and complicit with the human world.

Living with Disorder

We also have relationships with the natural world through the ways our innate urges for territory, dominance, survival, food, sex, transcendence, and bonding are caught up in moral systems and behaviours that aim either towards good or away from it. We can abuse the natural world for our own ends. But we can also worship the natural as if it were God, or an aspect of God, rather than as an aspect of God's creation. When we confuse creation with Creator, we fall into idolatry. Spiritualizing the natural merely creates ideologies of Romanticism. Rather than finding God through nature, we try to find God in nature. The natural, which includes spiritual forces, finds its fulfillment in the divine, just as one form of creativity of the divine is the natural. To live in the natural as just natural is ultimately frustrating and subversive. To live the natural as spiritual is radically limiting to our identity to be in relationship with the divine. Moreover, it distorts our real relationship with the natural.

Yet often we unconsciously do just this. Most of us would like to believe that, as civilized persons, we have achieved some form of transcendence of the natural. We see then that we are not purely natural – though we are still creatures. That is good. When that transcendence is short-circuited, we fall into more civilized forms of disorder. Then the natural is subjected to other forms of ideology. It is treated as distinct from us and becomes a thing to be used and manipulated. We enter the world of privilege. Technology seeks to dominate or reconfigure the natural. Cosmetics abort the aging process; commercial forms of energy pollute the environment.

We cannot escape this disorder that is woven into the very fabric of our lives. Our personal disorder is part of and contributes to social disorder, which in turn is part of and contributes to cultural disorder. Cultural disorder is a part of and contributes to the disorder of the human race. The human race is contextualized in the natural and the cosmic. We are all part of creation. We act on it and it acts on us. But we can only find out how this operates if God, who is beyond creation, shows us. This second exercise directs us to ask for and to seek such a revelation.

We usually receive this understanding when we enter into all the dimensions of our lives. This inner journey of self-discovery leads to an outer journey, where we find our place in the universe and in God's love.

We must learn these things from our own lives. No one else can teach us. Let us try to enter these places now.

In this prayer period, we explore where we are in our relationships with others, with creation, and with God. We ask for the grace to see how we affect others and are affected by them. At the end of the prayer period, have a conversation with Christ, as the Word through whom the Father creates the universe, about whatever arises from the prayer or your concerns.

Questions for Prayer and Reflection

1. How was this prayer different from the previous three prayer periods?
2. Did anything come together for you in this prayer period – in terms of insight or emotion or your relationship with God?
3. What was the most consoling moment in this prayer? What did it mean for you?
4. What was the most desolate moment in this prayer period? What does that mean for you?
5. What is happening to the ways in which you understand yourself?
6. What is happening to the ways in which you understand the relationships and moments in those relationships that have come up in your prayer?
7. How do you experience the world in this prayer period?
8. Is there any healing you would like to see happen to you now? In your own life? In relationships that have shaped you? In the way you deal with the world and the world deals with you?

3rd Exercise: Destruction

Scripture verse

Out of the depths I cry to you, O Lord!
Lord, hear my voice!
Let your ears be attentive
To the voice of my supplications!
If you, O Lord, should mark iniquities,
Lord, who could stand?
But there is forgiveness with you. (Psalm 130:1-4)

From the Spiritual Exercises

I will conclude with a colloquy, extolling the mercy of God, our Lord, pouring out my thoughts to Him, and giving thanks to Him that up to this very moment He has granted me life.
(Sp. Ex. #61)

Grace to be prayed for

This is to ask for what I desire. Here it will be to ask for a growing and intense sorrow and tears for my sins, emerging from a love of God rather than from self-pity.

The third exercise asks us to examine thoroughly the ways we have been actively or passively involved in, or have contributed to, the destructiveness of sin. Ignatius asks us now to pray for "a growing and intense sorrow and tears for my sins" (#55:2). The thrust of this exercise is to break down the defenses of the ego so that it becomes aware of its limitations and defects in contrast to the goodness, mercy, wisdom, and life-giving creativity and generosity of God. We realize here that we are not God; we are not the centre and the meaning of the universe. God, the centre and meaning, cares for our true selves, and sustains, maintains, and cherishes them. This exercise focuses on the mercy of God as realized by our new and growing understanding of our sinful nature. It aims at developing from our side the relationship with God that we have neglected or displaced.

People falling in love usually share their deepest and darkest secrets with the other, almost to test if the beloved could bear to love them in their darkness. In this exercise, we are encouraged to share those secrets: not to debase ourselves but to confirm to ourselves that we are loved to the core of our being, and that we can be held in love even as we admit those moments when we were unloving, unlovable, and unloved.

To do this we will spend some time with the Beatitudes of Matthew's gospel, since praying with them opens the prisons that prevent our hearts from contacting the intimate love God has for each of us.

In Matthew's gospel, Jesus says,

Blessed are the poor in spirit, for theirs is the kingdom of heaven.
Blessed are those who mourn, for they shall be comforted.
Blessed are the meek, for they shall inherit the earth.
Blessed are those who hunger and thirst for righteousness, for they shall be satisfied.
Blessed are the merciful, for they shall obtain mercy.
Blessed are the pure in heart, for they shall see God.
Blessed are the peacemakers, for they shall be called children of God.
Blessed are those who are persecuted for righteousness' sake, for theirs is the kingdom of heaven.

(Matthew 5:3-10)

We journey towards God in our daily lives. God also journeys in us to the depths of our being, where we are open and intimate with that compassionate mercy. As the lover and the beloved come close to each other, both are changed. We become more human, and we discover God as if for the first time. The journey through the Beatitudes is a journey into spiritual intimacy, into becoming more and more alive, and into discovering the power of God who desires to let us see and know and love ourselves the way the Trinity sees and knows and loves us all.

In this journey, we are liberated from whatever traps us in false self-images, in destructive relationships, or in stories that distort the truth of our lives. As we walk that pilgrimage, we discover the real cost to ourselves of the malign power in sin and evil. We also become aware of that constant, involved, and creative mercy of God incessantly labouring for us, and for all of creation, to return to intimacy and right relationship with Him. God does not wait for us to return to Him because we have lost the way. God comes seeking us in ways that give us our freedom and reconstruct our integrity.

This intimacy breaks down the false defenses of the ego so that we become aware of its limitations and defects in contrast to the goodness, the mercy, the wisdom, and the life-giving creativity and generosity of God. The path of the Beatitudes reveals the mercy of God in our lives and invites us to share that mercy with whomever we meet.

Because this exercise is difficult, breaking it up into separate parts is helpful. We will use the path through the Beatitudes in Matthew's gospel to discover our poverty of spirit and God's overwhelming love for us in this state. We will look at the ways we destructively compensate for that poverty of spirit. To experience God's love, we are called to enter into those tragic dimensions of our lives. When we do this prayerfully and patiently, we discover the transforming power of God's love. The Beatitudes, which embody the Christian vision, are a powerful way of opening ourselves to conversion. Most of us live out of our hurts. Praying the Beatitudes transforms those hurts into encounters with God's compassionate mercy. This journey will carry us to experience passionately a love that embraces us into the fullness of life. It is the essence of the First Week of the Exercises. The personal dimensions we encounter here embody the very brokenness of our lives and God's invitation to hold them up to the power of resurrection.

In Matthew's gospel, Jesus Christ is presented as the new Moses leading his people out of slavery through the desert into the promised land. Praying the Beatitudes carries us from the bondage of whatever stops us from being free, with its illusions about freedom, to a life that rejoices in a personal intimacy with God.

To enter the Beatitudes and be carried by them, we must spend time with the first one. This allows us to experience both the degree to which our lives are beyond our control as well as how much we are held and cherished by God. The unfinished business that arises in our prayer from each beatitude carries us in an intensely personal way to the next one. This path leads to an ever-deeper awareness of the presence of God in our lives. Allow enough time to enter into the dynamics of each beatitude. Each is a blessing that reveals its depths only in patience and prayerful reflection. The love that surrounds us will reveal what we need to know and do. This first beatitude describes the human condition and God's gift to us as we truly are.

[1] Blessed are the poor in spirit; theirs is the kingdom of God

Spiritual pilgrims follow the path of Christ. We realize that our lives are handed over to the mystery we call God, not in some abstract way, but here and now, concretely: not only with who we are, but who we are with, and in the situations within ourselves, within our immediate communities, our families and friends, and within the manifestations of the Church today. To realize this is to realize our poverty.

We have little control over these areas of our lives. Often we prefer to hide from this poverty and from the fact that we are truly broken people. We are broken intellectually, physically, emotionally, spiritually, communally. Today we are asked to take time to acknowledge the brokenness in our lives – the brokenness that is our life. We put aside, gently but firmly, the illusions we have of being whole, and stop pretending that we are God. Truly we are the emptiness that only God can fill.

Before we can be filled, we must admit our poverty. When we do this, we open ourselves to the path that leads to the kingdom of God. Instead of viewing our poverty as a horror and a burden, we may see it as a door that we need to walk through. We need to be led and carried by our poverty to wounded places where we are raw, vulnerable, naked. There we contact our own poverty, other people's poverty, and the poverty of the world. Poverty allows us to discover community, which is the kingdom of God in our midst.

Poverty of spirit is the radical awareness of our nothingness and of our dependence on Divine Providence for health, approval, image, identity, friendship, even life itself. To enter into poverty of spirit is to enter the realm where we are stripped of illusions – even the illusions of our illusions. Poverty of spirit sentences us to death, beyond the awareness of our mortality. When we live out of that poverty, the unexpected happens. We see every moment as a gift, a luxury. Every moment is one of pure wonder. Such poverty cuts a lot of nonsense out of our lives. Because we cannot compromise that poverty, we do not need to defend ourselves, or sacrifice ourselves to maintain false images. We can be simple and tolerant in our suffering and the suffering of others.

The discipline of poverty is to remain empty. In that emptiness comes the presence of God as God in the surprising forms of Divine Providence. There the scandal of the cross is transformed into the awe of the resurrection. To live in that emptiness is to change our self-image and our expectations of others. It changes the way we imagine the world. We become so open that the energies of God can flow through us into the world.

Poverty of spirit is liberation from illusion; it is the ground of detachment. Here we can simply and shamelessly be passionate with God, and God is simply and shamelessly passionate with us, even in our bodies. Right here and right now.

Questions for Prayer and Reflection

1. What are your gifts? How do you use them? How are you trapped by them?
2. What are your poverties? How do you hide from them? What happens to you when you enter into those areas?
3. What are the areas in which you do not believe in yourself? What are the areas in which you do not believe in others, or in God?
4. Where do you feel threatened? Where does your body tell you that you are threatened?
5. How are you threatened by God? by your family and friends? by your community? by yourself? by your prayer? How do you experience that threat in your body? [that feeling is the first embrace of God – the fear of God is the beginning of wisdom]
6. What are the areas of vulnerability in your life?
7. What are the areas that can humiliate you?
8. What are the areas in which you are humbled?
9. Poverty takes only what is needed from this world, nothing more. Can you distinguish between what you want and what you need? To know what that is requires discipline, spirit,

wisdom. Can you pray for that grace – generally, and in specific instances?

10. What aspects of your own poverty of spirit do you feel called to spend some more time with? How will you do that? Can you sit in the presence of God and allow God to encounter your own poverty of spirit? What happens when you do that?
11. Our poverty of spirit never goes away. As the Buddha's First Noble Truth has it, everyone suffers. How can we suffer and yet be in the kingdom of God? Simone Weil says that when we follow false gods, suffering is transformed into violence; a true God transforms suffering into pain. Where does your violence come from? Where does the violence inflicted upon you come from? How has that suffering been transformed into pain? How is your suffering to be transformed into pain?

Scripture Passages for Prayer

"Blessed are the poor in spirit, for theirs is the kingdom of heaven." (Matthew 5:3)
Psalm 136:34
Isaiah 41:17-20; 55:1–56:9
Luke 1:5-38
Phillipians 2:1-11
Revelation 3:14-22

When we enter our poverty of spirit, we discover that there are aspects of our lives that trap us and stop us from living joyfully, simply, and compassionately. We need to be liberated from these. The second beatitude offers us the next step in that liberation.

[2] Blessed are those who mourn, for they shall be comforted

To mourn is to acknowledge death and the call to a life beyond death. Mourning is the movement to resurrection, where we are saved, not by anything we have done or can do – not even by our hope – but by the generosity of God. In mourning, we let go of our dead into the shaping spirit of the One who forms us all. Mourning is our responsibility to the dead. In mourning them, we are present to them and allow God to reach through us to touch them. Mourning reminds us that we, living and dead, are still being created. That process of creation is a constant transformation. When we hold onto the dead, or allow the dead to hold onto us, we stop that work of transformation and creation. We reject God's gift of creativity in our lives and in our world.

To mourn, then, we must first acknowledge the presence and effect of the dead in our lives. To only remember the dead as they were is to create a tomb; it equates this life with all that they are. But that is not all they are. They are now embraced by a love that transforms them as they accept it. If we fail to believe this, and so often we do, then we fear to mourn, and we hold on to a rotting corpse. We seek ways to pretend that what is dead is alive. The only way this is possible is to become dead ourselves. We become trapped by a past that gives no life. So imprisoned, we deny life to ourselves and to those around us. By pretending that the dead are alive, we repress death and enter into a false freedom where the dead possess us unconsciously because we have not released them into the power of resurrection. Then they shape the path we walk. Our fear of abandonment, our desire for the security we once knew, is a form of despair that, in reality, death is the end. We can be so blinded that we cannot see the corruption and the stink we carry. Yet it manifests itself in our cynicism, our despair, our rigidity, our self-righteousness. Then we do not bring life to others, but rather take it away. The basis of this is fear. Such a fear denies that God is stronger than death and more compassionate and life-giving than we are.

We must first look at the ways we are trapped by fear. This can only be done in the context of a love that holds us securely. Our prayer at this time offers us that love. Then, we can become conscious of the ways the dead influence our perceptions, our ways of thinking and acting. We can fight against this awareness or we can welcome it. In so doing, we begin to realize how our traditions – personal, family, cultural, religious – affect us. Tradition is the handing on of life and of spirit. Some aspects of our tradition free us; other aspects do not. We are asked always to choose life and to hand on life. We are asked to hand over to resurrection what traps us in death. Then we will see death as part of life, rather than living life as part of death. When we acknowledge the presence of the dead and their effect on our lives, we become aware of the work we must do in our desire for liberation. We note that we ourselves cannot transform death into life. Resurrection is always a gift from God. But we can dispose ourselves for resurrection by accepting the love that raised Christ from the dead. That love did not resuscitate the dead Christ, but transformed the dead Christ into a new creation. This same love does not bring our dead back to life, but transforms our dead into a new life. Our work is to bring the dead to that transforming love.

We offer the dead our mutual path to the resurrection, where the fullness of life is possible only when all of creation comes together as one in joy and in the shared gratitude of being redeemed into a common life. For to mourn is to enter into community; the comfort offered to those who mourn is the growing realization that the very act of mourning is also the act in which resurrection happens. Mourning creates joy. Mourning transforms grief into hope. In grieving we become aware of loss and of the fragility of the "world" in which we live and find our meaning. We admit our inability to maintain that world. And in grieving, we live with the fragments of that world and with the empty spaces between those fragments that nothing can fill. Grief kills. Mourning brings life. When we mourn we bring all our grief to God. There we abide in the lived consolation of being companions together in this dreadful adventure, and wait in prayer for the tombs to open and the new life we call resurrection to occur.

Questions for Prayer and Reflection

1. What are the dead of your life? What are the things you despair over, believe are unchangeable, in your life, in the life of families, in the larger communities? How do these things relate to your poverty of spirit?
2. What are the dangers you encounter in your mourning? For example, how do you distinguish between mourning and being critical? Can you distinguish between "coming back from the dead" and "resurrection"?
3. How does your grieving alienate you from others? What happens when your identity becomes fixated in grief or nostalgia?

4. Who, or what, have you found personally helpful in your process of mourning?
5. Do you have any instances of resurrection in your life? How were you surprised? How have you shared the resurrection you have received?
6. What things, places, works, and/or people in your life would you like to experience resurrection? What ways have you tried, or do you try, to promote resurrection to these? Another way of asking that question is, How do you comfort others?
7. What is the difference between solitude and loneliness?
8. Can you experience solitude without being lonely? How is this possible?
9. What illusions has your personal encounter with death removed from your life? What illusions has that encounter provoked?
10. Heidegger says we are beings thrown towards death. How do you live in this radical contingency that questions every aspect of your life?
11. Our relationship with Christ does not allow us to evade death. We must all die. How do you experience that relationship with Christ in the face of death? How do you experience your relationship with the Father in the face of death?

Scripture Passages for Prayer

John 11:1-45
Luke 7:11-17
Matthew 9:1-7
Matthew 17:1-13
Luke 4:14-30
Luke 23:50–24:11
John 20:11-18

When we mourn, we discover a certain liberation. This manifests itself in a loss of fear, a certain flexibility in our attitudes, the ability to delight in what is given as gift without clinging to it. But we also discover those elements in our lives that refuse to let us be free. They do violence to us, and we are tempted to do violence back to them in our struggle to be free. Because we are not always conscious of them, they also incite us to be violent in our relationships with other people. The third beatitude addresses this issue of violence. Violence destroys the community love seeks to create.

[3] Blessed are the gentle; they shall inherit the earth

We are all vulnerable. If we were to meditate on our vulnerability, we would discover in ourselves opposing tensions in our living out of our vulnerability. Such vulnerability can breed fear when we internalize the forces that threaten us. The fear creates alienation when we understand the "other" to be inimical to our well-being, and the alienation manifests itself in violence as we try to defend that space in which we find our identity. Then "the kingdom of heaven is taken by violence and the violent destroy it" (Matthew 11:12).

But there is another approach to being vulnerable. Vulnerability opens us to the dimensions of Divine Providence in our lives when we realize, in examining our very histories, that we are not destroyed, but instead are saved in spite of ourselves. The awareness of our lives being held in God's care moves us to gratitude, especially when we grasp how easily we can be destroyed. This spirit of gratitude manifests itself in the gentleness with which we deal with ourselves, others, and the world. We do not have to be violent to maintain ourselves. God's power comes "to save all the meek of the earth" (Psalm 76:10).

To be gentle is, first of all, to face not only our vulnerability, but also the horror, the abject nakedness, and the blind misery that masquerade as the powers of this world, without becoming paralyzed or trapped by fear – our own or others'. To be gentle calls us to be attentive (as opposed to blind) to the forces that comprise our world; to be discerning, insightful, political, and flexible in dealing with these forces; and to be responsible – rather than reactive – for the transformation of the oppressor and the oppressed. To be gentle calls us to dance in the flames, and in the ashes, and in the hard places of this life. The witness of this gentleness lies neither in our devotion to an ideology of social justice nor in withdrawal from the arenas of social effect. It lies in the manifest joy of knowing with our own body the presence of the powers of good that are holding, protecting, affirming, and guiding us along the path that is salvation.

This joy allows us to see, in the cracks and the terrors of this world, the promise of paradise. It invites us to co-operate with the powers of good by being present, humbly and gratefully, at precisely those places, so that through our simple presence, the mystery we call God can enter the world.

Questions for Prayer and Reflection

1. What are the areas of violence in your life [individually, communally]?
2. In what ways does your lifestyle create violence to your integrity, to your family, to the larger community?
3. How do you feed your violence, communicate your violence – in your silence, apathy, speech, narcissism, and in the practice of your daily life?
4. What difficulties do you have in reconciling your notions of gentleness with your idea of what it means to inherit the earth?
5. What possibilities of transformation open up when you do not assert your self-righteousness?
6. What comes to you when you pray for the grace to be gentle?
7. How can you affirm others in being a person for/with others in the context of your limited resources?
8. Moses was called "the meekest of men" (Numbers 12:3). How does this give you some indication of what meekness is? Can meekness then be seen as a disposability to the will of God, as opposed to pride, which makes you the centre of meaning and creation?
9. How is gentleness different from apathy, conformity, weakness, powerlessness, cowardice, passivity, victimhood?
10. How do the meek attract the heart and open it? What in you cries out to be opened now?

Scripture Passages for Prayer

Matthew 27:15-23
Matthew 11:25-30
Matthew 7:7-12
Isaiah 29:13-21
Isaiah 61:1-4
Psalms 37; 75; 131; 138

It is always shocking to discover the violence in us, and the violence around us. In fact, we have become so accustomed to violence, we might consider it a normal part of living, and characteristic of being human. But when we discover how much of our lives is caught up in violence, from which there seems to be no escape, we feel helpless and overwhelmed. We cry out for a different reality. We cry out for conversion. Those who hunger and thirst for such a transformed world, and who place themselves on the path to such a life, enter into the work of the fourth beatitude.

[4] Blessed are those who hunger and thirst for justice; they shall be satisfied

The practice of freedom lies in the midst of evil, not beyond it. If our choices enslave anyone, we are not free. The freedom that liberates is generated through God's saving activity and our abiding intimacy in that relationship, which God's constant creativity establishes and maintains here and now, even in the midst of suffering caused by the aggressions of narcissism. God's love for us sets us free. When we are rooted in that love, we may strive for the justice that liberates all. True justice comes only from justification. As we accept that everyone is loved – even when we sin – we approach what it means to be justified. Otherwise, our understanding of justice remains fallen, defined in terms of recompense, and of contract and social norms. Then our commitment to justice, on whatever level – personal, communal, social, or cultural – is maintained within the boundaries of self-knowledge and self-interest. This is the position of the Pharisees and the Zealots. It is the position of those who destroy others, and even themselves, to maintain what they think is right.

Such a position denies the depths of what it means to be human. First, it denies the pervasiveness of sin in our lives, so that we are blind to our blindness. Second, below the manifestations of that sin, it denies the constant hunger we *are* for God. Moreover, it manipulates people's hunger for God into accepting cult and ritual through guilt and repression. But we are not saved by the word of the law, whether religious or secular. We are saved only by the Giver of the spirit whose gift finds some inadequate expression in the law. Our hunger is not satisfied by the law, but in a relationship with the living Word under whose cross we find our life. To hunger and thirst for salvation is to commit to that life, not only for ourselves, but for all. It is to experience the agony of the passion as we struggle with all of our energies so that the fullness of life may be tangibly present to all in the sacrament of daily life.

On the cross, Christ is at his most creative. In this act, he overcomes those powers that, in their blindness, self-service, and malice, attempt to prevent life from being given to all who desire it. When we hunger and thirst for God, we hunger and thirst for a set of relationships for everyone in which the only criterion is mutual love. In John, Jesus prays to the Father for his companions, "that they may be one even as we are one, I in them and thou in me, that they may become perfectly one" (17:22-23).

The justice we embody is the witness of the justification we experience. How we treat ourselves and others manifests not only *what* we love, but *how* we love. That love is where we put our lives. Ignatius says that "love ought to manifest itself in deeds rather than in words"; he continues, "the lover gives and shares with the beloved what he possesses" (Sp. Ex. #230:1, 231:2). When we hunger and thirst for justice, we live our poverty in a way that allows the mercy of God to be manifest through us. We experience that desire even in our bodies, for our bodies are how we are in this world. We incarnate our desire with our bodies. Our desire is for the community of love that includes all without exception. Our desire is met and embraced by God's desire to create that community of love. That passion the Father has for the world makes us also his living words in the circumstances in which we find (and lose) ourselves.

We desire to be saved because we cannot save ourselves. When we follow the path of that desire, we allow God to come to us, and through us, into the world. The joy and gratitude we experience when that happens embolden us to continue God's mission in the world, because we discover we are all one.

Questions for Prayer and Reflection

1. Can you accept that you are loved? What stops you from accepting this?
2. What areas in your life are silenced, not believed, oppressed, marginalized, colonized? How are they to be loved into life?
3. What are you passionate about?
4. What is the connection between the way you see social justice and the way you experience God?
5. How do you inflict alienation on others? Do others experience you as an open door to the mystery we call God?
6. In what ways do you need to be more joyful?
7. What subverts your creativity into anger, or apathy?
8. What excites your creativity? What affirms your creativity in the present situation? In what ways can you commit yourself to your creativity?
9. What happens when you allow yourself to be passionate for God, and allow God to be passionate with you?
10. What happens when you ask for this in prayer?

Scripture Passages for Prayer

Psalm 130
Matthew 5:20-28
Luke 18:1-14
Romans 8:1-39
Romans 12:9-21
Exodus 3:1-18

When we experience the gift of being loved, we start to see how destructive violence is. We realize how that love loved us even when we were unloving, even when we were violent in our inability to love. This is the experience of mercy. It renders us merciful to those we encounter who have not yet experienced this gift. We give what we have received. In that giving, we enter deeper into the kingdom by making it more available to all.

[5] Blessed are the merciful, for they shall obtain mercy

Mercy is absurd. It is neither prudent nor politic. It has no aims, expects no rewards, and is not self-congratulatory. It strives to love its enemies, expecting nothing in return. In this it imitates God, who is "kind to the ungrateful and the selfish" (Luke 6:36). The merciful are always aware that God is good to us even as we sin, and so come to realize that God's justice is his mercy, his constancy of help, and his patience, which manifests itself in the gift of time. That mercy is not pity, which sees the suffering of the other and is only interiorly moved by it. Human mercy, like divine mercy, goes out of itself to transform the suffering of the sinner. Human mercy flows as an act of gratitude at having experienced divine mercy. That gratitude covenants God and man. That spirit of gratitude does not abet sin, but strives to bring those trapped in sin to the truth of their lives – the acceptance of the fact that they are loved, and that, in the circumstances of their lives, they can be loving.

The merciful are not judgmental. They know what it is to be trapped and what it is to be freed from those traps, and how easily, but for the constant support of God, they may be trapped again. Their personal history makes them attentive to the broken of the world, whether rich or poor, powerful or weak, shamed or shameless. It gives them the lived experience from which they can distinguish between "want" and "need," and allows them to respond to the need in people's lives. They realize the interconnectedness of all life, and the desire of all to be rooted in that interconnectedness. It is to realize that everything concerns us and evokes our compassion.

Yet we cannot do everything; the attempt to do everything denies us mercy. We can do only what we have been gifted to do. Our gifts are at the service of those we meet on our daily path. We are to be as open doors through which the world's needs meet God. In every encounter, that need is manifest, because no one is fully saved until all are fully saved. The preferential option for the poor recognizes the poverty in everyone and addresses it as Jesus did in his gospel life, scandalizing the self-righteous, who were blind to their own needs and thus blind to the needs of others (Matthew 25:34-40).

We can never be as merciful as we would wish, but we can be merciful as we are, with the little we have. In sharing that poverty, we discover what it means to be human. For the hard heart which cannot be hurt cannot love, either. To be merciful is to take the risk that one will be taken advantage of, be made a fool of. Indeed, this is often the case if we are concerned with self. But if we give what we have been given, this is never the case. It is easy to abuse God's gifts. Human history is the history of such abuse. Yet God does not stop giving; our history is also one of salvation. Mercy is rooted in the absurdity of love – of being loved and of being offered the opportunity to love. It is expressed as gratitude for that felt knowledge.

Questions for Prayer and Reflection

1. Have you ever received mercy? Have you ever offered mercy? What was the experience like – then, and now as you reflect on it?
2. What are you truly grateful for? What do you accept as your right? What is the difference? What do you reject out of that sense of your rights?
3. What gifts can you offer others now?
4. What gifts can you offer your community? What do you do if your gifts are not accepted by the community?
5. How do you deal with rejection?
6. What can you risk to create community? What do you risk to create community?
7. Have you ever been trapped? How did you become free of that trap?
8. How do you direct your energies towards the life given you, rather than in building your defenses against that inevitable last breath?
9. What are the things that stop you from being merciful? Is it the fear of being used, of seeming weak; is it simple blindness; is it your preoccupation with your own needs?
10. How does your understanding of righteousness in your daily life stop you from being merciful?

11. How do you distinguish between mercy and pity? Why is mercy the expression of our common, naked vulnerability?
12. At this moment, where do you need mercy? Can you ask for it? At this moment, where can you show mercy? Can you give it? Is it to yourself?
13. What moves you as you stay with this prayer?

Scripture Passages for Prayer

Psalms 22 and 23; 86; 88 and 118
Luke 6:27-38
Luke 18:9-14
John 8:2-11
Luke 23:32-46

We are never fully converted, and will never be until every aspect of creation is fully united to God, because every aspect of creation, including ourselves, is interconnected. But we are on our way, and along our way, through our acts of mercy, we offer to all the gift of living in God. When we live this way we are turned towards God. Then we desire God and we desire to find God in all things and all persons, and in all the circumstances of our lives. To live this way is to be pure of heart. Jesus, in the sixth beatitude, assures us that as we live our lives this way, as we walk this path, we shall embrace God, our beloved.

[6] Blessed are the pure in heart, for they shall see God

Our deepest desire is from God. Our deepest desire seeks God in all things. That desire directs our spiritual path. In the course of living our lives, we discover that we are shaped by many desires, and we seek discernment: which desires lead to the building up of the kingdom of God and which do not? The manifestations of our deepest desire move us to be companions of Christ. Those other desires are energies, or patterns of energy, that have somehow become detached from our deepest desire and lead a separate existence. They can be identified by that separation. Consolation occurs when our desires harmonize with the energies of the Spirit; joy occurs when our energies harmonize with those of those around us; happiness occurs when those energies surrounding us harmonize with ours; pleasure occurs when those energies submit to us. The range between consolation to desolation is from community to narcissism.

To be pure in heart is to be on the path to integration where all the energies of our life – spiritual, social, communal, personal, emotional, intellectual, sexual – are woven together by our deepest desire. That deepest desire carries us beyond our present sense of self into truer and more intimate modes of being with others. The focus of that path is on relationship rather than ritual, on prophecy rather than professionalism. The integrity of the weave of those energies makes no distinction between private and public, between self and other. To be pure in heart is to realize the unity of all that exists and to value all that exists. This unity includes the energies that comprise the self, and this unity manifests singleness of purpose. As we move on the path of purity of heart, we discover a singleness of purpose that makes us flexible to the Spirit. That union of spirit – the passion for community – carries us to those places where displaced and separated energies come to light. Then we endure the exorcisms of encountering a love that reweaves those straying energies into a simpler and more integrated life

The trials of living this way embody the struggle between narcissism and community. As we walk the path and struggle for that more total integration, we discover that nothing human is foreign to us. Such self-awareness makes us humble; in that humility, we become more and more disposed to the dance of the energies, more open to the darkness in which God dwells, where we see first not with the eyes, but with the heart.

What the heart sees is that everything that exists is holy. To be pure in heart is to enter into the struggle of creation, in which everything is involved. It is to realize that call to holiness in all the circumstances of life. Evil is fragmented holiness; the task of the pure in heart is the careful gathering up of those fragments into unity – the unknotting of the tangled energies that hold us in the bondage of compulsion and oppression. The pure of heart, by the simple act of being present, heal the afflicted, bind up the brokenhearted, give sight to the blind, set free the enslaved, and announce to the world the presence of God among us, so that they can freely enter into the play and the delight of the life where God dwells.

Questions for Prayer and Reflection

1. What are the current divisions in your personal life? in the life of your community?
2. How do those divisions affect you? What are you concretely doing about them?
3. What are the difficulties you encounter as you strive to witness to the integrity of God?
4. Can you discern between passion and compulsion? Between indifference and apathy? Between pilgrimage and forced marches?
5. Where are the freedoms in your life? How do those freedoms come together? What aspects of your life are in pilgrimage (as opposed to bondage and its forced marches)? Where do you celebrate? How? With whom?
6. What is the witness of our life? Who witnesses God to us?
7. Purity of heart just opens the doors of perception. Purity of heart does not create what is perceived. What is given to the pure of heart is a gift. It sees what has always been there waiting to be celebrated. What has been given to you in your own vision quest?
8. Have you ever had an experience that you considered a personal revelation? How has it shaped your life?
9. Can you talk about the stages of your spiritual journey that led to an encounter with the divine?
10. Can you talk about the stages of your spiritual journey after that encounter with the divine?

Scripture Passages for Prayer

Genesis 22:1-19
Psalm 116
Romans 8:1-39
Matthew 4:1-11
Mark 5:1-20
Revelation 19:9-11

As the pure of heart walk towards God, they gather up the broken, the disaffected, the alienated, and the fearful, along with the rich, the powerful, the gifted, the lucky, in an open community of common affection, mutual sharing, and respect. It is the work of the peacemaker to help create and maintain such communities. They are the kingdom of God on earth.

[7] Blessed are the peacemakers; they shall be called the children of God

Hatred destroys not only the other, but also us. In maintaining hate we sacrifice ourselves to the lie that the enemy deserves to die. This war, breeding more war, "is only a cowardly escape from the problems of peace" (Thomas Mann). The only way to overcome an enemy is to make the enemy a friend. The problem of peace is *how* to make an enemy a friend. To make peace is to move beyond apathy or tolerance. To make peace is to create community. Community is created when we live in such a way that the energies of all are allowed positive expression. It is a question of imagination. Because we live in imagined worlds, what we imagine as real defines how we relate with others. When we indulge ourselves to imagine the world, instead of allowing ourselves to live as God imagines us, we follow the path of fantasy. And, as Yeats, in his poem "The Stare's Nest by My Window," observed of those fighting against each other in the civil war in Ireland,

> We had fed the heart on fantasies,
> The heart's grown brutal from the fare ....

Before we can create community, we need to ask what fantasies shape our lives and, further, what forces in our lives maintain those fantasies. If we see only through the filter of our hurts – rather than the call to creativity that gives us our vision – we project onto those we hate what has hurt us and what we deny in our own lives. We know these exist because they trap us and we experience feelings of hate.

We become peacemakers only as we makes peace with ourselves, only as we acknowledge the hurt in our life, through a healing of memories and sensibilities within the vision that gives our life meaning. That vision emerges when we accept that we are all held in the compassionate mercy of God, and that no one is outside of that mercy. This meaning becomes real in our lives. not in terms of satisfaction. but through the modes of consolation. In consolation we are redefined, not according to fantasy, but through an immediate openness to God. That state "without any previous cause" moves us beyond our boundaries to a new awareness of reality in which what we consider impossible is possible. In this openness, the enemy can become the friend. This openness does not manipulate the other into becoming a friend. The other is always free to choose. Even self-sacrificing love – radical openness – does not make the other free. But it is the most we can do. We can love our enemy without indulging our enemy's destructiveness, and hope for the best. This is our calling as human beings. We love each other, or we die.

Christ, the peacemaker, comes to show us how to reconcile ourselves to God, to each other, to ourselves, and to all the forces of creation. Reconciling the estranged is Christ's mission. He does it by showing that we all have a common source, the Father, and that we are all one in that same Father. We, Christ's companions, inherit that same mission from God, according to today's beatitude. Community can be built only if persons share a common vision in which everyone maintains a common good. That common good is manifested differently according to different gifts, but underlying these differences is the same spirit and a common vocation. The dynamics of integration required to be a person of peace are also necessary to be a community. Prayer, dialogue, openness, intimacy, and celebration create life. The path of the peacemaker leads to the broken and hard places of our own life, community, and world. It takes up the Standard and Cross of Christ, our brother. We stand in those places, simply and humbly, as open doors, in our poverty of spirit. As open doors, we allow the mercy of God to enter the world, and allow the pain of the world to pass through us to be held by that transforming love of God.

Scripture Passages for Prayer

John 14:15–15:17
Galatians 5:13–6: 2
Ephesians 2:8-22, 4:1-16
Romans 5:1-11
Daniel 10:15-19
Isaiah 11:1-11

Questions for Prayer and Reflection

1. Who is your community – the ones you share your life with? Why do you think so? How did you come to those relationships?
2. How do you find your community? Does it support your integrity? Are you inspired by the community, the society, the culture you live in?
3. What ideals of community life do you hold that alienate you from the people you live with?
4. Do you know the estranged parts of your life? Do you know the integrated parts of your life? Do you live out of alienation or integration with yourself, with your community? How do you realize, individually and collectively, your call to be a peacemaker where you find yourself now?
5. Who is not your community? Why do you say that? How do you treat those others?
6. What boundaries do you impose upon the way you imagine yourself? Are those boundaries open or closed?
7. How do you experience yourself, and others, as mystery? With whom are you intimate?
8. How are you intimate with yourself – in terms of self-awareness, self-knowledge, being comfortable with yourself, loving yourself into transcendence?
9. How are you intimate with others?
10. How are you intimate with God, so that God can be fully present, through you, in the world?
11. What difficulties do you have with intimacy? What stops you from trusting? What concrete elements stop you from risking

– that movement beyond trust into the darkness? What forms of fear, of established positions, of power, of disillusionment possess you?

12. Where do you find life? Where do you give life? Where do you take life?
13. To whom, and with whom, and for whom do you feel responsible even with your very life?
14. Can you distinguish between peace-lovers, peacekeepers, and peacemakers? Where do you find yourself as a member of a common humanity? of a common culture? of a common church? as an individual?
15. What do you do to bring about the kingdom of God in your daily life?
16. How is this beatitude a manifestation of the gospel reality of the passion of Christ?
17. How does your prayer on this beatitude reveal to you your own divided heart, the ways in which you are invited to do good, and the ways in which you succumb to evil?
18. In your conversations with God at the end of your prayer, what manifested itself to you?

Scripture Passages for Prayer

Blessed are the peacemakers, for they shall be called "children of God."

John 17:6-26; 1 John 1:5–2:17
1 Corinthians 12:1-14
Genesis 22:1-14
Genesis 32:24-31
Song of Songs 3:1-5; 8:6-7
Revelation 21:1-8
John 14:15–15:17
Galatians 5:13–6:2
Ephesians 2:8-22, 4:1-16
Romans 5:1-11
Daniel 10:15-19
Isaiah 11:1-11

To be a peacemaker is to enter the dark and dangerous places of life where there is conflict, violence, separation, and distrust, and to allow ourselves to be an instrument of God's mercy there. It is to be a prophet. The hope and life offered by peace run counter to the powers of evil that seek destruction and despair. They turn against the peacemaker in violence. Because evil is not creative, the pattern of its destructiveness is the same throughout the ages. The lives of prophets witness their intimacy with a power greater than evil. They have found that intimacy by walking the path of the Beatitudes. They have found a love they offer to the world.

[H] Blessed are those who are persecuted for righteousness' sake

When our hearts are filled with longing for the kingdom, that longing shapes everything we do. We hold values different from the world's, trust what the world neither sees nor believes in and, then, because we are judged as "other," we become the objects of derision, or fear, or hatred. A Hasidic tale tells of a house where there was a wedding festival. The musicians sat in a corner and played their instruments, the guests danced to the music and were merry, and the house was filled with joy. But a deaf man passed outside of the house; he looked in through the window and saw the people whirling about the room, leaping, and throwing about their arms. "See how they fling themselves about!" he cried. "It is a house filled with madmen!" For he could not hear the music to which they danced.

To be possessed of the desire only for God is to be judged crazy or eccentric, like Francis of Assisi stripping naked in the public square of his father's town. It is to be accounted dangerous by the moral guardians of society, as when the Inquisition imprisoned Ignatius of Loyola, who asserted that God could be found in this world. This hunger for God makes us fools for Christ's sake, and lets us share in the passion the Father has for his Son and in the passion the Son has for the Father. That passion to say yes to life, to make the leap of faith in every moment of life, and to return to the marketplace bearing gifts is the Spirit.

The path of the Beatitudes always returns us filled with the Spirit to a world to be transformed. We leave that world because it does not satisfy our needs; in that journey, we discover the dead we carry with us and experience the humility of the powerless who have been saved. The zeal our transformation engenders is tempered into a mercy that makes us one with God in compassion for the world. Living compassionately in this world, we manifest the prophetic presence, being living words of God, companions of Jesus. In each stage of the path, there are trials to be endured. Each stage brings a death and a resurrection. Then, like Paul,

> We rejoice in our hope of sharing the glory of God. More than that we rejoice in our suffering, knowing that suffering produces endurance and endurance produces character, and character produces hope, and hope does not disappoint us, because God's love has been poured into our hearts through the Holy Spirit that has been given to us. (Romans 5:3-5)

Through the Beatitudes, our devotion becomes the sacrifice making the world holy, and unites us in the embrace of God. In living that embrace, we live not for ourselves or through ourselves. When we fully commit ourselves to life, the lives we lead are Revelation for others. Then, Christ lives in us and through us.

> You are the salt of the earth; but if salt has lost its taste, how shall it be restored? It is no longer good for anything except to be thrown out and trodden under foot. You are the light of the world. A city set on a hill cannot be hid. Nor does anyone light a lamp and put it under a bushel, but on a stand, and it gives light to all in the house. Let your light shine before all, that they may see your good works and give glory to your Father who is in heaven. (Matthew 5:13-16)

Our desire is that all may have life and have it to the fullest. In that desire for fullness of life, every death is embraced so that it becomes the door to a deeper and fuller life. This life is a gift always offered to everyone.

Questions for Prayer and Reflection

1. How are you to live here and now?
2. What do you need to live that life?
3. Which beatitude gives you the greatest consolation? Which beatitude challenges you the most? What does this tell you about your path and about your shadow?
4. How do the people you admire live the Beatitudes? How do you live the Beatitudes?
5. What is the concrete relationship between the Beatitudes and your daily life, the way you see yourself and others, the ways you share life and make decisions?
6. Where are you now?
7. What work needs to be done to continue your experience of being loved into life by God?

Scripture Passages for Prayer

Psalms 42 and 24
John 21
John 1:13-23
Luke 21:1-4
Acts 2:1-28
Mark 3:13-35

Oscar Wilde, in his essay "The Soul of Man Under Socialism," says, "A map of the world that does not include Utopia is not worth even glancing at, for it leaves out the one country at which Humanity is always landing."

Every true map of the world contains utopia. We set off looking for it, and when we arrive, we find that that it is not what we desire. And so we set off again. We are driven by desire. Do we know what we desire? How do we satisfy our desire?

Do we think that the kingdom of God is just a utopia? If we cannot satisfy our desire, can we allow God to do so? How can we do that?

Questions about the Beatitudes

1. Journeying through the Beatitudes carries us out of one story into another. We move from one set of desires to another. What are the elements of the old story (call it Act I), that you experience in your life?
2. What do you imagine the new story to be like?
3. Why do you not know the new story as yet?
4. What happens when you project (call it Act II) the dynamics of the old story onto the new story?
5. What has to be given to you to start the new story?
6. What elements of that new story have already been given to you? What do you desire now, having gone through the Beatitudes?
7. What desires you?

Question about The Path Through the Beatitudes

The eight Beatitudes are listed below, along with some statements you've been given about them.

A: *The poor in spirit*:
"We are broken intellectually, emotionally, spiritually, communally."
"Poverty of spirit is liberation from illusion."

B: *Those who mourn*:
"Acknowledge the presence of the dead in our lives."
"Become conscious of the ways the dead influence our thinking and acting."
"To mourn is to enter into community."

C: *The gentle*:
"Face our own vulnerability and also the powers of this world, without becoming paralyzed or trapped by fear – our own or others'."
"To be gentle calls us to be attentive and to be responsible for the transformation of the oppressor and the oppressed."

D: *Those who hunger and thirst for justice*:
"Commit to life, not only for ourselves, but for all."
"How we treat ourselves and others manifests not only *what* we love, but *how* we love."

E: *The merciful*:
"Mercy strives to love its enemies, expecting nothing in return."
"To be merciful is to take the risk that we will be taken advantage of."

F: *The pure in heart*:
"Our deepest desire is from God and moves us to be companions of Christ."
"The pure of heart, by the simple act of being present, heal the afflicted."

G: *The peacemakers*:
"To make peace is to create community."
"The path of the peacemaker leads to the broken and hard places of our own life, community and world."

H: *The persecuted*:
"When our hearts are filled with longing for the kingdom, that longing shapes everything we do. We hold values different from the world's."
"That passion to say yes to life and to return to the marketplace bearing gifts is the Spirit."

The Path

When we enter our poverty of spirit prayerfully, we move towards liberation. In that movement we discover the traps that stop us from experiencing gratitude at being embraced by God. So we pray to be liberated from those traps, the deaths that take away our joy. As we pray to mourn, we discover more freedom. That freedom allows us to admit that there are still areas in our life where the dead have taken over and we are possessed by violence. We pray to have that violence transformed into creativity, and discover the creativity that seeks conversion of heart. When we discover our lack of conversion in so many areas, we cry out to God for mercy. Knowing what it is to be a sinner, we judge no one else. In fact, we then work to bring ourselves and all to that simple path where we acknowledge that not only we, but all, are loved and lovable. This purity of heart makes us peacemakers, makes us willing to enter into the struggle for a world where all can live their identities as "the beloved." Such a struggle is not without its sufferings, but we accept those sufferings in union with Christ and all who do good, because that creativity is the expression of our identity. It witnesses to the meaning of our lives. It allows us to restore, and re-story, the world as imagined by God.

The path through the Beatitudes makes us co-creators of the community that extends through all time and all space, and incorporates everyone and everything. Here all are loved and can share love freely and simply and joyfully. To walk this path is to open and live the gift of intimacy with a God who desires us.

4th Exercise: Repetition

Scripture verse

O Lord, you have searched me and known me,
You know when I sit down and when I rise up;
You discern my thoughts from afar.
You search out my path and my lying down,
And are acquainted with all my ways. (Psalm 139:1-3)

From the Spiritual Exercises

This exercise will consist in repeating the Previous Exercises. In doing this we should pay attention to and dwell upon those points in which we have experienced greater consolation or desolation or greater spiritual appreciation.

(Sp. Ex. #62)

Grace to be prayed for

A deep knowledge of my sins and a feeling of abhorrence for them; an understanding of the disorder of my actions, that filled with horror of them, I may amend my life and put it in order; a knowledge of the world, that filled with horror I may put away from me all that is worldly and vain. (Sp. Ex. #62)

The Three Goals of Repetition

Ignatius, as you will soon discover, uses repetitions of previous prayer materials to reinforce a point, or to achieve depth, or even to move the retreatant to a different place by exhausting his or her sense of curiosity. This allows the deeper elements of the prayer exercise to emerge.

This exercise asks you to repeat the most significant points you have discovered in the previous exercises. You need to examine what you have found in yourself, and what you need to do with what you have found. This is not an issue of mere technique. It is one of intimacy. Sin makes us avoid intimacy. There is a way of becoming disciplined so that we can enter into intimacy and maintain it. Intimacy transforms us.

The easiest way to do this is to ask what has been the most significant moment in the previous exercises, and to stay with it in prayer. If there were several significant moments, you will need to spend prayer time with each one before moving on.

The second way is to ask what has brought you closer to God (note that this does not necessarily mean what has been pleasant) in each prayer period that you have had so far, and what has taken you away from God (e.g., distractions, boredom, agitation, daydreaming, pleasant or otherwise). Going back to those moments brings us to intimacy. In the first instance, we go where the intimacy invites us to deeper intimacy. In the second instance, we return to the place where intimacy needs to happen because that experience has triggered a flight from intimacy.

Let us consider the movement of the Exercises so far. We might think of them as opening up with a wide-angle shot from a camera that slowly zooms in. It opens with cosmic disaster, the sin of the angels. Then there is the middle shot, the sin endemic to the human race. Next is the tightly focused shot, where one human sin is explored. In this exercise, the sin of just one human – you – is exposed. But this foreground shot can be seen only in the light of the background of God's passionate love for all of creation, for all of humanity, and for each of us personally. We can become truly aware of this disorder only if we are given a perspective from which to comprehend it. That perspective comes from the growing realization of the love that works to sustain creation and us as we struggle for identity, meaning, and satisfaction. Repetition aims at bringing to our consciousness this dual awareness of our sinfulness and of how we are loved. The gift of love allows us to examine our very selves with increasing close-ups, without collapsing back into that very self that is disordered. Love makes us aware that we are more than just that disordered self. Love makes us desire to shun the habits and patterns of that disordered self and of the disordered world that feeds it. And so this repetition aims for three things.

First Goal

First, it aims to give us a deep experience of our own disorders, from the new perspective of intimacy with God. We do not have to reenact or re-engage in them, but we do feel abhorrence for them. Sin traumatizes us by defining us in an obsessive-compulsive way, and by desensitizing us to the horror of what we have done. We need to re-enter those moments of trauma – this time from the context of being held in God's love – and walk through each trauma with God or Jesus as our companion. The love we now experience will make us aware of the destructive nature of what we have done, and give us a sense of horror at its effects.

Second Goal

Second, this exercise aims to help us understand those disorders – how they arise, what triggers them, how we manifest them. Filled with a horror at them, we might amend our life and allow it to be renovated by God's love. It is one thing to re-experience those moments and patterns of sin from a self-conscious perspective of being loved by God, even as we sinned, and to recall those sins. The deeper level is that of integration. That level seeks to understand the reasons why we sinned, and the patterns underlying our actions.

Third Goal

Third, this exercise aims to give a true knowledge of the nature of the world and how, filled with a horror at it, we put away from ourselves all that tends to destructive worldliness. Here we look at the ways of the world that seduce us into sinning, or trap us in sin. At this level, we ask for the grace to find out how that world operates and how we are rendered complicit in its activities.

Breaking the Cycle

These three goals ask us to look at our actual experience, at our inclinations and habits that dispose us to sin, and at the disordered contexts in which we live. We don't do this to save ourselves. We cannot, nor can we save anyone else. What we can do is pray for the grace to have a firm purpose of amendment. We pray to find ourselves so caught up in love that we can resist our inclinations to live out of any lesser desire than the desire for God. That purpose resolves itself in a hatred for what we have done, a desire to discover why we have done it so as to avoid repeating it, and a resolution not to do it again. Even if we have been sinned against, we seek to end that cycle of sin and destruction and to ask God's grace in doing this. We hold it up to be redeemed, and to transform what is destructive into what gives life. We also must understand the nature of the world that drives us to such a condition, and find out how it makes us complicit in its activities. These are the graces we pray for as we consider, at a deeper level, not our sinfulness in itself, but how we can co-operate with the merciful love of God in re-creating the world and the relationships we have damaged. This is the first step in responding lovingly to the love that we have discovered.

Ignatius does something interesting in this exercise of repetition. He encourages us to call upon those forces of love that have rejected the sin of the cosmos and the sins of humanity to intercede for us. In the spirit of humility, we first ask Mary, the Mother of God; then Jesus Christ, the Messiah; and finally, the source of life itself, the Father. Our alignment with the forces of God and the good occurs when we seek their help to obtain the graces we pray for in this exercise.

Questions for Prayer and Reflection

1. What were the significant moments of the previous prayer periods for you?
2. Can you divide these moments into consolations and desolations?
3. What happened in these prayer periods when you prayed over each of those moments?
4. Did you find you were receiving the three graces you asked for?
5. What are the sins of your life? How does sin operate in your life? How does the corruption in the world affect you?
6. What happens when you discuss the answers of these three questions with Mary, with Jesus, and with the Father?

5th Exercise: Repetition

Scripture verse

> You shall love the Lord your God with all your heart, and with all your soul, and with all your mind. This is the great and first commandment. And the second is like it, You shall love your neighbour as yourself. (Matthew 22:37-39)

From the Spiritual Exercises

> We are created to praise, reverence, and serve God our Lord, and by this means to save our souls. The other things on the face of the earth are created for us to help us attain the end for which we are created. (Sp. Ex. #23)

Grace to be prayed for

> To see, know, and love ourselves the way God sees, knows and loves us and to see, know, and love all others the way God sees, knows, and loves all.

Being Named

Ignatius asks us in this prayer period to repeat the third exercise. This repetition carries us further into self-disclosure. Maybe we need to pray to be disposed for that gift of self-recognition. Such naming is not applying a label to ourselves, nor is it accepting the labels others apply to us. It is something that reaches up from the depths of our being as it encounters a love that has been searching for it since the beginning of time. We need to sit in that profoundly contemplative space and allow that connection to be made. The naming, if it is done, is often beyond words or images. It simply resonates with a felt intimacy. Deeper than the original sin that traps us is the original grace in which we were created. More profound than the social sin that takes away our freedom is the gift of the Spirit, which is not blocked by such disorder. More creative than the power of death that destroys our bodies is the glory of the resurrection which is God's constant gift to us. We come from God and we return to God. The desire that names us is the desire for life. If we sit with our sin in prayer, we discover the life that is our life. Buddhism asks this question: What is your face before you were born? At this level of Christian prayer, we discover the answer. The experience of life is our true nature. That life is experienced as the simple, profound, and all-encompassing relationship we share with God.

We can abandon ourselves to that awe we experience there of being fully and truly known. That is the naming on the level of experience. We find ourselves as the beloved whom God desires and calls.

We find ourselves being called "the beloved." That is the naming on the level of concept. This echoes the Easter Vigil liturgy, which sees the sin of humanity, rendered archetypically in Adam and Eve, as "O happy fault," because it brings into our lives the human embodiment of God in the form of Jesus Christ.

We can find our naming in the response we now offer to the love that has found us. This can be manifest in an attitude of humility and gratitude towards this awesome mystery, whose sole desire is that we come to life and its fullness. The humility emerges from the profound awareness of our limitations, blindness, and destructive actions. The gratitude comes from that profound awareness that we are always held and loved into being.

We may also find our naming in what we do. The life that names us also defines us by what we do. The choices we make define our identity. As the famous prayer of Fr. Pedro Arrupe, a recent Father General of the Jesuits, puts it,

> Nothing is more practical than finding God,
> that is, than falling in love
> in a quite absolute, final way.
> What you are in love with,
> what seizes your imagination,
> will affect everything.
> It will decide what will get you
> out of bed in the morning,
> what you will do with your evenings,
> how to spend your weekends,
> what you read, who you know,
> what breaks your heart,
> and what amazes you with joy and gratitude.
> Fall in love; stay in love,
> and it will decide everything.

Finally, we can live love, in all of its mysterious complexity and simplicity. We let love name us and guide us in the very depths of our being. Of particular use here is the eight-fold noble path of the Buddha. Centuries before Jesus, the Buddha, following his enlightenment, devoted his life to promoting his insights into living correctly. We adapt the Buddha's insights here for a Christian context, because those insights represent eight interrelated approaches that create a wholesome spiritual path. To live an integrated life, one must have the following: right view; right thinking; right mindfulness; right speech; right action; right effort; right concentration; and right livelihood. We look at these here to clarify those aspects of our lives that are out of sync with who we are called to be. With that clarity, we can see where we still need to pray to experience God's compassionate mercy.

The Eight Practices of Wisdom

- *Right view* reminds us that we are rooted in God's love: that we are all lovable and capable of loving, no matter what situation we find ourselves in. St. Paul puts it this way: "Nothing, neither death, nor life, nor angels, nor principalities, nor things present, nor things to come, nor powers, nor height, nor depth, nor anything else in all creation, will be able to separate us from the love of God in Christ Jesus our Lord" (Romans 8:38-39).

- *Right thinking* refers to the process of reflection that arises from the experience of God's love for us, as opposed to those negative tapes of conditioning that debilitate us and alienate others. Right thinking does not ignore the real presence of evil, but knows – as Julian of Norwich knows – that "all shall be well and all manner of things shall be well." It knows that good overcomes evil and transforms it. It knows that fundamentally we are aligned to good. It knows that forms of evil, because they have separated themselves from the creativity of God, are basically deceptive.

- *Right mindfulness* is being attentive to the truth, and so discerns truth from illusion. It seeks to find God in all situations and to live in the love the Christ has for the Father. In practising right mindfulness, we have the same focus and desire as the Christ, and live fully in the gift of this presence.

- *Right speech* speaks the truth lovingly. Truth without love is a lie; and love without truth is sentimentality.
- *Right action* manifests itself in a reverence for life through generosity, responsible gestures (a gesture is an act of homage to God performed in this world), and the way we place our body as incarnate spirit. We practise right action conscious that we are the beloved of God.
- *Right effort* examines how we spend our energy. We can achieve correct effects by incorrect means. To live out of the right effort is to use correct means. As evil seeks to ensnare us ever more tightly in the webs of narcissism, right effort struggles against those ego-limitations to embrace ever more comprehensive and life-giving relationships within our communities.
- *Right concentration* is a spiritual calm that acknowledges both what passes and what abides at the same time. It is the Ignatian "indifference" that values everything as a response to God's love.
- *Right livelihood* is having an occupation that fosters our vocation to be a witness to that love.

Along with these practices is *right community*. We are not isolated individuals, but need the support of others who share our vision. The above eight practices of wisdom allow for the creation of community, which is not a given – like an address, or a selection of cronies – but allows unity in diversity.

We can make a fundamental option to live in this way, but how that will be concretely and existentially realized in our daily life will emerge in the path of intimacy we are walking. At the moment it is enough to acknowledge, joyfully and gratefully, that we have let ourselves be found by God. We can relish the delight in being found. This is the first stage of intimacy.

Questions for Prayer and Reflection

1. Where has your prayer led you?
2. Using each element of the eight-fold noble path, examine your life to see where you stand; where you are called to grow; where you are invited to be disciplined; where you need, because you may still be trapped, God's help and mercy.
3. What has been the consolation of this set of prayer periods? What does that tell you?
4. What were the desolations? What does that tell you?

6th Exercise: Hell

Scripture verse

> Whatever overcomes a person enslaves that person.
>
> (2 Peter 2:19)

From the Spiritual Exercises

> I shall also thank God for this, that up to this very moment He has shown Himself so loving and merciful to me. (Sp. Ex. #71)

Grace to be prayed for

> I should ask for what I desire. Here it will be to beg for a deep sense of the pain which the lost suffer, that if because of my faults I forget the love of the eternal Lord, at least the fear of these punishments will keep me from falling into sin.
>
> (Sp. Ex. #65)

Understanding Mysteries

This is a meditation on hell. We are asked to enter as fully as possible, imaginatively, into the realm of hell from our present perspective on life, and to use our senses to become aware of the pain that the lost suffer. From medieval times to today, popular preaching uses graphic depictions of hell as a motivation for upright behaviour. Ignatius is no different. He notes that "if because of my faults I forget the love of God, at least the fear of the pains of Hell will keep me from falling into sin." The question is this: How can a loving God allow hell to exist? The following question is similar: How can a God of love allow evil to exist and allow the effects of evil to attack the innocent? These are big questions. They raise the very real issues of our image of God, our understanding of love, and, even more radically, the limitations of our understanding to comprehend these mysteries.

Before we can enter into this meditation, we need to examine the ways we experience hell on earth. Wars and famine abound. Oppression and the brutality of self-righteous power are rife. People torture each other and treat others with disregard and prejudice. Some people find their food in garbage dumps. People experience despair, self-pity, and meaninglessness. Anger, malice, confusion, abuse, and neglect are rampant. Some practise idolatry by expecting the world to be God and sacrificing themselves to that world. We do not have to conjure up some Gothic scenario to know this. It is part of our world, our culture, our lives, and, if we dare acknowledge it, even our own hearts.

This exercise attempts to bring to light those areas in our own lives, in our own hearts, in our predispositions that prefer to accept the disorder of a fallen world and its implications rather than accept and live out of the mercy of God. Inasmuch as we live in this world, and we accept this world as it is, we not only live in hell (and, at times, hell can be comfortable), but also we contribute to it. When we experience love and reject it, or manipulate its free gifts for our own ends, we are in hell. Hell is nothing but the rejection of love. The passion of God's love is everywhere. Hell is filled with the love of God, but the lost refuse to acknowledge that love, and thus experience their rejection and the torments of that rejection. The mystery is not that hell exists, but that we can prefer to live out of such a rejection. And that is the mystery of the freedom that God offers us in his love. In fact, on whatever level it happens, falling in love is the path to becoming free.

Those Without Love

In this exercise, Ignatius asks us to consider those who have never experienced love; those who have been offered love but chose otherwise; and those who have been offered, have accepted, and have experienced love, but later reject it. One might want to consider child soldiers, whose only experience of life is brutality; or those in our culture who prefer success to relationships; or those who become afraid of intimacy and so retreat into the self-destructive security of narcissism.

But, more important, we can consider how these three dynamics operate in our own lives and look at the effects of living in such destructive ways. The prayer attempts to flush out any residual resistance we might have to accepting God's love. Of course there is resistance. If we are honest, we will realize that we will always be resistant and continue to live destructively in ways beyond our control. We can admit this. In the end, we fall upon the mercy of God, who is always willing to embrace, support, encourage, and purify us to a continually deepening love.

In becoming aware of this mercy, of allowing ourselves to experience and accept it, and in opening ourselves up to it at deeper and more comprehensive levels, we increasingly occupy the posture of gratitude and thanksgiving.

Ignatius suggests that we conclude this prayer period by allowing ourselves spontaneously to express that thanksgiving to the mystery of God we call "Abba," and to conclude with the recollected praying of the "Our Father," which expresses our relationship to the One who loves us.

Questions for Prayer and Reflection

1. Where is hell in your life?
2. How do you experience it?
3. How do you respond to it?
4. What happens when you find yourself in contact with it?
5. How does it affect you?
6. Are you helpless in those moments and situations?
7. What can you do?
8. Where is Christ in all of this? (Here you may want to recall the Elie Wiesel story of the Jewish prisoner being beaten to death in one of the prison camps while the rest were forced to watch. In one of the lines a voice whispered, "Where is God now?" Another voice answered: "Here He is – He is hanging here on this gallows.")
9. Where is the Father in all of this? Why don't you ask him where he is?
10. Have you ever experienced the mercy of God? Where? How?
11. How do you experience the mercy of the Father now?
12. How does that mercy feel?

7th Exercise: Death

Scripture verse

> God so loved the world that He gave his only Son that whoever believes in him should not perish but have eternal life. For God sent the Son into the world, not to condemn the world, but that the world might be saved through him.
>
> (John 3:16-17)

From the Spiritual Exercises

> This is to consider how God works and labours for me.
>
> (Sp. Ex. #236)

Grace to be prayed for

> To experience oneself deeply as a loved sinner.

Death Is Our Friend

Ignatius suggests two other exercises to help us experience the loving mercy of God: one on death and one on judgment. These two exercises reinforce the graces of the First Week and so are included here.

We will all die. In fact, we are dying at this very moment. Heidegger says we are being thrown towards death, and nothing can stop that process. Often our life is an attempt to ignore or deny death. The exaltation of youth as the standard for beauty, accruing power as symbolic of life, and the refusal to recognize how we deplete resources in our effort to maintain extravagant and vital lifestyles are just three ways that human beings, individually and collectively, maintain a deliberate blindness to the life cycle in nature. Such blindness leads to aggression, then frustration, and then despair. Out of that despair comes the malice of self-hatred and of vindictiveness towards others.

But we need not regard death as an enemy. Constant awareness of death allows for a calm indifference to "the slings and arrows of outrageous fortune." It allows us to examine our values and to commit ourselves to the most important ones. It helps us to relish the beauty in what is transient. It encourages us to seek for what abides under the transient. Death shows us that, ultimately, we cannot hold onto life. In Western mythology, the vampire is the one who, in trying to hold onto life, instead becomes a living death, corrupting everything and everyone who crosses its path.

But if we enter into the mercy of God, we discover that death can be a friend. Rather than being the final destination of an inconstant life, death becomes a doorway towards a greater life – resurrection, even. Moreover, as we relax more fully into the mercy of God, we begin to discover the many smaller deaths that are stations in our life so far. For example, each stage of our spiritual development involves rites of passage. In each of these pivotal moments, we leave behind the old and enter into the unknown and its uncertainties. We risk our very lives in those transitions, because we do not know what will emerge. But we emerge from that darkness and slowly become familiar with a new state of life. We establish relationships according to that new state of life. And then we are called once more to give up what was familiar and to journey forward again into the darkness, becoming light. Our spiritual journey into intimacy calls us ever forward beyond ourselves into greater life. That calling turns us always to the darkness, and the deaths it contains.

Transition Points

In this meditation, you can consider any one of those transition points in your life, and the ways you have negotiated the significant moments in that transition. You may even want to re-enter prayerfully into that time, especially if it was a difficult one, or if it left you with scars that are not yet signs of the resurrection. When you re-enter these moments, do so conscious of the mercy of God present there. Ask to be held and transformed by that mercy as you allow those images, sensations, and memories to emerge.

One significant way of entering this contemplation is to imagine our own death. We can imagine our fading powers and our growing dependence upon others; we can imagine moving beyond their phsyical help; we can imagine our own abandonment to our helplessness; we can imagine the body's struggle beyond our will to maintain itself; we can imagine its exhaustion; we can imagine it stopping. Death. But we can also imagine being surrounded by God's love, manifested in God's tangible mercy. We can imagine being supported by the saints and angels and all the powers of good, by all the people we know and love who have gone before us. They all encourage us to become one with that love and that sense of compassionate presence, which desires only the fullness of life for us.

In this prayer, we can sink into that sense of presence that shows us that no one dies alone, and that this death is a time to lay down all our burdens. It is time to trust that the Divine Presence, who has cared for all from the beginning of creation, will kindly take care of all our unfinished business. We dwell in this warm, embracing sense of presence, with its sense of light entering into the depths of our being. We allow what emerges at this time of simple dwelling to be the matter for reflection and discussion with God, who desires only that we come to the fullness of life.

Questions for Prayer and Reflection

1. How do you deal with death?
2. What experiences of death have you had?
3. How do you experience death in your world?
4. How do you react to that experience?
5. In what ways has your denial of death shaped the way you live? How has it influenced your projects and plans?
6. How have you negotiated the significant transition points of your life?
7. Is there a common pattern of behaviour to those experiences?
8. Is this the way to deal with your death?
9. What would you wish to be different? What would you keep the same?
10. Is death a friend for you? Or an enemy?
11. How can you make death a friend?
12. What happens when you imagine yourself surrounded and penetrated by God's love and light as you lie on your deathbed? Is there any unfinished business that you want God to take care of for you? Is there anything you would like to tell God or the people in your life, past and present? Is there anything you wish you had done? or left undone?
13. How do you experience God's mercy touching those areas in your prayer?

8th Exercise: Judgment

Scripture verse

> Now the word of the Lord came to me saying:
> Before I formed you in the womb I knew you,
> And before you were born I consecrated you.
>
> (Jeremiah 1:5)

From the Spiritual Exercises

> The lover gives and shares with the beloved what he possesses, or something that he has or is able to give; and vice versa, the beloved shares with the lover. (Sp. Ex. #231)

Grace to be prayed for

> To experience God's healing love pouring into the broken and damaged places of our life transforming them and integrating them into the community that is the fullness of our life.

The Lies of Evil

God has an abiding judgment of us. God judges that we are lovable and capable of loving. In all of his dealings with us, God has never deviated from that judgment. God creates in love, with love, and through love. At our very essence we are love incarnate, for we are made in God's image and likeness.

It is evil that judges us as other than God's creation, God's creatures, God's delight. In the beginning of the book of Job, Satan is described as "the accuser." It is the evil one – or, as Ignatius so aptly calls him, "the enemy of our human nature" – who judges us negatively and asks us to judge ourselves as incapable and unworthy of love.

From the life we have lived on earth, the choices we make show whether we agree with God or with Satan. In Christian mythology, at the judgment we encounter after death, we find ourselves in the presence of God. There we experience the freedom and the self-image that we have shaped with our choices in this life. We may experience ourselves as a mass of obsessive-compulsive behaviours that manifest our narcissism, or we may find ourselves acknowledging with our very lives that we are children of God, seeing God in everything and in each other and in ourselves. We may be astonished at this self-revelation and ask, "But Lord, when did we see you?" And he will reply, "When I was hungry and you fed my hunger; when I was lonely and you became community; when I was with the oppressed and you struggled to set them free; when I was with the joyful and you celebrated life with us; when I was with those who risk themselves in creating and you did not abandon me." For truly God is in all places and all times and with all peoples. Nothing and no one is left out, for God chooses freely to be committed to us.

What we see now and at the judgment emerges from who we are. At that judgment, we shall experience God as God, and we shall experience ourselves as we truly are. We can rejoice because we are finally found and are finally coming home, or we can be like Adam and Eve in the garden after they ate the forbidden fruit, hiding from themselves and from God. Even there we can trust either in our egos or in the mercy of God.

Surrounded by Saints

For this meditation, imagine that you are already dead and are surrounded by the dynamic, compassionate love of God; surrounded by all the saints and the powers of good who pour out their energy and love into us; surrounded by all those whom you love and who love you and desire only what is best for you. Allow yourself to enter into that embrace, and allow that embrace to enter into the very depth of yourself. Deeper and ever deeper. Just remain in that state of acceptance and see what happens, and how you respond. Allow whatever emerges in your awareness to come, and, without holding onto it, offer it up to that mercy who transforms everything into life. Stay with that state of presence until it ceases.

Have a conversation with the Father about what happened in that prayer period. Allow yourself to express all the things that you experienced, and discuss what you experienced with the Father. Close with the "Our Father."

Questions for Prayer and Reflection

1. What self-image do you hold now?
2. Where does that self-image come from?
3. The medieval mystic Meister Eckhart says, "The eye by which I see God is the eye by which God sees me." What do you think he means?
4. How do you experience God seeing you?
5. How do you experience God?
6. What was significant in the prayer?
7. Why was this significant?
8. What does it tell you about your relationship to God? your relationship to yourself? God's relationship to you?
9. What are the crucial elements in a relationship for you?
10. Do you experience God trusting you? How do you experience that? How does it feel?
11. How do you respond?
12. How did the prayer experience reveal you to yourself?

9th Exercise: Summary of the First Week

Scripture verse

> We know that all things work for the good of those who love the Lord. (Romans 8:28)

From the Spiritual Exercises

> [The Spiritual Exercises have] as their purpose the conquest of self and the ordering of one's life in such a way that no decision is made under the influence of any inordinate attachment. (Sp. Ex. #21)

Grace to be prayed for

> To ask the Father to show you your life as He sees it, and to rejoice in the life and in the path that is one's life.

Finding the Pattern

You have just been through the rather intense experience of the First Week of the Spiritual Exercises of St. Ignatius of Loyola. Before we continue on this spiritual journey, it is helpful to reflect on what has happened and how it has affected you. A simple way of doing this is to ask yourself the following questions:

- What has changed in me because of this experience?
- How was I before entering this journey? How am I now?
- What accounts for the difference?
- What have I learned from this experience?
- What are the graces I was given by God by opening myself up to these exercises?

Take some time to reflect on these questions before you proceed to the outlook presented below. Write your responses in your journal.

The aim of the First Week is to experience the mercy of God and achieve some self-awareness about being a sinner and yet being loved at an intimate and personal level.

This conversion dynamic seeks to liberate the self from the constraints of the ego as defined by sin operating on cosmic, human, and personal levels. What is brought to light are the illusions of the illusion that we hold to be the self. Those illusions encompass our self-image and our deeply rooted ways of seeing the world, our relationships, and even God. Some of the ways this false self we hold instinctively to be ourselves are deconstructed include the questioning of the self that is part of every exercise. This allows the prayerful reconstructions of a self exposed to God's love. What follows is our growing self-acceptance as defined by God, rather than by the traumas that create self-consciousness. Thus we pray to see, know, and love ourselves as God sees, knows, and loves us. While God calls us back to be faithful lovers, we experience ourselves as loved sinners.

People experience this pattern differently. Some find the experience of confronting themselves to be a source of desolation; others find it a relief finally to abandon the project of creating the self and to rest in God's creative mercy. Many move from desolation to consolation in this set of exercises. At first, there tends to be both conscious and unconscious resistance to the transformation that occurs as we open ourselves to God's love. There, we experience the ways the self is imprisoned, and we resist accepting those unredeemed areas of our lives. The love we encounter challenges the sense of comfort and the habitual by which we maintain our ego.

When the prayer invites us past these boundaries, we often experience as threatening or overwhelming the fear of what is "other." At the same time, we have a profound sense of entrapment and bewilderment. We are asked to remain in that sense of the unknown until we realize that we are neither destroyed nor overwhelmed by it. If we can do this, we experience both a liberation of those trapped energies and the consolation of being loved and accepted beyond ourselves. We sink into God's love and discover a renewed sense of being alive and of being amazed at the life that is given to us.

But what does all of this mean in terms of grace? First, we discover the truth of our very self, and the dynamic context of love in which all of our lives are held. We find ourselves falling in love with a God who has fallen in love with us even before we knew it. This awareness of being loved also makes us realize that we are not God, and so we become aware of our boundaries, our limitations, and our constant need for God's mercy. Moreover, as we sink into that love, we are invited to continue that journey towards even greater intimacy. The journey is both inward and outward at the same time. Inwardly, we discover more and more aspects of ourselves being loved into life. Outwardly, we are invited to share in the work of that creative love seeking to transform the world. What we discover in all of this is how we are relationship: we are related to everything, and everything is related to us. St. Ignatius had this insight when he notes that in saving others, we save ourselves. The journey into intimacy encompasses all of creation opening out to God, and experiences the love of God unceasingly at work in that creation.

Questions for Prayer and Reflection

1. How helpful has the description of the First Week been for you?
2. How has it illuminated your experience and self-understanding?
3. What was different in the description from your experience?
4. How do you explain this difference?
5. In what ways does the mystery of God remain a mystery?
6. How comfortable are you in living in such a mystery?
7. What do you feel called to do next?

Part 2

The Second Week: The Path of Spiritual Intimacy

1st Exercise: The Kingdom

Scripture verse

Happy is the one whose help is the God of Jacob,
Whose hope is in the Lord, our God,
Who made heaven and earth,
The sea and all that is in them:
Who keeps faith forever;
Who executes justice for the oppressed:
Who gives food for the hungry.
The Lord sets the prisoners free;
The Lord opens the eyes of the blind.
The Lord lifts up those who are bowed down;
The Lord loves the righteous.
The Lord watches over those who journey;
He upholds the widow and the orphan
But the ways of the wicked he brings to ruin. (Psalm 146)

From the Spiritual Exercises

Eternal God of all things, in the presence of your infinite goodness, and of Your glorious mother, and of all the saints of Your heavenly court, this is the offering of myself which I make with Your favour and help. I protest that it is my earnest desire and my deliberate choice, provided only it is for Your greater service and praise, to imitate You in bearing all wrongs and all abuse and all poverty, both actual and spiritual, should Your

> most holy majesty deign to choose and admit me to such a state and way of life. (Sp. Ex. #98)

Grace to be prayed for

> Here it will be to ask of our Lord the grace not to be deaf to His call, but prompt and diligent to accomplish His most holy will. (Sp. Ex. #91)

Becoming Engaged

We are all called to love. It is our very nature. Our very nature – who we truly are, and how we are situated in relationship to God, to others, and to the rest of creation – finds its fulfillment in loving and in being loved. It is only when that first step is radically settled and affirmed in our lives that the next step on our spiritual journey appears. How are we to manifest the love we have received that calls forth our own loving in the concrete situation of our daily lives?

At this point we may be tempted to think we can make that decision by ourselves. We figure: I have experienced the love that loves me no matter what, so whatever I do will be all right because I am doing it in love. This temptation is very subtle and insidious, because there is much truth and value in it.

But it is not the whole picture. Think of yourself as driving a car that is a wreck. You take it to a garage where it is fixed, serviced, and refuelled. Now you are on the road again. "The open road … freedom … yes, this is the life!" you might say to yourself. This analogy might describe your situation when you discover you are loved. But just because the car is now roadworthy doesn't mean your worries are over. You can still have engine trouble. You can still hit potholes. You can still fall asleep at the wheel. The idea that whatever you do will be okay is problematic for three reasons. First, it presumes that you no longer need God's grace. Second, you do not know the route that will make more effective your new-found desire to be more loving. Third, you do not yet know how to communicate with the God who loves you into an ever fuller life. Now that you are in relationship with God, you need to consult God on how to live the rest of your life. Think of this present stage in your spiritual journey in terms of a formal engagement between a couple who have fallen in love, but who still need to figure out how to live that love concretely.

During the engagement period, each learns more about the other, and accommodates plans and projects to include the other. In this stage of our journey, we risk our new-found lives to God, and God risks his fullest manifestation in creation to us. The grace we seek at this time is to enter into this developing relationship as deeply as possible. Ignatius puts it this way: "Here it will be to ask of God the grace not to be deaf to His call, but prompt and diligent to accomplish His most holy will" (#91). This is very much the stance of the lover asking the beloved, What do you want? What do you want of me? What do you want with me? What do you want for me? What do you want us to do together in this world in which we find, and lose, ourselves? We desire to give of ourselves in any way that might help.

The Cost of Loving

To enter into this contemplation, Ignatius asks us to consider how we might relate to someone who is obviously doing God's work. Ignatius believes that such a person must be "chosen by God Our Lord Himself" (#92). Many projects and enterprises claim to be from God. Many leaders use spiritual, religious, moral, and ethical arguments to validate their ways of proceeding. Often these seem persuasive; they may have the weight of public opinion or tradition on their side. But this does not necessarily make them God's chosen. In fact, when we read the Scriptures, we discover that God often chooses those who run counter to establishment values. The prophets were such people, as was Jesus. Ignatius insists that it is God who must do the choosing, not humans. Humans might try to conscript God into their own projects and dramas, but God's ways are not human ways, and the Spirit blows where it wills. The qualities we consider important – gender, religious tradition, political subscription, intellectual acuity, ethnic nationality, economic or social status – in service to God do not matter to God. Indeed, the history of God's choices shows a significant indifference to race, creed, colour, academic giftedness, sexual orientation, or economic status. What that history does show is how the chosen people give witness to the same values as God's chosen, the Christ.

All of God's chosen leaders offer a sharing of the life of service to the Father. This life of service follows the same pattern as the life of Jesus Christ. It is a life of creativity that labours and suffers, as

Christ did, to allow people to experience themselves as lovable and capable of loving. Ignatius knows that such a labour, while it gives a joy the world cannot offer, also involves suffering as we work against the forces of disorder present in ourselves, our circle of relationships, our culture, and our world.

Indeed, Ignatius does not cover up the cost of engaging in such an enterprise. This kind of love in action is not sentimental or occasional. It is battered by forces from within and without. It is hopeful without being naive, faithful without being irresponsible, compassionate without being weak. It is human with all the flaws and glories of being human, when being human asks us always to go beyond ourselves, and to move from sincerity to authenticity. We are sincere when we trust ourselves and remain within ourselves; we are authentic when we trust beyond ourselves in such a way that we are brought to a deeper and truer sense of ourselves. Our spiritual journey calls us beyond sincerity to authenticity. A spiritual leader, such as Moses guiding the Israelites out of Egypt, is one who leads us to authenticity.

Love calls us to authenticity. Love calls us to love. Love calls us to God, who is manifest in love.

Such authenticity is not possible by ourselves. We need friends, companions, partners, lovers, spouses. We need others who are committed to the same path. But more than them, we need God.

We cannot respond to God and offer ourselves to God by ourselves. We need God's constant presence and the constant presence and support of the company of those who have committed their lives to God's service. We can then make that offering of ourselves, knowing deeply and passionately that we are never alone in the struggle to bring life to a disordered time and to a disordered world.

Ignatius asks us to contemplate those whose lives witness to such a dedication. He asks us to consider how we feel when we take some time to examine one such life. He also asks us to experience our sense of a common mission with such a life, and the resulting sense of community that involvement in a common mission gives to us. He suggests that we conclude our reflection with a prayer offering ourselves to be part of that mission and community.

> O most gracious God, source of all life, I can only make this offering with your grace and your help. I make it aware of

your constant loving goodness and in the presence of all those who have dedicated their lives to you – all the forces of good in all times and in all places throughout creation, and all the saints of every tradition. My deepest wish and desire, only if it serves to build up the community of all creation, infinitely open to your never-ceasing love, is to become an intimate companion of your Son, the Christ. Then, I desire to be with him wherever he is and goes, and to share his life, his joys and sorrows, and, like him, bear all injuries and wrongs, all abuse and poverty, actual as well as spiritual, if doing that helps build up your community of love. I desire this only if you desire to choose for me such a way of life, and to receive me into that life, and, because I am weak and fickle, only if you be with me strongly in such a life.

Questions for Prayer and Reflection

1. What do you value now at this stage of your life? How are those values expressed in what you do, whom you associate with, how you plan for the future? Do you experience any tension in your values?
2. What elements in your life are in conflict with your deeper values?
3. How do you resolve these conflicts?
4. What happens when you let yourself experience the desire to do something of greater value with your life?
5. What stands in the way of your doing this?
6. When you contemplate the Christ speaking to you, what does he say and do?
7. How do you feel about that?
8. How do you see yourself as a companion of Christ, as one who shares his vision and work of being the compassionate and creative presence of the Father in the world?
9. What would your prayer of self-dedication be? (Let this come out of your prayer, rather than out of some idealized way you might see yourself or want to see the world.)
10. What is possible given your real circumstances?

2nd Exercise: The Incarnation, The Annunciation

This exercise has two parts: the Divine Presence's concern for the world and their decision to do something at the right time; and the human response of Mary at the Annunciation.

(1) The Incarnation

Scripture verse

Who is like the Lord, our God,
Who is seated on high,
Who looks far down
Upon the heaven and the earth?
He raises the poor from the dust,
And lifts the needy from the ash heap,
To make them sit with the rulers,
With the rulers of his people.
He gives the barren woman a home,
Making her the joyous mother of children.

Praise the Lord! (Psalm 113)

From the Spiritual Exercises

The Three Divine Persons look upon the whole expanse or circuit of all the earth, filled with human beings. Since they see that all are going down to hell, They decree in Their eternity that the Second Person should become man to save the human race. (Sp. Ex. #102)

Grace to be prayed for

This is to ask for what I desire. Here it will be to ask for an intimate knowledge of our Lord, who has become human for me, that I may love Him more and follow him more closely. (Sp. Ex. #103)

Imagining the World

The Spiritual Exercises of St. Ignatius expand our understanding of how we are present to ourselves, to others, and to the world. It does this is by expanding our imagination, allowing us to experience it not just as the producer of fantasy and images, but as the producer of all that is. The Hindu Scriptures say that we are like the spider. We weave our life and then move along in it. We are like the dreamer who dreams and then lives in the dream. This is true for the entire universe (Aitareya Upanishad). We live in our imagined worlds as if they were real. The First Week of the Exercises brings us to some awareness of how our imagined worlds are misconstructed by sin. The work of that First Week is to free us from the power that destroys seeing and being. The work of the Second Week of the Exercises, the Week we are now beginning, is to reconstruct our world as a companion of Christ. But to do this we first need to realize that it is within our power to do so.

If we look around, even where we are now, everything we see or feel or hear was first a product of the imagination. The process of transforming that imagined entity to a sensible reality also requires an imaginative process. When our imaginations are frozen, we end up with the notion that reality cannot be changed. When our imaginations are subverted by evil, we create distorted forms of reality. But when our imaginations are liberated by God, we imagine as God imagines, and create as God creates.

When we are trapped by sin, all we can see is sin, and the way we imagine we can free ourselves is in itself sinful. Ignatius starts his Exercises by showing us how sin traps us in ways beyond any form of self-help. One of the first steps in our liberation is realizing our radical helplessness. We cannot save ourselves. When we accept this fact, we grow to understand that, despite our helplessness, we are not destroyed. We see that there is a power at work in our lives and in our world that is larger than the forces of destruction. It is the power of love. The work of love is to liberate those trapped energies of our imagination so that we can see and experience ourselves as God sees and experiences us.

This liberation is present in the first part of this second exercise, where we are asked to imagine being in the very presence of God as the three persons of the Trinity contemplate the disordered state of our world. The divine energies of love, manifest in the Father, the Son, and the Holy Spirit, are not detached, dispassionate omni-powers. They are the fullest manifestations of an involved and concerned Love that creates constantly, sustains without ceasing, and redeems always by entering into the traps of sin and death to bring all, in Their patient wisdom, to the process of resurrection. God knows that we, and our worlds, are still being created. We are invited to co-operate in that creation. That process transforms evil into good by entering into the afflicted dimensions of creation.

Seeing as God Sees

In this contemplation, we are asked to share the perspective of the three Divine Persons of the Trinity as they look at the state of the world. They are not filled with moral disgust at the desperate state of humanity; rather, they determine the best way for us to be saved is for one of them to become one of us. In this way we can see that it is still possible – despite the terrible straits we are in, and the illusions to which we enslave ourselves – to realize our union with God. The deceptions we are mired in either suggest to us that this is not possible, or offer erroneous ways to achieve that reality. These only increase our frustration and despair. As we have already discovered, we cannot liberate ourselves. How can we be human without being mastered by sin? The question is this: How can we be ourselves and yet be beyond ourselves?

The Trinity's solution to this question is the Incarnation. God enters into the human condition, into created history, to show us that we can enter into God's condition, God's creativity, and God's very life. The Trinity offer us the gift of themselves, and they offer the way for us to receive and open, live and share that gift. They show us how to be most fully human.

Because of this action of God, we are given the opportunity to become most truly ourselves by going beyond how we see ourselves. We see ourselves with the possibilities God always sees in us and calls us to. The gift of the Incarnation, of God becoming human, allows us to become fully human. We do this by becoming companions and intimates of that human God. The gift of love, when we accept it, makes us truly loving. In love we grow in our connection to ourselves, to all others, and to God.

Questions for Prayer and Reflection

1. Do you think that reality cannot be changed? Is that because you confuse the familiar with the real?
2. What aspects of your reality would you like changed? How would those changes concretely help build up a more compassionate society?
3. Given your present situation, what are the necessary steps to do that? Are those ways within your power?
4. What would you need to help create that more human world? What gifts would those be?
5. How do you receive gifts?
6. How do you open gifts?
7. How do you use gifts?
8. How do you share your gifts? Have you ever been given a gift that you did not know existed? That you did not know how to ask for? What was it?
9. Have you ever been in love?
10. Have you ever loved anyone – not for yourself, but just for that other person?
11. What is/was it like?
12. How does it keep changing your life?
13. In this prayer period, what does it feel like to enter into the imagination of God?
14. How do you feel as you become a part of the Trinity's decision not to give up on humankind? If you were to talk to the Trinity about their decision, what would these conversations and your concerns be about?

We are invited to co-operate with God for good to happen in this world. God does not choose to work without us. Have we ever felt invited to such a thing? God enters the world through human faces, hands, and works. When God enters our world through the nativity, it happens because a human being, Mary, said yes to God's invitation. Before we consider the Nativity, we need to look at the Annunciation, which made the Nativity possible.

(2) The Annunciation

Scripture verse

Mary's prayer:

You come to me, O mysterious One, as Desire
To My deepest Desire
and I, thus found, am lost
in Your Love
You take from me All I know
except your Love
calling me beyond my life
into Your darkness
to trust you and you alone
You open my life
as a beggar's bowl
and I am attentive to what is daily given
such riches
I have not imagined
I offer what is given
the life that flows
through my emptiness
water to the thirsty
food to the hungry
a home to the dispossessed
all because I said yes
to your, first, Yes

(adapted from Luke 1:46-55)

From the Spiritual Exercises

Consider what the persons on the face of the earth do, for example, wound, kill and go down to hell. Also what the Divine Persons do, namely, work the most holy Incarnation, etc. Likewise, what the Angel and our Lady do; how the Angel carries out his office as ambassador; and how our Lady humbles herself, and offers thanks to the Divine Majesty.

(Sp. Ex. #10)

Grace to be prayed for

Here it will be to ask for an intimate knowledge of our Lord, who has become human for me, that I may love Him more and follow Him more closely.

The Risks of God

In the narratives of the Bible, God constantly risks his plans and desires with his human collaborators. This begins in the Old Testament with Adam and Eve, then moves through Abraham and Sarah, Isaac, Jacob, Joseph, Moses, David, and the chosen people. They all agreed to the covenanted relationship, but they all broke it. God chose each of them in love, and kept on risking his life with each of them. Nevertheless, God did not give up on them, and God does not give up on us. God also constantly risks his plans and desires with each of us.

In the New Testament, God's risk-taking reaches new levels. The Three Persons of the Trinity commit all of their creative plan to the free response of a politically, socially, and culturally insignificant young woman in a small village in a war-torn and occupied territory in the Middle East. They desire that she become the mother of the Word made Flesh. This has never happened before in human history. The God of all creation asks Mary, who is engaged but not yet married to Joseph, to break all the codes of orthodox religious behaviour and consent to a plan that challenges the boundaries of established sanity and conventional wisdom. The story is told in Luke 1:26-38.

In today's contemplation, you are asked to enter into the dynamics of this mystery.

The iconic depictions of Mary's response presented in Luke's gospel have been refined in order to express post-resurrection theology. But imagine a young girl's crisis when she finds herself unmarried and pregnant. How can she explain the pregnancy to her betrothed? To her family? To his family? To the village? Historically, young girls have from time immemorial become suddenly pregnant. The excuses have varied, but the reality has remained the same, and the punishments in the Middle East, as in many other cultures of the world, for bringing such shame upon one's clan are brutal.

Even before Mary agrees to co-operate with God's plan, the implications of such an act weigh in. Mary has the freedom to accept or to decline. God neither seduces nor rapes. For Mary, this is not a moment of reckless romantic abandon that no afterlife of prudent consideration will compensate for. She does not hurl herself into this act unthinkingly. Neither does she bargain. What shapes her answer is her own love story with God. Her love for God frees her to trust her entire being, and her future, to that One from whom she has accepted the gift of being the beloved. She agrees to become the mother of the Messiah.

Opening to Love

In this contemplation we are asked to do two things. First, we are asked to be as fully present as possible to God's incredible vulnerability and trust in offering the deepest mystery of his love to one of his creation. Second, we are invited to enter into Mary's profound sense of self-offering as she says yes to God's invitation. In doing so we may feel ourselves being opened by love to our very depths. We may choose in the prayer to behold Mary with God's eyes, and find ourselves profoundly grateful for that love that says yes to what it does not understand, a yes to an intimacy that will carry it to places beyond its imaginings. We may even choose to enter into the role of the angel who mediates between God and Mary, and experience what it means to be missioned and to find one's life, joy, and meaning in that service. Our entry into our annunciation is to let the desire that is our life encounter the Desire who desires us to the depths of our being. We, like Mary, or God, or the angel, experience annunciation as the expression of desire. We are asked to allow ourselves to acknowledge ourselves as that desire that wells up in us and manifests itself as the profound longing to love, and to give our lives in service to that Love who passionately and profoundly desires us. When our deepest longing encounters that simple and all-encompassing love, we enter the state of intimacy called annunciation.

To facilitate this contemplation, you might want to read the passage in Luke's gospel that describes this scene (Luke 1:26-38). Spend time with the encounter. Allow the energies of the Annunciation to touch your own energies in their desire to be part of the ongoing incarnation that occurs when we open ourselves to God in love.

The love affair that we are invited to here is willing to risk itself for us and in us. It invites us to respond – not impetuously, but freely. Where we are free, we experience love. Where we are not free, we experience the tug of compulsion. We can offer only what we have. This love, which has waited since the beginning of time for Mary to appear and to be ready, now waits for us.

Questions for Prayer and Reflection

1. Have you ever felt called in love to do something?
2. How was this different from being compelled?
3. Do you know the difference between passion and intensity? Passion calls us beyond our egos; intensity inflates those egos.
4. Have you ever waited on someone in love?
5. What is it like?
6. Have you ever experienced someone waiting on you in love? What was that like?
7. Our lives are filled with moments of annunciation. Identify some of these moments and enter into those experiences again.
8. What was the prayer you just experienced like?
9. What did it reveal to you about yourself? about God? about your path in the world?
10. If you were to have a conversation with Mary about her experience of annunciation, what would you say? What do you think she would say to you?

To say yes to love opens us up to an incredible level of vulnerability – both God's and our own – and often in contexts that are destructive. Here we are asked to trust in the Divine Providence that does not seek to have us destroyed. We must be discerning so that we can distinguish between what is good and what only appears to be good. In saying yes, we maintain our integrity in the face of the seductions towards the lesser good.

In the Nativity, we see God's providence at work in a world alienated from the greater good that desires the fullness of life for all.

3rd Exercise: The Nativity

Scripture verse

> She gave birth to her first-born son and wrapped him in swaddling cloths, and laid him in a manger, because there was no place for them in the inn. (Luke 1:7)

From the Spiritual Exercises

> Consider what [the Holy Family] are doing, for example, making the journey and labouring that our Lord may be born, in extreme poverty, and that after many labours, after hunger, thirst, heat, and cold, after insults and outrages, He might die on the cross, and all this for me. (Sp. Ex. #116)

Grace to be prayed for

> This is to ask for what I desire. Here it will be to ask for an intimate knowledge of our Lord, who has become human for me, that I may love Him more and follow Him more closely. (Sp. Ex. #104)

The Illusions of Christmas

We have sentimentalized Christmas. We have made it pretty and politically correct. We are trapped in the tug of unreality this creation imposes upon us with its saccharine depictions of peace, family harmony, Victorian cheer, and nativity crèches of pious and frozen poses. Prayer does not support such illusion; instead, it puts us in touch with the truth, of which those illusions are fragmented distortions. The contemplation on the nativity of Christ allows us to experience the mystery of the divine love, and of various forms of human love present to each other in mutual dependence in the most difficult of circumstances. It invites us to share in that reality as we now read and contemplate prayerfully Luke 2:1-14.

Between the Annunciation and Jesus' birth, Mary's life has not been settled. She has told Joseph of her condition. He decides to break their engagement quietly, and is only dissuaded from this plan by a dream. He has not been involved in Mary's original decision, yet his life, too, is turned upside down by these unique events, about which he has to make choices and commitments. Then Mary leaves to visit Elizabeth, her kinswoman, who has become pregnant in her old age. Mary cares for her and then returns home, only to set out for Bethlehem to register in the Roman census with her husband and his family. Her baby will be born soon. There, in spite of the cult of hospitality, her condition and the shame it brings upon them affords her and Joseph no space in his family homes. There is no mention of care or concern from those quarters. There is not even room in the inn. It is in the place where animals are stabled that the Christ is born.

Caring for God

Ignatius asks us to enter into that human drama of struggle and sacrifice so that love can be born. In our contemplations of the sequences leading up to and including the birth, he suggests that we make ourselves "poor, little, and unworthy servant[s] [of the holy family] gazing at them, contemplating them, and serving them in their needs ... with all possible respect and reverence" (#114). In this poverty, we imitate the Divine Word, who "did not count equality with God as something to hold onto, but emptied himself, taking on the form of a servant" (1 Philippians 2:7). That second person of the Trinity becomes poor and humble in the service of a love that desires to save us and all of creation. As we enter into that love, we find ourselves taking on its characteristics.

Mary and Joseph also take on those characteristics of self-emptying. One of the points of this contemplation, Ignatius tells us, "is to behold and consider what they are doing; for example, journeying and toiling that the Lord may be born in greatest poverty; and that after so many hardships of hunger, thirst, heat, cold, injuries, and insults, he may die on the cross! And all this for me!" (#116).

In this contemplation we witness that self-emptying love in Mary and Joseph and in their relationships with each other. Mary gives up her own personal interests and desires because of that love. God does not abandon her after the moment of annunciation. His love remains active in her world. When Joseph wants to dismiss her, God intercedes with him in his dreams, and Joseph takes Mary as his wife. That same God protects the family in their trials when the political forces of the day seek to destroy Jesus. But even with this help, their lives are not easy; rather, their lives are rooted in a love for God that goes beyond their self-interests. They respond to God's love, which, in its mysterious ways, chose them to be part of its merciful providence.

When we enter into this contemplation, we enter into all the aspects of that journey to birthing God in this world. We go with Mary and Joseph on their journey, and make it our own journey. We are present to the perils and the uncertainties of that journey, present to the care and concern they show to each other. We are present at the birth of Christ, the miracle of seeing God fully human and fully vulnerable, needing us. We can ask to hold that child and that love in our arms, in our hearts, and with our lives.

We conclude this prayer period with a conversation to the Trinity, to the Christ, or to Mary about what stirs in us during the contemplation.

Questions for Prayer and Reflection

1. How did you find this contemplation?
2. What happened to you in this contemplation? Where did it take you?
3. What was deeply personal for you in this prayer?
4. How did it feel to hold the child Jesus?
5. What did the prayer confirm in you?
6. What was the conversation at the end of the contemplation like?
7. Is there any part of the prayer that you feel called to return to because you know there is more in it for you?
8. Did you find any part of the prayer difficult or dry? Why do you think that was so? What does it tell you about yourself?

4th Exercise: The Early Life of Christ (I)

Scripture verse

> Jesus increased in wisdom and in stature, and in favour with God and man. (Luke 2:52)

From the Spiritual Exercises

> I will make myself a poor little unworthy slave, and as though present, look upon them, contemplate them, and serve them in their needs with all possible homage and reverence.
> (Sp. Ex. #114)

Grace to be prayed for

> This is to ask for what I desire. Here it will be to ask for an intimate knowledge of our Lord, who has become man for me, that I may love Him more and follow Him more closely.
> (Sp. Ex. #104)

The First Ones to See Jesus

Ignatius divides the early incidents of the life of the Christ child in the following sequence: the angels' announcement of the birth of Christ to the shepherds (Luke 2:8-20); the circumcision of Christ (Luke 2:21); the visit of the three kings (Matthew 2:1-12); the purification of Our Lady and the presentation of the Infant Jesus (Luke 2:22-38). Normally, each one of these incidents would be a prayer period in itself. The intent of each section, and of the whole sequence, is to proclaim God's mercy to the human condition. In our contemplations we are asked to find ourselves in that mercy, and so we always pray during this Week of the Exercises for that grace of "an interior knowledge of Our Lord, who became human for me, that I may love him more and follow him more closely" (#104).

It is helpful to unpack the gift we are asking for in these prayer periods. We seek an intimacy with the Christ first of all. That intimacy goes to the source of our being, where we are rooted in God. It is out of this rootedness that love flows, and it is out of this love that we discover how to follow Christ in service. The love does not create the intimacy; the prior intimacy manifests itself in love. Ignatius believes we are all mystics since we are all rooted in the mystery we call God. Sin deceives us into living out of the false notions of who we truly are. But as we enter the path of the Incarnation, we return to our depths, and there we discover our union with God, who has always been united to us. The journey through the Exercises is the path to an intimacy that includes, but goes beyond, the sensible, the emotional, the social. It is a journey that allows us to seek and find God in all that we encounter. The God we discover excludes nothing and no one.

A Politically Incorrect God

The shepherds were the first to be shown the birth of Christ. Shepherds, in Christ's time, were regarded as depraved, corrupt, and outside of the Law. They were social outcasts and considered to have less value than the animals they protected. Shepherds were the poorest of the poor. When you are poor, no one believes in you; you do not even believe in yourself. Yet it is to these that the angels came with the news of Christ's birth, and they were the first outsiders to see him in the flesh. At this point it is helpful to remember the gift of the First Week, when the divine mercy comes to those who are alienated from themselves and from others. The love we experience in this contemplation is the same love that goes out to the shepherds. Divine love desires that nothing and no one is left out of its embrace.

That divine mercy calls to all: poor and rich, wise and unlearned. It calls to the magi – those wise ones from a religious tradition other than the Jewish faith. Following their hearts' desire and using the knowledge available to them, they, too, encounter the Christ child; they worship and they offer their gifts to this tiny human manifestation of the divine. On their journey to Bethlehem, they also encounter Herod, the duplicitous, who seeks their knowledge for his own ends. But because they are under the divine mercy, they escape his wiles.

For Ignatius, God's love is not exclusive or otherworldly. It concerns itself with everyone, no matter what their state of life. The nativity story reveals a God who touches the lives of a variety of people to affirm, protect, or rescue them, or to answer their needs. Inasmuch as we, too, are touched by that divine mercy, we see, as the

Trinity does, everyone in need of love. In our desire to be one with that love, we offer freely to all, here and now, what has been given to us freely and joyfully. That love is the witness of the intimacy we share with God. The witness does not come from obligation or compulsion or ideology. It flows out of a covenant – a *cum-venio* – the coming together of God and ourselves.

Circumcision is the sign of the covenant between the Jewish people and God. When Christ is circumcized, he witnesses to that covenanted love. In being named "Jesus," he becomes the embodiment of that naming that "God saves." Where we place our bodies witnesses to what we value, and how we place our bodies incarnates those values. Among the Christmas names of Jesus is "Emmanuel" – God is with us. In the Christ child, we see a God who is one with humanity, who in human form is still the second person of the Trinity. We experience the value God places in us: he enters our human condition so that one day we can enter into God's own life. In these prayers, we ask to experience ourselves as ones who are so valued. The contemplation asks us to enter into that experience of being so valued, not just intellectually, but intimately and with all of our senses and desires. It asks us to relish that intimacy and to rest in it.

The Patience of Hope

It is this intimacy that Simeon and Anna relish when they encounter Joseph and Mary as they bring Jesus to present him in the temple. Both Simeon and Anna were devout people. They had lived through the trials of a Roman occupation and through the corruptions of Herod's religious politics without abandoning hope that one day they would experience the deliverance of Israel. They always remained faithful to God's promise, not knowing when it would be given or what form it would take. God is gracious to them in their patience and humility and long suffering. That long waiting on God teaches them discernment. It lets them see what is from God and what is not from God. Because their eyes are so opened, they can see in the ordinary baby the promise of God. That day at the temple, God rewards their patience and fidelity. They know Jesus to be that lived answer to their hope and their faith. They feel, touch, see, and hold their hearts' desire. Too often we give up our heart's desire. We accept what the world has to offer as the only reality. But our desire never gives up on us, for to do that is to die. If in this contemplation we can open ourselves to our deepest desires, to the pain and the longing, and to its promise, we, patiently waiting, discover, like Simeon and Anna, a gift that answers that longing. It is the Christ. Let us relish that gift in this contemplation.

Questions for Prayer and Reflection

1. In the contemplation, which incident was particularly meaningful for you? Why?
2. How does it feel to enter into Christ's life during your contemplations?
3. How does it feel to have Christ enter into your life during these contemplations?
4. What does this tell you about your developing relationship with God?
5. What comes up as significant in your conversations with God, or with Mary, or with Jesus at the end of the prayer period?
6. Does anything disturb you in the prayer? What? Why do you think that happens?
7. How is your prayer influencing the rest of your day or week?
8. How is the time out of prayer affecting your contemplations?
9. Do you think you are getting the grace of an intimate knowledge of the Christ from your prayer?
10. How does that grace affect you?

5th Exercise: The Early Life of Christ (2)

Scripture verse

> An angel of the Lord appeared to Joseph in a dream and said, "Rise, take the child and his mother, and flee to Egypt, and remain there till I tell you; for Herod is about to search for the child, to destroy him." (Matthew 2:13)

From the Spiritual Exercises

> It is characteristic of God and His Angels, when they act upon the soul, to give true happiness and spiritual joy, and to banish all sadness and disturbances which are caused by the enemy.
>
> It is characteristic of the evil one to fight against such happiness and consolation by proposing fallacious reasonings, subtleties, and continual deception.
>
> (Sp. Ex. #329)

Grace to be prayed for

> This is to ask for what I desire. Here it will be to ask for an intimate knowledge of our Lord, who has become man for me, that I may love Him more and follow Him more closely.
>
> (Sp. Ex. #104)

The Human Cost of Love

Until the beginning of Jesus' public life, the Scriptures mention only three incidents after the presentation of Christ in the temple. Ignatius cites these as the flight into Egypt (Matthew 2:13-18), the return from Egypt (Matthew 2:19-23), and the finding in the temple at the age of twelve (Luke 2:41-50). All three show the human cost of love: the way those who commit themselves to the Divine Life are treated in the world. Innocents are slaughtered because they are suspected of being a political threat. Jesus and his family become refugees and lead lives abandoned to Divine Providence. The contemplations based on these scripture passages destroy the notion of a sentimental God as a divine Santa Claus. They show, instead, the power of love in hard times, in the face of absurdity and worldly malice. The focus of that love is always on the primary call of the divine.

The Powers of the World

In secular terms, where reality is understood only as a worldly construct, any claim to power or authority is a challenge to the rulers of the time. Such is the case with Herod when he hears the news of Christ's birth. He is dominated by his desire to eliminate what he sees as a challenge to his authority. As local king, he orders the death of any male child born in and around Bethlehem around the time of Christ's nativity. Christ escapes that slaughter because Joseph is told in a dream to take his family and flee into Egypt. Here Matthew's story echoes the story in Genesis of Joseph the dreamer, who is sold by his brothers into slavery in Egypt, where he eventually rises to power and rescues the Israelites in a time of famine. Egypt, as we note in the book of Exodus, is place of exile and slavery. Matthew's Joseph and family become refugees, aliens in an alien land. Their commitment to God, and God's commitment to them, prevents them from being destroyed, but it does not prevent them from suffering loss, hardship, and exile. Moreover, the story also tells us the tragic cost to those families with children around Jesus' age. The presence of God's mercy in this world provokes the powers of this world to act with outrageous cruelty. No one, not even the innocent and the unwitting, are uninvolved in this cosmic human drama. All are involved, all are consumed. We, too, find ourselves in this sphere of action.

In this contemplation we encounter the forces of the divine and the energies of the despotic. We can ask, in the midst of human suffering, "Where is God?" God can also ask, "Where are you in all of this?" God shows us where he is: he is the life in the midst of death. We are asked to follow the Christ.

The return from exile occurs when Herod dies. But the hope for homecoming is dashed when Herod's equally corrupt son assumes the throne. Instead of being able to return home, Joseph, once again warned in a dream, withdraws with his family to Nazareth in Galilee, where Jesus grows up.

The Sacred Space in Every Exile

It is the dream of every exile to return home. Exiles define themselves by memory. They long for the place and the people they remember as their own. They suffer from a homesickness caused by too long an absence from all that roots them and gives them their identity. That dream and that desire become a passion – at times, even an obsession. This passion provokes a fanaticism for a homeland free of foreign influences. In Joseph's case, despite that dreadful and raw need, he remains faithful to the covenant promise of a Messiah to restore the fortunes of Israel. He waits, open to the mystery of God's provenance. His new home, he discovers, is within the relationships of Mary and Jesus, and not within the pre-established norms of clan, culture, and land.

When we enter into this contemplation, we enter into a sacred space where our own dreams and energies are realigned from clan and culture, ethnicity or ego-orientation, to our deepest passion: to be one with God. We acknowledge both what we desire from our human point of view and what God is giving us.

Even Mary and Joseph endure this human tension. They have sacrificed everything for the sake of the one they call Jesus. Yet, when the time for his ritual entrance into adulthood comes, at Passover, the twelve-year-old Jesus leaves them behind to stay in the temple. As he later tells them, "Did you not know I must be in my Father's house?" (Luke 3:49). Jesus' passionate desire is always for the Father; everything else finds meaning only in that relationship. The story foretells another Passover, some 21 years later, when the Christ's passion for his Father, and the Father's passion for the Christ, reach through the boundaries of human life and human relationships – death – to resurrection. The focus on Divine Providence that underlies the early life of Jesus, as well as his family, sets the stage for his public life and ministry.

If the earlier parts of this prayer period reveal the focus of love in a corrupt and cruel world, the prayer ends with that focus bearing in on the intimate relationships within a small family centred on the Christ. The pattern is the same: the relationship with God is of the utmost importance. It is only that intimacy that allows us to live a life of love in situations that mock the reality of a God who cares. The prayer does not lead us away from those terrible situations. Rather, it invites us to seek and find God in those places where Jesus finds himself, and us.

In this prayer you are asked to enter more and more deeply into that relationship by contemplating the early life of Christ in the world of his time.

Questions for Prayer and Reflection

1. In these prayer periods, you have been asking for the grace of "an interior knowledge of Our Lord, who became human for me, that I may love him more and follow him more closely" (#104). How has this grace been given to you?
2. What has been revealed to you about the nature of the world? How do you react to that spontaneously? How do you react to it when you travel with Christ?
3. What was the most consoling thing about this prayer? What does it tell you about yourself and about your relationship with God?
4. What has been the most negative thing about this prayer? When did it occur? What does it suggest about your values and relationships?
5. Have you ever had an experience of being alienated or separated from the people or the places you loved? How did you survive that separation?
6. Are any aspects of your life like being in exile, being a refugee, or being the pawn of forces greater than you? What are they? What forces exile you?
7. How do you deal with those aspects and those forces?
8. Can you bring those forces and those aspects to your contemplation, or to your dialogues with God?

6th Exercise: The Hidden Life

Scripture verse

> In the beginning was the Word, and the Word was with God, and the Word was God. He was in the beginning with God; all things were made through him, and without him was not anything that was made. In him was life, and the life was the light of men. The light shone in the darkness, and the darkness has not overcome it. (John 1:1-5)

From the Spiritual Exercises

> In souls that are progressing to greater perfection the action of the good angel is delicate, gentle, delightful. It may be compared to a drop of water penetrating a sponge.
>
> The action of the evil spirit upon such souls is violent, noisy, and disturbing. It may be compared to a drop of water falling upon a stone. (Sp. Ex. #335)

Grace to be prayed for

> This is to ask for what I desire. Here it will be to ask for an intimate knowledge of our Lord, who has become man for me, that I may love Him more and follow Him more closely.
> (Sp. Ex. #104)

Waiting for God

The following exercise may well be one of the most enigmatic of the prayer periods that St. Ignatius asks us to engage in. We are asked to contemplate the hidden life of Christ from age twelve to the beginning of his public ministry, when he sets off for the Jordan and is baptized by his cousin John. Nothing is written of these years except a general statement in Luke: "Jesus increased in wisdom and stature, in favour with God and man" (2:52).

People have different prayer experiences when they ask Jesus to reveal that hidden life. What is fairly common to all is that what is given deepens their personal relationship with Jesus. Each person receives what he or she needs to continue this spiritual journey to intimacy with God.

Up to now, the material of the Exercises has been contained in scripture or in a personal history. Now you are asked to enter the contemplation, in the hope that something will be given to you. This must come from God: it cannot be created by the one doing the Exercises, and yet it must completely involve that person's particular energies and concerns. It is just like someone falling in love saying to the beloved, "Tell me about yourself; tell me what you have never told anyone else." What is given is not conjecture to be verified against possible historical evidence. Its truth lies in the intimate weaving of the personal with the divine within the depths of the psyche, and is experienced through the contemplative imagination.

There is a level of intimacy in love that allows personal questions to be asked. The level of trust established allows those questions to be answered in such a way that the answer reveals both the lover and the beloved.

Here the unknown becomes known; here God makes the incarnation personal.

The relationship with God requires trust. This contemplation is about trust. From the time of the finding in the temple, when Christ announces to his world that he is about his Father's business, Christ waits on the Father to reveal how that business is to take place. At a time when young Jewish men first assume the responsibilities of their maturity – having a job, a vocation, a family of their own – Jesus waits on the Father to reveal to him the next step. He waits eighteen years. He learns to wait. This experiential learning allows him to withstand the temptations in the desert and to wait on the Father's will. That learning continues on the cross, when, in his passion and death, Christ waits on the Father to reveal his love. That revelation is resurrection. But here, in the hidden life, we contemplate a young man's waiting. And we enter into our own waiting.

Learning to Be Ready

There are many ways to wait. We can "kill" time with distractions; we can freeze time in boredom; we can suffer time in anxiety as we search for meaning, purpose, fulfillment. We can slowly learn that the patience of God is time, and so become attentive to time, like Simeon and Anna, to what is daily given. We learn to cherish each moment without grasping it. In this we learn indifference, that basic stance of doing what we can to the best of our nature, and trusting that what we do reveals our acceptance of the constant mercy of God. Through this learning, we become instruments of God, attuned to God's will. This is what it means to be contemplatives in action. It is not pious and sentimental, or intense and willful. We learn to be flexible and open so that we can delight in what is joyful, mourn with what is sorrowful, revere what is holy, shun what is destructive. We learn to live fully in the world without becoming trapped by the world and its values and judgments.

In this contemplation, we discover how Jesus learns and how he grows into that state of readiness that will allow him to hear and accept his call by the Father at his baptism in the Jordan.

What is happening to Jesus is also happening to us in this contemplation and in these Exercises. When we become intimate with Christ, we share his relationship with the Father. Like him, we grow in awareness of what that relationship is.

Questions for Prayer and Reflection

1. What happened when you entered into this contemplation? What surprised you about it?
2. What were the consolations and desolations of this contemplation?
3. How did the grace of intimacy with the Christ manifest itself to you?
4. How do you generally wait?
5. How do you view the future? with trepidation? with worry? with calm? with curiosity? with joy? How do you feel when you wake up in the morning?
6. How have you experienced time? your history?
7. How do you find your relationships with people?
8. How do you find your relationship with that mystery we call Father?
9. How do you experience your sense of sinking into an intimacy with God?
10. How does that affect you?

7th Exercise: The Two Standards

Scripture verse

Beloved, do not imitate evil but imitate good. (3 John 1:11)

From the Spiritual Exercises

St. Ignatius recommends that

1. We should approach our Lady asking her to obtain for us from her Son and Lord the grace to be able to follow Him.

2. We then ask her Son to obtain the same favour for us from the Father.

3. We beg the Father to grant us the same graces.

(Sp. Ex. #147)

Grace to be prayed for

This is to ask for what I desire. Here it will be to ask for 4 things. 1. a knowledge of the deceits of evil and how I am caught by them, 2. help to guard myself against them, 3. a knowledge of how to live truly, as shown by Christ, and 4. the grace to be like Him. (Sp. Ex. #139)

The Human Struggle

In the middle of the Exercises, when we contemplate Jesus' life and how he operates in his world, Ignatius pauses to ask us to consider how we, personally, operate. He states, "While continuing to contemplate His life, let us begin to investigate and ask in what kind of life or in what state the Divine Majesty wishes to make use of us" (#135). He suggests that we do this by first looking at the ways Christ operates and the ways "the enemy of our human nature" operates. To this end he proposes a meditation on "Two Standards" (#136). First he looks at the way we are seduced and trapped by evil. Then he looks at the way Jesus operates and asks us to follow that way. When we do evil, we operate under the Standard of Satan; when we do good, we operate under the Standard of Christ. Ignatius adapts this military image from his years in the army, where soldiers declared their allegiance to a particular cause by serving under its flag or standard.

This is not an abstract process of reflection. Ignatius realizes that we need help in discovering these things. We cannot abstract ourselves either from our good or our bad orientations to achieve these insights. And so he names four graces to pray for during this period to hammer home the individual patterns of our personality dynamics: 1) a knowledge of the deceits of the evil leader; 2) help to guard myself against them; 3) a knowledge of what gives genuine life as shown in Jesus; and 4) the grace to imitate him.

In this exercise we are not asked to choose one way of proceeding over another. Ignatius realizes that, even as we orient ourselves towards God on the path of intimacy, there are still forces, habits, and dimensions in our own lives that turn us away from the love that desires us.

People of the Lie

The simplest way of getting these insights is to consider how you behave when you feel vulnerable. We have two opposing ways of being in those situations: the way of the evil one and the way of Christ. The way of the evil one appeals to our strengths, so that we achieve the prestige and honour that the world bestows because of our own strength; this reinforces the pride of our ego. For example, when I enter a social situation where I feel uncomfortable, I withdraw into a posture of witty cynicism that comes easily to me. People react to my comments and I become the centre of attention. This justifies my belief that I need only depend on myself.

Ignatius says that we are tempted first to covet riches, so that we might more easily attain the empty honours of this world, and thus develop overweening pride. "Riches" may be material wealth. But riches also include any talent or gift or any other created thing that we have or desire and that we can use for our own ends in order to live in a way that maintains our ego. For Ignatius, the movement to narcissism keeps us from being fully human. No one is ever free from this temptation. Ignatius does not claim that riches, strengths, or gifts in themselves are bad. But holding onto them and using them to boost our self-image is dangerous. This movement and direction, which we find in ourselves and which carries us to a self-enclosed ego-maintenance, is destructive. For Ignatius, there is no such thing as a static state of being; we are all moving either to spiritual intimacy or to more and more radical forms of self-enclosure and fragmentation. We are either moving towards God or away from God. But even when we are moving towards God, we are still attracted to selfishness

In the meditation on the Two Standards, evil is shown to operate by terrorizing us and then offering us a way of coping with our terror by seductive techniques of ego-maintenance. This meditation offers us a way of discovering how our own personality dynamics respond to being presented with situations that elicit our fear.

It is very useful here to examine our personal histories to see the pattern of our basic disorder at work, and to discover how we become complicit in destruction. Awareness of this dynamic can help us overcome it. But we also need to learn other techniques to counteract these spontaneous tendencies. Ultimately, we realize that we cannot do this by ourselves; we need God's constant help and mercy. Ignatius knows, from personal experience, that this help and mercy is constantly and freely given. He knows that we are loved even when we sin, and even when we are trapped and blinded by sin. This love stops us from further self-destruction.

The Hard Road

Opposed to the seductions, manipulations, and entrapments of evil is the hard road to freedom offered by Christ. Ignatius's Christ and his followers "spread His sacred doctrine" to all, "no matter what their state or condition" (#145). Religion is not just for the rich, or just for the poor. It is for all. Everyone needs God's love. Christ's teaching and ways of life cut across any form of exclusivity. The sacred doctrine he presents is God's incarnate mercy. There is a pattern to embodying this mercy, and it all depends on God's own desire. For Ignatius, nothing should be done unless God desires it. The principle of all human action, in freedom, is God's desire. Such freedom is different from liberty. Liberty is doing what we like; freedom is living in a relationship that carries us to the fullness of life. That relationship is with God. What is to be done? The answer is "Inshallah" – "as God desires."

Within the scope of that desire, the path Christ offers is through spiritual poverty, which leads, in this world, to desire exactly what this world does not desire. In response to a life lived as the desire for God, rather than for the world, the world offers insults and contempt. Rejected by the world, we discover humility (#146). Humility is not spiritual self-abuse. Humility is living out our life in the right relationship we have with God – living in constant intimacy with a God who has created us, sustains us, protects us, loves and redeems us. When we live truly, we discover we can do nothing without God. That discovery reveals us as the poor in spirit in our utter, passionate dependence upon God. In our love affair with God, we desire only to be as his Beloved, the Christ, is, and to live the life and the path of the Beloved. This is the path of humility.

From a worldly perspective, both humility, where we reject the affirmation of the world, and spiritual poverty are difficult to desire. We are so caught up in this world that even asking for them seems masochistic, inhuman, and unnatural. The truth of the matter is we are totally and utterly dependent on God. But as our time in the First Week showed, we generally live our lives away from this basic truth. We come to that truth when we realize our radical spiritual poverty. Too often, we are so caught up with running from that understanding of ourselves that we also forget the God who creates, sustains, and redeems us. This Love does not desire our harm, but only that we be happy and become fuller and yet fuller manifestations of that love. The way we can witness to that love, and to our loving and trusting that love, is by living out of the poverty in our lives, should God so desire it. As Ignatius puts it, the call Christ makes to those who love him is that they "seek to help all, first by attracting them to the highest spiritual poverty, and should it please the Divine Majesty, and should it please Him to choose them for it, even to actual poverty" (#146).

Living Our Poverty

We do not offer to God the gift of our poverty, spiritual or material. The reality of our spiritual poverty is the human condition; the gift of actual poverty is what God also offers to some. This gift is not the imposition of poverty through personal misfortune, social injustice, the economic imbalance of nations, or the results of global imperialism. Those are evils. Actual poverty is the choice of a lifestyle we make freely, desiring only God's love and to live out of God's loving providence in this world. We choose this only if we are confirmed that God desires this for us. Anything else is spiritual pride masquerading as poverty. Should God desire it, we are offered the option of choosing actual poverty. We do not let poverty choose us. In choosing actual poverty, freely, we witness to the world that we are willing to be radically dependent on God for all we need to live joyfully in this world, knowing fully well that such poverty leaves us open to be trampled by those forces that strive to dominate the world.

When we live out of the very poverty that is the centre of our being, we quickly discover that we do not live out of the values of this world. In fact, our path becomes offensive to the world. It responds with pity, condescension, contempt, insults, mockery, neglect, abuse, abandonment. Instead of the trappings of honour and prestige that the world so delights in, some wear the tatters of humiliation. In this they identify with Jesus, who was also insulted, treated with contempt, humiliated. This identification with the beloved is important. We do not choose insults and reproaches, we choose Christ. We choose to be as Christ was and is in this world. We choose to be with the poor of Christ in this world. They are our community because they share with us the vision and the desire of a radical intimacy with God.

To look for insults and injury while we maintain purely worldly values is to be sick and self-destructive. That is not what God desires. God desires that we be holy. Holiness comes when, instead of fleeing from the full awareness of our poverty, we embrace it, and through it see our path to God with new eyes. We have, in the examples of saints and holy people of all spiritual traditions, this rejection of the values of the world while living in the world. And we have the long tradition of their ill treatment at the hands of the world throughout human history in various cultures and religions.

That ill treatment from the world engenders a profound humility. In humility, the ego does not have to defend itself. In humility we live every day totally and intentionally dependent on God and on the compassionate manifestions of goodness in the world. We wait on God, and on the providence of God. We see everything given as a gift to be opened. We discover the presence of God. Every moment offers an entry into the divine. Then our lives become an open space through which God enters into the world, and the pain of the world encounters the compassionate mercy of God. In humility, we accept that we are God's beloved and we live our lives in that love.

In the eyes of the world, this is sheer folly. But we celebrate our gift of being God's fools.

The Pattern of Our Choices

The meditation on the Two Standards allows us to see graphically in our own lives the choice that opens to us at every moment of our life, whether we are conscious of it or not. In our vulnerability, we can take up either the standard of evil or the standard of Christ. If we take up the standard of evil, we are led through coveting riches to honour and pride. If we accept the standard of Christ, we are offered poverty and, through that, the displeasure of the world, and so reach humility. The choice is ours.

Ignatius realizes that this is a difficult and subtle meditation. He suggests that we do it four times so we can realize the graces we are asking for in this prayer. Those graces are first, to understand truly how we get trapped; second, to receive help to escape those traps; third, to understand how Christ behaves; and, fourth, to ask for and receive the grace to follow him.

This prayer is not a pious exercise. It seeks to reveal the dynamic core of our being and our behaviour patterns. The resistance to that revelation is strong. God's love for us, however, is stronger.

We need to draw on all the help we can to achieve the graces we seek in this prayer. The Spiritual Exercises suggests that we seek the help of Mary, the mother of Jesus, then Jesus, and finally the Father, by discussing with them what we need and what arises when we enter fully into this prayer.

Questions for Prayer and Reflection

1. How do you spontaneously react when you are vulnerable?
2. What are your "riches," "honour," "pride"? How do they manifest themselves?
3. What is your "poverty"? How do you deal with your poverty? Have you ever found God in your poverty?
4. What happens when you pray to be identified with Jesus as he is insulted and held in contempt?
5. How do you live your humility? How does it shape the way you see and deal with others?

6. How does it affect your relationship with the things you possess?
7. What happened in your prayer that was consoling? What does this tell you?
8. What happened in your prayer that was negative? What does this tell you?
9. What happened in your conversations at the end of the prayer with Mary, Jesus, and the Father?
10. As you prepare to repeat this prayer, what areas do you feel the need to focus on?
11. Were the graces you prayed for given? How? How did you receive them?
12. How does this prayer relate to your earlier prayers of this Second Week?

8th Exercise: The Three Classes of People

Scripture verse

> Behold, I have set before you an open door, which no one is able to shut; I know you have but little power, and yet you have kept my word and have not denied my name.
>
> (Revelation 3:8)

From the Spiritual Exercises

> Here it will be to behold myself standing in the presence of God our Lord and of all His saints that I may know and desire what is more pleasing to His Divine Goodness. (Sp. Ex. #151)

Grace to be prayed for

> Here it will be to beg for the grace to choose what is more for the glory of His Divine Majesty and the salvation of my soul.
>
> (Sp. Ex. #152)

Our Choices Define Who We Are

In spiritual terms, people can be divided into three groups: a) those who do not care one way or the other about God, b) those who want God to support them in their schemes, and c) those who desire to follow God. Each of us combines elements of all three types. Depending on the circumstances, we behave in one of these three ways. This is because our lives are fragmented. The path of intimacy that we are walking seeks to orient all aspects of our lives in one direction: facing God. Each of us must decide in the choices we make how we will relate to God. It is not what we have, but the choices we make with what we have, that define who we are. Those choices show how we embody our deepest desire in our daily lives.

Let's look a little more closely at these three different types of people. The first group does not pursue a relationship with God, for a variety of reasons, some of which are valid ones. So the relationship never gets expressed. It is rather like being in love with someone and not admitting it to yourself, not declaring your love to that person, not doing anything about it. The relationship remains unacknowledged and undeveloped. People who live this way are not concerned with sincerity or authenticity. They operate according to an existential pragmatism that asks and answers these questions: What is the next step? What is to be done? Other people function simply to facilitate that next step.

The second type of person admits to being in love, but that love is defined only by personal needs. This person is sincere, and so, being true only to the self, lives to satisfy those needs and demands. The beloved must do and live only as the person in love wants the beloved to live. This type of love manifests itself in jealousy, or narcissism. The beloved has no individual life, but instead must live as the lover's idealized projection. Abusive relationships often arise from such selfishness. This second type of person treats others, and God, as objects to be manipulated for immediate satisfaction. Often we think God treats us in that same way. That is because we do not allow ourselves to experience the freedom God gives, which includes the choice to turn away from God. If it seems that God acts as this second type of person does, this means we are the same type, and have projected upon God our own notions of relationship and intimacy. We avoid, then, the mutuality of a love that allows both God and ourselves to be free.

The third type of person is committed to the beloved and lives out of that commitment in a responsible way. People of this type "seek to will or not will as God our Lord inspires them, and as seems better for the service and praise of the Divine Majesty" (#155). Because of the mutuality of the intimacy they share with God, they enter the process of discernment about their choices. They seek to love responsibly in the concrete circumstances of their lives so that neither they, nor anyone else, nor the witness to God's love are destroyed as a result of their choices. Their intimacy with God gives them a spiritual literacy. They discover how they speak to God, and how God speaks to them. Together they develop ways of communicating with each other and of being together that allow choices that build up the community of love we call the kingdom of God.

Of course, all of us would claim that we want to love in a way that brings life to those involved with us. "Love" is a much overworked word. It means different things to each of these three types of people we have been reflecting on. Each would claim to act lovingly. For each, the greater good has different connotations. It really is difficult to achieve true self-awareness of what we mean by "love" in our daily lives. Ignatius suggests that instead of looking at love, we look at how we would use riches – money or talent – that we have received. Cunningly, Ignatius suggests that we consider the means by which we have acquired those riches, to be disposed for the love of God, to be somewhat suspect (#150). Those riches are not ours by natural right or by law. Ignatius knows that our gifts are just that. They are not us. They are distinct from us, and the distance between us and them means we have to make conscious choices how to use them We know we should use them for good, because we do not want to be selfish. Having completed the First Week of the Exercises, we know selfishness traps and destroys us, and we want to avoid that trap. But we also know we are not free from the tendencies to selfishness.

Facing Selfishness

The first type of person, unable to decide how to avoid being selfish, does nothing and so remains selfish. The second type of person makes the decision to be selfish and seeks to have God justify that selfishness. The third type of person is concerned only with making the best use of the gift. If the best use is seen as selfish by others, that is not their concern. If that best use is seen as wonderfully philanthropic by others, that also is not their concern. That person wants only to better serve and praise God as a gesture of gratitude for the love freely given and received. The person here does not act out of contractual obligation or moral duty. The intimacy in the relationship sees the giving and receiving as a gift.

This exercise is not about making a decision. It is about the intimacy needed in order to make a correct decision. St. Augustine sums up this attitude in his precept "Love and do what you will." St. Ignatius asks, "But what do you love?" What you will shows what you love. Your will-ing is your love in action. When you see where your will has led you, then you will see whom and what you love.

Whom you love and what you love may not love you. In fact, the expression of your desires may even destroy you. This is what happened to Christ. Why you love what you love is crucial. Jesus loves us as an expression of his love for the Father. In his love for the Father, who loves us to the depths of our being, Jesus is willing to be fully present to the alien forces of creation that seek to destroy us. He chooses a path that leads through death, not out of a love for death, but out of his passionate desire to show us that same path through death towards the fullness of life. So it is not just a question of loving, but of loving for the right reasons. We love as an expression of spiritual intimacy. The grace we seek in the present stage of the spiritual journey we are on is for "an intimate knowledge of our Lord, who has become man for me, that I may love Him more and follow Him more closely" (Sp. Ex. #104). This intimacy manifests itself in a love shown in concrete acts of service.

If we are passionate for God and allow God to be passionate for us – as Christ is passionate for the Father, and the Father is passionate for Christ, and for us – then we become indifferent to all created things. We desire only what God desires. This does not mean we are passive or wishy-washy. It means we see and hold all things within the dynamism of that love that loves us intimately and totally.

While we may agree wholeheartedly with this approach, and find it very moving, it is very difficult to give up our self-will and to value things and other people only within the mutual love between God and us. St. Ignatius suggests that when we find this difficult, we should beg God to give us the freedom and the grace to work against those desires that limit us, and to come to the position of loving as God loves.

Questions for Prayer and Reflection

1. When have you been unable to make a decision? Why did that happen? How did it affect you?
2. When have you spontaneously expected the world, others, and even God to agree with your plans and desires? How did you try to manipulate those situations to meet your own needs? What happened when things did not go according to your plan?

3. When have you given yourself over unreflectively to a mood, a situation, another person, a political position, or social or cultural values because you felt it was the right thing to do?
4. In what ways have you loved? In what ways have what you loved not been in your best interests?
5. Have you ever loved in a way that you found life and brought life to one or more persons?
6. Did that loving involve any sacrifice? How did you deal with that sacrifice?
7. If you are in a relationship now, how do you communicate with each other? How do you make decisions together? What are the tensions in that relationship that create difficulty in making decisions together? How do you resolve those tensions to make good decisions?

9th Exercise: The Three Degrees of Humility

Scripture verse

> Have this mind among yourselves, which you have in Christ Jesus, who, though he was in the form of God, did not count equality with God a thing to be grasped, but emptied himself, taking the form of a servant, being born in the likeness of men. And being found in human form he humbled himself and became obedient unto death, even death on the cross.
> (Philippians 2:5-8)

From the Spiritual Exercises

> I desire and choose poverty with Christ poor, rather than riches; insults with Christ loaded with them, rather than honours; I desire to be accounted as worthless and a fool for Christ, rather than be esteemed as wise and prudent in this world. So Christ was treated before me. (Sp. Ex. #167)

Grace to be prayed for

> They should beg our Lord to deign to choose them for this third kind of humility, which is higher and better, that they might the more imitate and serve Him, provided equal or greater praise and service be given to the Divine Majesty.
> (Sp. Ex. #168)

Being Human

The word "human" comes from the Latin word *humus*, meaning earth or soil. The word "humility" comes from that same root. To be human is to be humble. To be demonic is not to be humble, for then one is filled with pride and sets oneself up as a god. To be humble is to understand ourselves profoundly as creatures, born of the soil but loved by God. How we live as humans depends both on our awareness of ourselves as creatures and on how deeply we love.

Ignatius asks us to consider this exercise as a development of the previous one, where he had asked us to pray for the grace to love.

In this exercise, he asks us to pray for the grace to love as deeply and passionately as Christ loves. He sees this approach, which he calls the third degree of humility, as the most perfect way of being human.

Love and Goodness

The first degree of humility is to love as a good person. That person lives with integrity, is respectful of other people and of creation, and loves God. Such an individual is ethical, moral, and upright; does not do wrong but lives in a way that maintains essential relationships; admits limitations and boundaries and lives within them. This, admittedly, is a very high standard of morality, and most of us, if we are honest with ourselves, reach this level of commitment only in certain areas of our lives and at certain times. For the rest, we find ourselves caught in ambiguity and compromise. We acknowledge we are sinners and, in spite of our occasional best efforts, get trapped by our own disorders and by the disorders of the world. We can even acknowledge we are so trapped as to be blind, for the most part, to the ways we destroy ourselves, others, or the world. For example, we can maintain a standard of living that does violence to the resources of the planet, or live a stressful lifestyle that damages our bodies and our spirits, and think this is normal or mature or acceptable. This is not to say that we are not good people. We are. We are good people living at the first level of humility.

Love and Detachment

The second degree of humility moves away from a certain lack of reflectivity that ignores a greater spiritual good. It seeks to become aware of what blinds us at the first level, and to try to become indifferent to those things that we would normally value as good. Ignatius gives us some examples of these. He says, "As far as we are concerned, we should not prefer health to sickness, riches to poverty, honour to dishonour, a long life to a short life" (#23).

Now, this is quite radical. No one wants to be sick or poor or despised or to die without having lived enough. What Ignatius knows, from his own life, and what we know from examining the lives of the saints, is that illness can be a blessing. It was only when Ignatius fell ill that he started his quest for God; indeed, illness shows us the radical limitations of the self to control and maintain life. Similarly, we can learn that riches cannot buy happiness, and that in poverty we may discover a freedom to use our energies in more life-giving ways. We will also find, as we mature spiritually, that loving relationships, not the prestige of the world, establish our identity, and a loving relationship with God takes away our fear of death.

Here Ignatius is not asking us to choose poverty, or sickness, or dishonour, or a short life. He is merely asking us to be indifferent to these things. To be indifferent is to be so passionate only for God that we desire only those things that will maintain that loving relationship. We value whatever we have only inasmuch as it helps that relationship deepen. It might well be that riches or health foster a vital relationship with God. In that case, we should actively cultivate them. The second degree of humility describes the attitude of mind that seeks only God, and seeks everything else only as it can help that relationship with God. This sensitivity is not just theoretical: it manifests itself actively in what we do and how we live.

Love and Passion

The third degree of humility is grounded on the first and second. It asks us not to be indifferent to poverty or dishonour, but to choose them: not for themselves (since they are just "creatures"), but in solidarity with Christ's poor and suffering, and in a lover's identification with the condition of the Beloved, the Christ, in this world. Moreover, that choice is made only if it gives greater praise and service to God.

This third way of loving is more than just a witness for God in a socially conventional manner. It means showing with our very lives our abiding trust in Divine Providence that the love to which we give ourselves will not abandon or destroy us. It means putting our lives where the beloved has put his life. Christ, the beloved, lives a passionate intimacy with the Father. In his daily life, public or hidden, he waits on the Father for all he needs. Similarly, in that mutual self-giving, the Father gives the Christ all that is necessary for him to walk his human path back to the fullness of life. We, too, in this third degree of humility, are invited to a similar path and a similar passion.

In the great hymn in Philippians 2:1-11, we are told that the Christ did not count equality with God as something to be held onto, but rather emptied himself, "taking on the form of a servant," and became one like us. He went even further, because as a human he "humbled himself and became obedient even unto death" – that shameful death on a cross.

Ignatius does not present an incarnate Christ who is a triumphalistic or autocratic human being. Rather, he presents a Christ who manifests himself in humble service to the mystery we call Father. He suggests that the highest form of human love is in identifying with the beloved in a similar manner. He offers to us the possibility of praying for that identification in the third level of humility, which says, "I want to be so like you that I am willing to live as you lived, love as you loved, suffer as you suffered." It says, "I am willing to share your life with those who are poor and suffering and dishonoured, neglected, mocked, ignored." It says, "I am willing, if you want me to, to become one of them and to live the fate of one of them because you loved me that much and because I, too, love you as you have loved me." This is not the path of the hero or the masochist. This is the path of the saint and the mystic. We are all called, every one of us, in our own ways, to be saints and mystics, for they express most fully what it means to be human and our response to having every aspect of our being loved totally, intimately, and passionately.

Questions for Prayer and Reflection

1. Have you reached even that first level of humility?
2. How do you respond to God's love knowing that you are a sinner?
3. Does an awareness of your sinfulness stop you from loving as fully as you dare?
4. How do you experience the urges to love more? How do you embody them without being imprudent or naive?
5. How does your culture condition you to accept yourself as it defines you? How do you break out of that conditioning? What helps you move beyond those definitions of yourself? How does it feel to live in those spaces beyond cultural definition?
6. Who are the saints that inspire you? How do they do that?
7. Who do you know who lives (or tries to live) that third level of humility today?
8. What happens to you when you consider living radically out of God's love?

9. What happens to you when you ask someone – such as Mary, the mother of Jesus, then Jesus himself, then the mystery Jesus calls his "Father" – for the love to live and love as fully as they love you?
10. What do Mary, Jesus, and the Father say to you in that prayer? How do you experience that prayer?

10th Exercise: Discernment

Scripture verse

None of us lives to ourself, and none of us dies to ourself. If we live we live to the Lord, and if we die, we die to the Lord; so then, whether we live or whether we die, we are the Lord's. (Romans 14:7-9)

From the Spiritual Exercises

In every good choice, as far as depends on us, our intentions must be simple. I must consider only the end for which I am created, that is, for the praise of God our Lord and for the salvation of my soul. Hence, whatever I choose must help me to this end for which I am created. (Sp. Ex. #169)

Grace to be prayed for

To seek to find and serve God in all things. (Sp. Ex. #233)

Seeking a Heart to Understand

We all want to love passionately and choose rightly. But we realize that not only do we lack all the facts necessary for the perfect choice, but also our perceptions of the facts can be biased by our disorders. Still, we must choose. Every day we make myriad decisions – major and minor – that determine the shape of our lives. With major ones, we become a little more conscious of the decision-making process. Each of us has our own way of making a decision. We collect facts, get insights, have intuitions, weigh the pros and cons, look for signs of rightness, ask friends for advice, or pray for God's help. We try to get into the right "space" to make a correct choice.

Sometimes, the right decision comes to us clearly and simply. Sometimes we have to find a quiet place and settle down to see what emerges from our deliberations. Sometimes we must project ourselves imaginatively into living that decision and foreseeing the outcome. Sometimes we ask God to show us the way. Whatever we do, every decision is a risk and a creative moment. We set out on a path we have not walked before.

What is a discernment and how does it differ from a decision? The two are different, even though the result might look the same. A decision is not necessarily a deliberate, self-conscious choice, and it does not necessarily occur in the context of prayer. Discernment does both. With discernment, we enter into a dialogue with God after establishing a right relationship. In that mutual sharing and trust, an answer emerges. Then we not only see as God sees, but we act as we believe God would want us to act.

So far in these Exercises, we have been establishing that right relationship with God, discovering how God communicates with us personally through our feelings and our history. We are becoming aware of how we operate, so that we know when we are being tempted to narcissism or being invited to self-transcendence. Now Ignatius is asking us to discern a life path, or a step on our pilgrim journey through life.

Making Correct Discernments

For St. Ignatius, correct discernments always move us towards God, community, and each other, as well as integrating the different aspects of ourselves. But, like any other discernment, we need to check them out to see whether they are valid or illusory. This takes time. The time given to us is the time of the retreat. If we have a decision we want to discern, we can take it with us as we journey through the rest of these Exercises. We can bring that decision into prayer and the reflection questions. Does that decision hold up to the relationship we form with Christ as we continue our journey? A good decision will draw us closer to Christ and identify us with him. A bad decision will alienate us from the Christ, put us at odds with our deepest desires, and separate us from the best elements in our community.

If we are called to make a decision at this moment, we might want to use some of the suggestions found at the beginning of this exercise. If we have made a decision and want to verify it, we can bring it along as we journey through the rest of the Exercises. This will transform the decision into a discernment. If there is no decision to make or verify, we can still deepen our intimacy with God as we continue. What we need to remember is that, as we are searching for God, God is searching for us. We will experience God's search for us in terms of that mercy and concern we can acknowledge in our path.

Whatever decisions we make, we are always held in God's loving mercy. That mercy has the power to transform the deadly effects of bad decisions into opportunities for resurrection. It has the power to affirm good decisions by celebrating the life it brings.

Questions for Prayer and Reflection

1. How do you generally make decisions? How have they differed from the discernments you have made? Has involving God made a difference?
2. How have you made significant decisions in your life so far?
3. Of those significant decisions, how have you made the ones that have brought you life? How have you made those that have been destructive?
4. What does this tell you about the way to make good decisions?
5. Is there any discernment that you need to make with God now? How will you two go about it?
6. Where does God feature in that process? How has God featured in your good decision-making process? Can you approach God in the same way this time?
7. When you pray about your life, what is God is telling you about it?

Discernments and the Path

We are on a spiritual journey. On that journey, different paths open to us. When we look back on our lives, we see that the choices we have made, and the choices that have been made for us, have led us to this moment. Those choices have made us who we are, and we are unfinished business. We are still in the process of being created. We can co-operate in that creation by what we do. Often our doing is not conscious. We operate by habit and by conventions. They set our attitudes, and our attitudes determine the possibilities open to us. At almost every moment of our lives we make choices, unaware that we are doing so. Sometimes our paths are determined by one of those moments. Only later do we see the significance of that moment.

At other times we are very aware that we have come to a place where we must make a choice. Choice implies risk. Because we then enter unknown territory, we become very attentive to the things around us and within us in order to ascertain the right decision. We know whatever we choose means giving up certain things and accepting others. Each possible path has advantages and disadvantages from our present perspective. But sometimes we do not even know whether something is an advantage or a disadvantage. Then we try to reach a level of awareness that allows us to see correctly, judge wisely, and choose what will satisfy our deepest desire. The choice is a door into the darkness. We do not know what we will encounter on the path that opens to us, and there is no turning back. We can and do make mistakes. But we know from experience that some of these choices have brought us life, joy, and freedom. So what do we do? How do we choose? What are we to hold as most valuable when we assess the pros and cons of possible decisions?

We know that ultimately God can transform even the effects of bad decisions, and we have already experienced the mercy of God in saving us even when we were in situations that were destructive. So what are we doing when we discern?

What discernments do, first of all, is witness to the relationship we have with God. They are covenant moments. The choices we wish to make will be the expression of our intimacy with God. We might simply think what we are seeking is what is best for us. But the best for us is what satisfies our deepest desire in concrete situations. These choices give "praise, reverence, and service" to God, but not in an ideological or programmatic manner that has as a propaganda slogan "This is being done for God!"

Rather, such choices reveal our attitude of being disposed to God and for God. As such they give praise. The praise they offer is that of a being willing to be disposed by God. The choice is a gesture towards God, acknowledging that I am a sinner. I can and do make mistakes. I often fall from the path. But I love you. What I choose to do in this situation, I do out of that love for you, knowing that you will not allow me to destroy myself. The gesture arises out of humility and a sense of dependence on God. It is carried out trusting God for whatever we need to live out the discernment. This attitude arises from the intimacy we have with God. The discernment is the expression of gratitude at having been found by God in this particular moment in our lives.

This attitude manifests itself in a stance of reverence and respect for God. The reverence here is a posture of seeking God in all things, and seeking to please God in all things. Like the widow putting her mite in the treasury, what we do is very little, but how we do it is important. How we behave in the world and in our daily life reveals our disposition to God. This creation is maintained by God's goodness. As creatures, we who are a part of that creation reveal our intimacy with God by the way we relate to his creation. The level of intimacy creates the posture we spontaneously assume. This is not a matter of liturgical correctness or cultural decorum. It is an act of adoration. It witnesses to the passion we, like Christ in the world, have for the Father.

We demonstrate that passion in acts of service that build up the community of love that is the Body of Christ. These acts of service that are the discernment in action say, "I am doing this because I believe that you, my God, has shown me this is the best thing to be done at this time in history in the ongoing struggle of good against evil." They manifest our commitment to that struggle as co-creators of the kingdom of God.

God's commitment in a discernment is to maintain the relationship with us as we live out our choice. This is the fidelity of God. We cannot undertake to live out our discernments by ourselves. That is impossible. Our commitment is also to maintain that relationship so that the discernment can take root and open further the path of intimacy. Sometimes we make a discernment, but do not maintain the intimacy with God in which the decision was made. Like Israel in the Old Testament, we break the covenant. We stray from that relationship or from the ways in which we might help maintain it. As a result, our commitment ceases, and our way of living changes. In this new state, we again find ourselves living in circumstances that call for God's mercy. Then we again seek to be redeemed. We may seek a new covenant in our changed circumstances.

We can make and live out correct discernments only in freedom, and those discernments can be effective only if we maintain the relationship with God in which they were made. When we discern, we have expectations about the way the discernment will work out in our lives. We often find that what happens as we live out of the discernment is quite different from what we imagined. This does not mean that the discernment was wrong. The meaning of the discernment changes at different stages of our journey.

We may fall in love and decide to live our life in a certain way. As we walk in that way, we change. We find that, from one stage to the next, we give up how we understand ourselves, or how we saw God, or even how we understood the meaning of the discernment. But we hold on to the relationship that allowed the discernment to happen. As the relationship changes, even our understanding of relationship changes. The intimacy of friends is different from the intimacy of lovers, and that is different from the intimacy of newlyweds. Their intimacy is different from that of a married couple with children, and an old couple understand and express their mutuality in ways that are different still from those bringing up a family. The same is true for the spiritual journey. The discernments that manifest themselves in covenant moments do not reveal their full meaning at those moments. As the journey progresses, the understanding of those moments changes.

Discerning does not guarantee us success in the eyes of the world, nor security, nor acceptance. Discernments do not make our path through the world any easier than Christ's. Discernments do not take away God's freedom or our own. What they do is open the path to intimacy where we discover, in new and often surprising ways, how we are God's beloved.

Questions for Prayer and Reflection

1. Can you recall covenant moments in your life? How have they defined your spiritual path?
2. Have these moments led to a greater intimacy with God?
3. How has your sense of intimacy changed because of them?
4. How does this manifest in your understanding of yourself? in your relationship with others?

11th Exercise: The Baptism of Jesus

Scripture verse

> This is my beloved Son with whom I am well pleased.
> (Matthew 3:17)

From the Spiritual Exercises

> It is more suitable and much better that the Creator and Lord in person communicate Himself to the devout soul in quest of the divine will, that He may inflame it with His love and praise, and dispose it for the way in which it could better serve God in the future. (Sp. Ex. #15)

Grace to be prayed for

> This is to ask for what I desire. Here it will be to ask for an intimate knowledge of our Lord, who has become man for me, that I may love Him more and follow Him more closely.
> (Sp. Ex. #104)

Living out of a Love that Trusts

All any spiritual discipline does is dispose us to God. It signals to God that we are willing to enter into a relationship with the divine. It cannot compel that relationship to happen. Similarly, spiritual techniques and rituals can facilitate the relationship with the holy, but they can never substitute for the holy. They cannot compel the holy to be present to us in ways we find useful. The same thing can be said about the Spiritual Exercises, or any other prayer. They do not make God present; they are merely a way of presenting ourselves to God. This is what happens to Christ. He loves the Father and disposes himself to the Father, but he cannot compel the Father to act before his time or in ways that are opposed to his mystery. Love does not force love; love trusts love and expects love to be loving. Christ lives out of that trust and that love.

After his presentation in the temple at age twelve, when he declares he must be about his Father's business, Christ receives no confirmation about what he is to do for the next eighteen years. He waits on God for the next step. He waits for God. We do not know just how that waiting shapes him. We can imagine him learning patience; putting up with the growing concern of his relatives that "he has not found himself"; and even working to understand what it means to be a just person in his religious tradition, without ever having affirmed at the root of his being what he intuits about himself. Because he is human, we can relate to his questioning who he is, his brooding about what others have told him about himself, his self-doubts, his sense of being special.

And then, one day, something happens. Jesus goes down to the river Jordan where his cousin John, an itinerant preacher, is preaching and baptizing. Jesus is baptized and experiences an epiphany. He receives his call when the Father says, "This is my beloved Son, with whom I am well pleased" (Matthew 3:13-17). The call is given not in terms of a plan of action, but as a relationship of love, of generation. Jesus is acknowledged as the Father's son, and as the beloved who pleases his Father well.

When we are called to love, we are called to relationship. Each of us is loved for who we are, not for what we do. It is the other in the relationship who acknowledges us. This is pure gift. We can dispose ourselves to the possibility of its happening, but how it happens, and when, where, why, and how, is beyond our control. We fall in love with someone and discover we are loved in return. We discover we are in love with God and experience God loving us.

What's in a Name?

Only after we have received that gift and accepted it can we name it, for it occurs at the core of our being. It takes time before we even realize what has happened. It takes more time to accept it and to live out of that wonder. It takes even more time to let that love name us and to discover our own name for that love, which now nourishes and enlightens us. It affirms that the core of our being is united to the source of all life, the Mystery Jesus calls "Father." That Mystery roots us. We know we are created by God, sustained by God, and transformed by God. But to be rooted is to be carried to deeper levels of relationship that struggle for words to express them. This is what Christ experienced at his baptism in the Jordan; God declares Jesus to be "my beloved Son." It is what we experience when God calls us by name. This naming does more than the names our parents and families bestow on us – it establishes our place in the structures and dynamics of creation. For this reason, names are sacred in spirituality: they tell us how we are holy.

In our lives, various incidents name us. When we are born, we receive not only our family name but "given" names – the names of ancestors, saints, or other significant people. We may have a confirmation name; friends may give us nicknames. Society names us with professional titles. The ones we love have pet names for us, intimate endearments that have secret codes of meaning. God also names us, and in that naming is our call. Thus, in Genesis, "Abram" is named "Abraham" by God; that naming publicly establishes their relationship (Genesis 17:1-14). A call is a vocation. Our naming shows us how we are to act in the world. Abraham's naming, for example, makes him the father of the Jewish people.

In Christ's baptism, he is named not only "Son" but also "Beloved." In the Second Week of the Exercises, the grace we pray for is a growing intimacy with Christ. As we are given that grace, we discover that we, too, are called "Beloved" and named as God's living Word in the world.

Rite of Passage

That naming is a transitional point in our lives. In biblical topography, the Jordan was the river the Israelites crossed to the Promised Land, the place where they could live out their covenanted relationship with God in community and in a land they could finally call their own. When we hear our call, we reach a transition point in our lives. At times that transition is difficult, as the Jordan was difficult to cross and treacherous in places. Often when we hear our call, when we experience our baptism, we find ourselves in a difficult place. We must give up the comfort of an old way of life. We must risk setting off on a new path. When we do, we find ourselves.

As you enter this contemplation of Christ's baptism, remember the times and places when you were named and given an identity. Recall the times when you were misnamed, given a false identity, and so lived in servitude. True naming emerges only in love and out of love. As you immerse yourself in the dangerous waters of transition, immerse yourself also in that love that surrounds you, cherishes you, and calls you "Beloved," in the passionate intimacy that each of us uniquely shares with the one we call "God." Ask for the grace to hear your naming.

Questions for Prayer and Reflection

1. What happened in this contemplation as you asked to share Christ's baptismal experience?
2. What has named and shaped you? How did these manifest themselves in your life?
3. What are your experiences of being known truly and lovingly?
4. Whom do you love so much that they learned to accept themselves, which changed the way they behave to others?
5. What risks do you take in loving, in giving love, and in sharing that love with others? Why do you take those risks?
6. What is the life you find as you risk in love? Does it sustain you? How?
7. When Jesus goes to the Jordan, he leaves home in such a way that he can never go back again. Have you ever left home that way? How did you deal with the resulting emotions? How can you bring those emotions to the prayer you are entering into?
8. How do you live out your being named "Beloved"?

12th Exercise: The Temptations in the Desert

Scripture verse

> Blessed be the God and Father of our Lord Jesus Christ, who has blessed us in Christ with every spiritual blessing in the heavenly places, even as he chose us in him before the foundation of the world that we should be holy and blameless before him. He destined us in love to be his own through Jesus Christ, according to the purpose of his will, to the praise of his glorious grace which he freely bestowed on us in the Beloved. (Ephesians 1:3-6)

From the Spiritual Exercises

> It is the mark of the evil spirit to assume the appearance of an angel of light. He begins by suggesting thoughts that are suited to a devout soul, and ends by suggesting his own. For example, he will suggest holy and pious thoughts that are wholly in conformity with the sanctity of the soul. Afterwards, he will endeavor little by little to end by drawing the soul into his hidden snares and evil designs. (Sp. Ex. #332)

Grace to be prayed for

> This is to ask for what I desire. Here it will be to ask for an intimate knowledge of our Lord, who has become man for me, that I may love Him more and follow Him more closely.
> (Sp. Ex. #104)

Living Vulnerably

Something dramatic happens in Jesus' life immediately after his baptism: "The Spirit immediately drove him out into the wilderness. And he was in the wilderness forty days, tempted by Satan; and he was with the wild beasts; and the angels ministered to him" (Mark 1:12-13). It is easy to think that when we are called and are filled with the Spirit, and have a profound confirmation of our identity, life will become easy and we will be spared its terrors. But that is simply not true. Rather, we immediately come in contact with malign forces – within us or outside of us – that try to make life unbearable, and we discover we are vulnerable to those forces. Yet we do not encounter those forces alone. Just as it is human nature to help someone who is in need or in trouble, it is God's nature to go to the endangered aspects of creation. When we are tempted, the illusion offered us is that we are alone. This is not true. Whether we feel it or not, we are held then, as always, in God's love. We are asked to rely on that love, rather than on our own abilities.

In the wilderness, Jesus is tempted to use his new-found identity to satisfy his ego. What the wilderness does for Jesus – as it does for each of us – is make us conscious of our vulnerability. In that vulnerability we have choices. We can rely on ourselves, or we can rely on God. The evil spirit suggests to us that we rely on ourselves. God asks us to trust in that Divine Mercy we have experienced constantly loving us.

More than an Animal

Thus, when Jesus is hungry, he is tempted to turn the stones into bread. He has the ability to do this, and he has a real need. But he responds by saying we do not live on bread alone but by every word that proceeds from the mouth of God. That all-creating word of the Father makes both stone and bread, but, even more important, it manifests itself in the mercy of Divine Providence. Jesus is willing, in his hunger, to trust Divine Providence rather than his own gifts. He chooses, in terms of the Two Standards, poverty rather than riches. We, too, are more than just the basic instincts for survival. We are asked to live, and to live in such a way that we aim for the fullness of life. Sometimes, this may mean giving up even basic satisfactions.

More than a Social Creation

Next, Jesus is offered the honour of the world (Luke 4:5-7). This he rejects by remembering that his basic identity comes from his relationship with God rather than with any aspect of creation. He affirms his basic stance of "praise, reverence, and service" to God rather than accepting the "authority" and "glory" of all the kingdoms of the world. In our culture today, we are led to believe that our identity comes only from our social milieu – family, friends, our jobs, the roles we are given in our society and culture. Often we try to live our lives to achieve the respect of others. We live as though their respect determines our self-worth. But there is a deeper level of our identity than these important factors. It is our relationship with God. In rejecting this temptation of being approved by the kingdoms of this world, Jesus affirms that his deepest identity comes from his relationship with God. He realizes that the powers of this world, then, as today, have abandoned intimacy with God. Often we, too, are seduced by our own needs to abandon that intimacy with God and to substitute for it the approval of others or the definitions of ourselves that the world tries to impose upon us.

More than Self-determined

In the final temptation, Satan wants Jesus to throw himself from a high place, the pinnacle of the temple in Jerusalem. He reasons that if Jesus is the Son of God, God will save him. But Jesus knows that he cannot flaunt the Father's gift to him as his right. He can only operate out of it as a merciful dispensation from the Father. Moreover, he knows who he is; he does not have to prove it to anyone. He replies, "You shall not tempt the Lord your God." Even though we are loved by God, we cannot do as we wish and expect God to acquiesce to us. We are made for God; God is not made for us. Our lives of love are in service to loving the world as God loves the world. Our lives of love are not the selfish exploitation of our gifts, or relationships with others, or our relationship with God. Should we do this, we become less than who we are.

The temptations ask Jesus to be less than who he is. They ask him to rely on his own gifts, to use the things of the world to maintain his own identity, and to use God to affirm himself. The temptations attempt to deny or distort his relationship with the one who has just called him his "beloved." In rejecting the temptations, Jesus shows himself content to wait on God to feed him, to affirm him, and to save him. Such waiting he learned in his hidden life; it will manifest itself again when he is on the cross.

To enter into a contemplation of Christ's temptations in the desert is to discover how our energies, now being woven together with Christ's energies, enter into temptation. We find, as we found in the Two Standards, that we are tempted by riches, honour, and pride. We want to rely on ourselves, to seek the approval of the world, and to set ourselves up as the centre of our universe. But if we journey with Jesus, we find we can overcome those temptations because our relationship with the Father, like Jesus', is stronger than our selfishness. We discover that, like Jesus, we are nourished and affirmed, and we find ourselves in that relationship. This manifests our call as companions of the Christ.

Questions for Prayer and Reflection

1. What happens when you read and contemplate the temptations of Christ in the desert?
2. What are your deserts? in your work? your family? your relationships? the society you live in? the world?
3. Is there a pattern to the way you are tempted?
4. How does the prayer affect the way you encounter temptation and deal with it?
5. What have been the consequences in your life of falling in love with God and allowing God to express his love for you?
6. What have been the consequences of not falling in love with God and of ignoring his relationship with you?
7. How does your intimacy with God express itself in your daily life?
8. How do you distinguish between being pious and being spiritual in your life?

13th Exercise: The Call

Scripture verse

The Spirit of the Lord is upon me,
Because he has anointed me to preach good news
to the poor.
He has sent me to proclaim release to the captives
And recovery of sight to the blind,
To set at liberty those who are oppressed,
To proclaim the acceptable year of the Lord. (Luke 4:18-19)

From the Spiritual Exercises

If a devout soul wishes to do something ... that may be for the glory of God our Lord, there may come a thought or temptation from without not to say or do it. Apparent reasons may be adduced for this, such that it is motivated by vainglory or some such other imperfect intention, etc. ... He should act against the temptation. According to St. Bernard, we must answer the tempter, "I did not undertake this because of you, and I am not going to relinquish it because of you."
(Sp. Ex. #351)

Grace to be prayed for

This is to ask for what I desire. Here it will be to ask for an intimate knowledge of our Lord, who has become man for me, that I may love Him more and follow Him more closely.
(Sp. Ex. #104)

The Nature of a Call

In the temptations in the wilderness, Jesus discerns how to behave in the world and returns to the world with that knowledge. He knows he is in communion with the Father and has the support of his family and friends. He knows he is not alone. But he realizes that if he is to share the mercy of the Father with the world, he needs others who are like him – who have seen the misery of this world and have encountered the traps and illusions the world uses to ensnare people. He needs others, who, like him, seek to do something, however small, to relieve that burden of mindless suffering, to enlighten the deceived, and to celebrate the life that comes from knowing one is rooted in love. First he calls people he trusts. Interestingly, he does not approach religious figures, but ordinary people, like you and me.

Each of us is, at the root of our being, a manifestation of love. It is our identity and we experience a sense of it only when we are in loving relationships. But, as we all know, there are levels to loving. There is the love that is not expressed, and there is the love that is expressed. After that there is the love expressed and received. Then there is the love shared. Finally, there is the love that is the expression and work of that shared love. Our call emerges when the love that is given to us is received, lived out, shared, and acted upon. Every call contains the forces of attraction, response, engagement, and commitment.

If we look at what we do with our life, we will see we live this way because of a call. Our behaviour is a response to that call. It may be a basic call to survival. It may be difficult or monotonous, but we endure it because we care about our family, or a particular cause, or a particular talent. Every call shows itself in what we value, because what we value is where we put our lives.

The call of Jesus to his disciples, and to each of us, asks us to put our lives beyond ourselves in trusting in a relationship with him. When we enter into that relationship, we are given a deeper access to the Father's mercy. But, like every relationship, it contains an element of risk. We give up our security to achieve our authenticity.

An Authentic Call

There is a story of an acrobat in a small circus whose single act was to walk a tightrope without a safety net. Above the middle of the high wire was suspended a ring made of rope, soaked in gasoline and set alight. At times he would climb the ladder to the roll of the drums and start his walk, only to turn back. The crowds would jeer. At other times, he would leap through the flaming circle. He said he was always scared, and the times he turned back were when his fear got the better of him. But when asked why he would attempt it in the first place, his answer was simple. He would say, "I know my life is on the other side."

When we follow our call, we give up our security, because our life is on the other side, in the living out of that call.

But how do we know we are called? In fact, we are called by many things, so the question is knowing what is the right call. A true call engages us fully, carries us beyond ourselves. It connects us, on a whole range of levels, with a reality that is both inviting and mysterious, compassionate and uncompromising. It is profoundly personal. It brings out the best in us and gives us a new and more realistic understanding of ourselves. But in answering a call, we also face our demons, as Christ did in the desert: we learn our limitations. We begin to appreciate what is given to us on our path and to be grateful for that path and for the companions and adventures we have along that way.

So how can we distinguish a true call? By the fidelity of the One who calls us. That One is true to our relationship in good times and in bad; does not judge us as anything less than lovable and capable of loving; respects our individuality; celebrates with us what is good in life; works along with us in transforming what is damaging in our world; gives us the strength and the courage to hold what is suffering or damaged; lets us experience our freedom to be creative. The one who calls us truly shares with us all that he has and is. When we are called by Christ, he shares with us the life and spirit he has with the compassionate and creative mystery he calls "Abba" … "Father."

Questions for Prayer and Reflection

1. When have you felt called to do something that you saw as significant? What were the stages of that experience? Looking back, what affirmed you? How did that happen? What forces worked against you? How did they manifest themselves? How did you overcome them?
2. Do the same exercise for two or three other significant life-changing experiences. Can you see a common pattern in the way you are called and the way you respond?

3. Read the call of apostles in the gospels (John ch. 1; Mark ch. 1; Luke ch. 5; Matthew ch. 4). Enter prayerfully and imaginatively into one of those scenes, giving the characters and yourself the freedom to say and do as they and you wish. What was significant in that scene for you?
4. Who in your world lives out such a calling within a family (such as a parent), a job (such as an artist), the community (such as an advocate for human rights), the international scene (such as a world leader), or a religious tradition (such as a saint, the Buddha, Rumi)? Have a conversation with that person about what moves you and what moved them to lead such a life.
5. Are you experiencing a call now? What form does it take? What are you doing about it?
6. In what ways are you a witness to life for others?
7. Not all of us are asked to be religious, but we are all spiritual by nature. In what ways does your intimacy with the spiritual manifest itself?

14th Exercise: The Cost of Discipleship

Scripture verse

> If anyone would come after me, let him deny himself and take up his cross and follow me. For whoever would save his life will lose it; and whoever loses his life for my sake and the gospel's sake will save it. For what does it profit a man, to gain the whole world and forfeit his life? (Mark 8:34-36)

From the Spiritual Exercises

> They will strive to conduct themselves as if every attachment ... had been broken. They will make efforts neither to want that, or anything else, unless the service of God our Lord alone moves them to do so. (Sp. Ex. #155)

Grace to be prayed for

> This is to ask for what I desire. Here it will be to ask for an intimate knowledge of our Lord, who has become man for me, that I may love Him more and follow Him more closely. (Sp. Ex. #104)

The Challenge of Living Authentically

A script we sometimes buy into suggests that implementing decisions is easy. But this is not so. Often the values of the world deride the decisions we make because this world's illusions are fickle and superficial. When we make a radical decision, even though we still live in the world, we do not live as the world proposes we live. For example, to enter into a life commitment flies in the face of overwhelming self-indulgence; to love what is broken transcends the lure of perfectionism; to believe in the power of truth destroys the convenient lie; to live spiritually exposes the shallowness of the materialism that surrounds us.

The Poor in Spirit

A call invites us to a deeper relationship with the divine. As we discovered in the First Week, when we encounter the divine personally and intimately, we discover our creaturehood. We experience that we are nothing in ourselves, and exist only because of the relationship God maintains with us, even though we might not be conscious of it most of the time. To exist consciously in that awareness is both liberating and terrifying. It is rather like discovering that the ground we have built our lives on, and our egos, with all of its assumptions and projects, is not solid after all. Until we learn intimately to trust the love that creates, maintains, and delights in us, what we hold to be real is just the product of habit and blindness. But when we love, we discover reality is mysterious. It challenges and delights. And, as we learn to trust that relationship with God, we discover that we are not destroyed by our sense of our nothingness. In fact, we become more joyful and free in learning that we are cared for by a Love that is bigger than we can ever imagine. That awareness allows us to see every moment as an entry into the divine.

Walking Through Our Deaths

That perspective is the basis of our discipleship. As we enter the journey to a closer union with God, we meet forces that prevent us from fully experiencing that love. To reach the life we desire, we must acknowledge and mourn the many deaths that keep us prisoner: the loss of innocence; loss of loving relationships; destruction of our ideals and hopes; despair that goes with accepting as reality that "things cannot change"; cynicism that is suspicious of any form of good. We have to find ways not to submit to these deaths. How do we do this? First, we can acknowledge them for what they are. They are moments in our path. They do not define us. Only God does. That awareness takes power away from them. Second, we need to be open about how they affect us. Often we close down in those situations that drain us of life. When we do that, we deny God the access into our lives to change them. Third, we can enter consciously into those deaths in prayer and ritual, and offer them up to that transforming power of love found in resurrection. That love seeks us just as we seek it. To be a disciple is to offer the deaths we experience to God, and so witness to our intimacy with the sacred.

Daily Gifts

In so doing, we discover humility. We experience our powerlessness in the face of the powers of this world and of our own disorders. We become sensitive to the forms of malign absurdity that seek to control even the most common and simple good. But we also become increasingly attentive to what is given to us daily and to the quiet and, often, small good that can be found and shared and celebrated in our lives. We discover that this is enough for the day and for our needs.

Hungering for Life

Yet we long for a just world, a good and meaningful life. We wish we could see, know and love the world and ourselves the way the Father sees and knows and loves us. This "more" we hunger for as we grow into discipleship becomes the consuming passion that God the lover has for us, the beloved. This passion shows itself in mercy.

A Compassionate Mercy

In our world, we strive to be merciful with our slender means as the Father is merciful to us. We give what has been given to us. We do this out of compassion, because we know what it is to be lost and lonely and unloved. But we also do it because the one who loves us behaves that way, and we desire to be one with the beloved in the ways that the beloved deals with the world. The disciple seeks at first to imitate the God who calls us all. In responding to that call, we discover that the journey to love slowly transforms the way of the pilgrim from imitation into identification. The mercy that finds us and that we accept slowly becomes our own life. The lover becomes the beloved in the world.

A Practical Love

In sharing the heart of God, we manifest Christ's love for the Father and the Father's love for his Son. This is not pious sentimentality or an otherworldly relationship of unnatural intensity. It is simple, direct, and practical. It sees what must be done and does it. It sees what needs to be done and does what it can. It manifests the quiet, ongoing creativity and the constant patient suffering of God. It says, as Paul says, "It is no longer I who live, but Christ lives in me" (Galatians 2:20).

Reweaving the World

The life of Christ that disciples witness to with their own lives is one of a growing spiritual intimacy. That intimacy creates community on ever more encompassing levels of relationships. There is the inner work of uniting the separated parts of the self, and, at the same time, the outer work of creating and maintaining bonds within families, communities, society, and nations. That intimacy reaches out to the broader dimensions of community, including the ecological and even the cosmic. This sense of unity is fostered by right relationships. The work of the disciple is to establish, preserve, and support relationships that give life and are rooted in the mystery of God's creativity.

But to live this way requires courage and a conscious rootedness in God's love, for such a life has to loose the bonds of oppression and unmask the lies that trap the human family. So we must be willing to speak for those with no voice and to share the life of these little ones in a way that convinces them of their worth and their goodness. Too often, such a life leads to suffering and persecution. The disciple knows that anyone in this intimate following of Christ will be treated in this world just as the Christ was treated.

Yet we are asked to live this way and on this path if we are to help transform this world into a place where good can be seen and cherished, truth known and upheld, and love become the basis of all action. The call to discipleship is primarily a call to such a deep intimacy with God that our lives manifest this intimacy in all we do and hold. Each of us is offered that call and that path. It is the path of the Beatitudes (Matthew 5:1-16).

Questions for Prayer and Reflection

1. This contemplation is a path through the Beatitudes and describes the life of a disciple. The Beatitudes were central to the First Week, to lead us to a spiritual freedom. Here the Beatitudes foster a deeper sense of intimacy with the Christ. This is the grace you are praying for. You might wish to pray your way through the Beatitudes as if Christ is journeying with you. Stay with each one until it moves you to the next.
2. In your journey through this contemplation, where did you find yourself stopping because something moved you, either positively or negatively? List those moments and go back to them one at a time, staying with each moment until you feel ready to move on.
3. Have a conversation with Christ about how your life resembles his. Ask him to show you how this is so.
4. What fears do you have about developing a closer intimacy with God? Where do these fears come from? What do they suggest about what you should do next? How will you deal with them?
5. What do you find attractive when you contemplate a closer intimacy with God? How do you know if this attraction is deceptive or not? How will you find out? What will you do next?
6. At the end of your prayer periods, do you find yourself being consistently called to pray about something? What? How will you pray about it? (Ask God to show you.)
7. At the end of your prayer periods, have a conversation with the Father, or Jesus, or his mother, or one of your favourite saints about what happened in the prayer.

15th Exercise: Christ Walks on the Water

(Matthew 14:22-33)

Scripture verse

> All things are possible with God. (Mark 10:27)

From the Spiritual Exercises

> God our Lord knows our nature infinitely better [than we do] ... He often grants us the grace to understand what is suitable for us. (Sp. Ex. #89)

Grace to be prayed for

> This is to ask for what I desire. Here it will be to ask for an intimate knowledge of our Lord, who has become man for me, that I may love Him more and follow Him more closely. (Sp. Ex. #104)

The Impossible Happens

In this gospel sequence, Jesus has just heard about his cousin John's execution by Herod. He withdraws to a quiet place to reflect on this news, but when the crowds see where he is going, they follow him. Feeling sorry for them, he heals the sick among them. In the evening, seeing that they have nothing to eat, he feeds them all from the little food they brought. Then he goes up into the mountains to pray. Late that stormy night, the disciples are in a boat on the lake. They see Jesus walking on the waters towards them and are afraid, but Peter says, "If it is you, let me walk on the waters to you." Jesus says, "Come." Peter climbs out of the boat and walks on the water, but, when he feels the force of the wind, he is afraid and starts to sink. He cries out to be saved. Jesus stretches out his hand and saves him, and they get into the boat. When the others see what Jesus has done, they acknowledge that he is truly divine.

When we enter into this contemplation, we feel very much as Peter did. In the midst of living out of our call, we are surrounded by alien forces beyond our control. The world situation teeters into instability, ecological catastrophes, nation in conflict with nation.

Closer to home, we experience family tensions, health concerns, financial stress. No one is immune to these issues, and the security we struggle to maintain is always fragile. In the midst of worries that sometimes threaten to overwhelm us, we forget our relationship with Christ, and try to save ourselves. When this happens, we do become overwhelmed. In desperation, we cry out for deliverance. When we do so, we see that help is at hand. God does not promise us security. He offers us a relationship that is not broken, no matter what dangers surround and infect us. In holding onto that relationship, we realize we are rescued from despair. We experience that ever-present mercy of God that calls us to go beyond ourselves and our resources to trust in him. He sustains and saves us.

Unfortunately, it often seems that we must find ourselves in such situations before we can accept that we are looked after. And, to be honest, in every new situation where we are surrounded by destructive forces, we forget the life lessons of being saved, and so we sink again. We sink until we cry out again in desperation to be saved, and again we are saved.

In following the path of the disciple, the ego never disappears; in situations of vulnerability it tries to rely on itself. It is the fallen human condition to rely on our own abilities in dire circumstances. We lose touch with that more deeply human aspect of ourselves that knows we live only in relationship and are most fully alive only in relationship with God.

Depending on God

To consider Jesus in his humanity and to see what he does in dire circumstances is also personally transforming. He had started his public ministry following John's example, but here Jesus sees what can happen when people witness in that way. The forces of the world destroy them. Herod kills John.

Jesus is grieved by the murder of a family member, but he also realizes the consequences of the path he walks. He withdraws, as in a retreat, to enter more self-consciously into that relationship with his Father, to be more deeply rooted and to take heart.

His desire for self-renewal is frustrated by the needs of the crowd. He puts aside his own ego needs in compassionate imitation of his Father. He heals the sick. Gathering the little food they have, he prays to the Father and experiences once again that mercy passing through him into the world. The loaves and fish are multiplied and all are fed. Even in his extreme need, Jesus depends on his relationship with the Father to sustain him and his mission. That love, which names him, as it names us, as the beloved, comes through. The people are satisfied.

It is only then that Jesus continues on his own project. He goes off into the mountains to commune with his Father. As we experience in the practice of these Exercises, Jesus realizes that he needs time to maintain his bond with the source of his life. He takes the time to do that. Out of this, he is renewed to continue his mission. He returns to those whom the Father has given him as companions for the journey, and he finds them in need. They are surprised at his mode of coming to them (as they will be surprised in the resurrection sequences) and wonder if it is not a figment of their frantic imaginations. Peter asks him to identify himself through his powers. Jesus accepts and calls him. In that personal calling, Peter is given the power to do what Jesus does. He walks on the water. When we accept our call, we are given the same power to do as Jesus does, and to live as Jesus lives. We set out, like Peter, with our eyes fixed on the Christ. It is when we leave our habitual forms of security and totally depend on Jesus that our faith falters and we become aware of our situation. We turn towards ourselves and break the relationship we have with the one who calls us. We sink.

We are rescued when we turn in desperation once again to God. The first time we turn is for proof; the second time we seek a deeper level. That first time is like the occasion when we make a discernment and some plan of action gets confirmed. The second time is like setting out on that plan, becoming overwhelmed by what we have to do, and falling back on our own resources. We discover that they are not enough. We panic and cry out to God as our last resort. By those saving acts, we recognize that neither ghosts nor illusions save us, but the Christ.

Many things happen to us in this contemplation. We recognize that the one who loves us is divine, and that this does not take away from his humanity, since he, too, suffers. We also learn to distinguish between the illusions that look like God and the real God, since only he can save us. We find out how vital is our relationship with God in living out our call, because we cannot do this on our own. We discover God's constant fidelity in taking the little we have and making it enough for what we must do. We learn that the Christ works to maintain his relationship with his Father, and that just as Christ responds to our needs, the Father responds to Christ's needs. We enter more deeply into that creative mercy witnessing to the Father's love for us and to Christ's love for us. We live out and share that creative mercy in our lives.

As we enter into this contemplation and open ourselves to being transformed by God's love, we become the disciples Christ gathers around him, as we are given that intimate knowledge that makes us his continuing presence on earth.

Questions for Prayer and Reflection

1. Read Matthew 14:22-33. Enter into a contemplation of it. Where were you? Were you an onlooker? One of those fed? A disciple on the boat? Peter? Jesus? What did the contemplation reveal to you about yourself? About your relationship to God?
2. Have you ever been in dire straits and then, through matters beyond your control, triumphed over that situation? When you relive such a situation, what does it say about your life and about God's presence in your life?
3. Are you in a desperate situation now? What is happening? What are you doing to emerge from this situation? How is God helping you to emerge?
4. In what ways can you be creative and joyful in your life in the midst of the unsettling times in which we all live?
5. When you read this exercise, what are the things that strike and move you? Stay with one of these and see how that gift opens. Stay with the others, one at a time, and see what emerges when we give ourselves time to think about them.
6. After you have reflected and prayed through these questions, how is your relationship to God changed? deepened? What areas of growth and challenge remain?
7. Are you still willing to walk with God in the midst of your incompleteness and your questions? Why? How?

16th Exercise: Jesus in the Temple

(John 2:13-22)

Scripture verse

> This people honours me with their lips,
> But their heart is far from me;
> In vain do they worship me,
> Teaching as doctrines the precepts of men. (Matthew 15:8-9)

From the Spiritual Exercises

> Consider how [the enemy of our human nature] summons innumerable demons, and scatters them, some to one city and some to another, throughout the whole world, so that no province, no place, no state of life, no individual is overlooked. (Sp. Ex. #141)

Grace to be prayed for

> This is to ask for what I desire. Here it will be to ask for an intimate knowledge of our Lord, who has become man for me, that I may love Him more and follow Him more closely.
> (Sp. Ex. #104)

Facing Hypocrisy

There is something dreadful when elements in religious organizations preach fear, control access to God through exclusivity, and set themselves up as the sole purveyors of salvation. It is even sadder when those same forces distort and restrict the message of God's compassionate mercy into systems of law, ethics, and theology. But saddest of all is the lack of the spirit of love, and the self-imposed blindness to that lack, when such figures present themselves to the world as authoritative voices for religious belief.

Then we have death masquerading as life. The same is true of social and political organizations that claim to maintain justice but create and uphold laws that favour the powerful, or that claim to search for and speak the truth but manipulate image and word for expedient ends. Jesus is fearless in the face of this hypocrisy. He condemns it.

And what about us, who see these things so clearly and are disgusted by them? What do we do? What do we do with ourselves when we find that we are no better than the institutions and structures we condemn?

This is a subtle and pervasive temptation in our time. Seduced by moral disgust, we either despair and do nothing, or react in a violent and destructive manner. If the previous exercise shows us how fear stops us from being intimate with Christ, this exercise shows us how both clarity and power are enemies of a full relationship with the One who invites us to share his life. With clarity we can see things as they are, but we react in a worldly way to what we see so clearly. With power we become presumptuous, and act out our desire to change what we perceive to be wrong in a worldly manner. Our journey now invites us not only to walk with the Christ, but to live and act as he does.

Creating a Sacred Space

In this contemplation, Jesus cleanses the temple by driving out those who corrupted that sacred space where we meet God. How are we supposed to act when we discover our sacred spaces are despoiled? We act not in slavish imitation of Jesus' actions in his time, but by putting on the mind and heart of Jesus. This crucial distinction points to the importance of a deep and lived personal intimacy with Christ. In that intimacy he reveals to us and shares with us his relationship with the Father, and invites us to be like him in living out of that relationship. So we act not out of our own perceptions and insights and inclinations, even though these may be valid, but rather out of the stance of being one with the source of all creation and creativity. This becomes our principle for discernment and action. Our role in the world when we act out of this stance is to maintain right relationships between everything and God. What Jesus did in the temple was to display the energy of righteousness against those who had made religion a business transaction rather than the expression of mercy.

In fact, all of Jesus' actions in the Temple – from his being found there by Mary and Joseph as a child, to his preaching there, to this final act – are manifestations of being about his Father's business.

That business is love – not a sentimental or pious love, not an escapist or exclusive love, not a passive or self-indulgent love, but a love that enters the world to bring everything and everyone into loving relationships with each other. This love has a reverence for life; it practises generosity by sharing time, energy, gifts, and resources; it sees itself as responsible for all of creation, human and otherwise; and it is full of care in the way it relates to others. In so doing, it acts as the Father acts towards creation. He has lovingly brought this creation into being; he maintains it and desires to transform it into a habitat where the destructive effects of sin are transformed into creativity and life.

Jesus turns his attention to the temple because for him, the temple is the meeting place between God and humanity. That meeting place had been turned into a place where transactions were commercial, political, and worldly. It was no longer a spiritual, open space where the sufferings of humanity met the compassion of God. And because the mercy of God refuses to be constrained by disorder, the Father creates a new temple to embody that compassionate love.

Christ is that temple, and his call to each of us is to become that sacred place where the world's pain and brokenness can, in humility, be met by compassionate mercy and held up to healing: to liberate the oppressed, and to celebrate community.

The Holiness of Everything

In his life, Christ restores sacredness to the desecrated. Our intimacy with Christ carries us along that same path. When we walk that path, we discover that everything that exists is open to the holy, and that everything we meet can invite us to encounter God in a deeper way. Evil, no matter how it is disguised as good, even as religious good, effectively tries to stop us encountering God. But when we have travelled a while with the Christ, as we have done in praying though these Exercises, we see through the illusions that pretend to be holiness. In relating to them for what they truly are, we take away their power over us and over those we care for, and whom we are now committed to cherish into the fullness of life. Like Christ, we are invited in love to restore a right order to creation.

When Christ cleanses the temple, he acts as a peacemaker. What is the difference between a peacekeeper, a peace-lover, and a peacemaker? A peacekeeper sacrifices everything to make sure that there is no disturbance in what is accepted as habitual. Fear and co-dependency underlie that position. A peace lover wants peace, but is not willing to commit to any actions that would remove or transform the forces that block right relations between different aspects of creation – people, classes, cultures, and nations. A peacemaker commits to establishing those right relations, which are found only when we take on the perspective and the work of the Creator. In cleansing the temple, Christ acts as a peacemaker, because his deepest desire is to do the will of his Father, and the deepest desire of the Father is that everything been seen as it is: holy. We are holy, our deepest identity is to live that holiness, and our mission in this world, no matter what we do, is to allow the holiness of everything to manifest itself in celebrating life.

Questions for Prayer and Reflection

1. How do you confuse religion with holiness? How does that restrict your deepest desires? How does it stop you from encountering God?
2. Pray through those manifestations of religion in your life that create a false image of God, yourself, and others by offering them up to the transforming spirit of the Father. What happens when you do this? How are you liberated?
3. How can you distinguish between your anger and God's transforming energy in the face of the world's oppressive forces?
4. How do you distinguish between self-indulgence and freedom in your life and in the world?
5. How do you feel when you discover that your growing intimacy with Christ asks you to take a stance in the world? In practical terms, what does that stance look like? (Remember that we are not asked to be seduced by our idealisms, our fears. We are simply asked to be where Jesus is.) When you ask the Christ in prayer where you are to be with him, what answers do you receive?

17th Exercise: The Raising of Lazarus

(John 11:1-45)

Scripture verse

> God shows his love for us in that while we were yet sinners Christ died for us. (Romans 5:8)

From the Spiritual Exercises

> Reflect how God dwells in creatures: in the elements giving them existence, in the plants giving them life, in the animals conferring upon them sensation, in humans bestowing understanding. So He dwells in me and gives me being, life, sensation, intelligence; and makes a temple of me, since I am created in the likeness and image of the Divine Majesty. (Sp. Ex. #235)

Grace to be prayed for

> This is to ask for what I desire. Here it will be to ask for an intimate knowledge of our Lord, who has become man for me, that I may love Him more and follow Him more closely. (Sp. Ex. #104)

Waiting on the Father

The Scriptures tell us that Jesus raised the son of the widow of Naim and Jairus's daughter from the dead. Jesus did not know either of these two people or their families. He simply acts out of compassion. Jesus also raised Lazarus. Lazarus was his friend, and Jesus knew the family very well. The odd thing about the raising of Lazarus is that Jesus knew that Lazarus was sick, and although he was not far away, he did not go and heal him. After Lazarus died, Jesus waited several days before even going to comfort the family, which seems unusual for someone who embodies the compassion of God. Jesus knew that the religious authorities were trying to kill him; was he afraid for his life? His previous actions indicate that he was not afraid of those authorities and often challenged them to their faces. We also know that his mission was to be compassionate even in the face of bodily destruction. So why did he delay going to Lazarus until it was too late?

In our own lives we experience instances of need. Even though we know that God is fully aware of our needs, nothing seems to be done. Others experience this as well. This is the reason many people do not believe in God. So at this stage of our spiritual journey through the Exercises, we raise this question: If this is the way you treat the person whom you say you love and whose life you share, how will you treat us, whom you say you love and ask to journey with you?

The answer lies in Jesus' relationship with the Father. Jesus does nothing apart from the Father's will, and his whole life is a manifestation of that will. He waited to be called at his baptism. He waits now until the Father tells him to go to Lazarus's tomb. He will wait for the Father to raise him from the dead. It grieves him to wait to rescue his friend and to comfort the family. In his waiting, he manifests that first commandment to "Love the Lord your God with all your heart and with all your soul and with all your mind, and with all your strength" (Mark 12:30).

In our deepening intimacy with the Christ, we, too, are asked to wait on the Father's will. It may grieve us to do that, for there are things we know we can do, and things we know need to be done. To seem to be doing nothing while others suffer and die, and to claim at the same time to love them, causes the Christ's followers to be deemed irrelevant, mindless, passive, or alienated from reality.

But Christianity is more than a program of social action. Waiting on the Father is not equivalent to inactivity. It is first and foremost a profound witness of our creaturehood. It is also a profound act of faith, hope, and love to wait in that relationship, knowing that something will be done, that it will be the right thing, and that what will be done and how it will be done will more deeply reveal God's selfless, constant, caring compassion. To wait like this in love is not apathy. It is leaning passionately into a relationship committed to making us fulfilled, comforted, and cared for. We expect it. We live out of it. And it comes.

The Greatest Gift

When Jesus goes to Bethany to Lazarus's home, Martha and then Mary meet him. Both upbraid him for not using his powers to save their brother from death. Yet Jesus' call is not to manifest his powers, but to live out his relationship with his Father. Jesus can raise Lazarus from the dead, as he raised two others. Like those two others, Lazarus will eventually die again. Jesus' own relationship with the Father allows for his resurrection, not resuscitation. That relationship manifests a love so strong that death cannot overcome it. Jesus enters into death, journeying towards a love beyond name and imagining, and that love enters into death to bring the beloved into that new creation called resurrection. That new creation is not the cyclical return of natural rhythms, nor is it the miraculous raising up of the dead back into earthly life. It is something new, and it attests to the transforming creativity of the Father. In the Lazarus story, Jesus gives some indication of that greater gift the Father has for us. This is not the gift of a life repeated. It is the gift of such intimacy that we will be like the Christ – not that we will bring the dead back to life, but that we will be resurrected. The gift does not ignore the wretchedness of a disordered world or the ravages of sin and death and their effects on all of us. Instead, it enters into those places of crisis and takes away their power, making them doorways – however painful and powerful – into new life. It is that greater gift that empowers us to be in the disordered places of our world as a transforming presence.

The risk the Father takes with Mary and Martha in denying them immediate access to Jesus' power is the risk the Father takes with each of us. If we are indulged with instant gratification because we know God loves us, and we love God, we reduce God to being a magician and ourselves to a narcissism that ignores the world's suffering. This approach overlooks God's mysterious will to enter into that suffering as a human being, and to endure it even to a humiliating and painful death on a cross. Reducing God to a magician does not admit that we are invited to follow Christ in living out his passion for the Father. Neither does it admit that our intimacy with Christ makes us *more* human, not less. So we are more aware of the destructiveness of evil, but also more aware of the depths of God's love.

When Jesus raises Lazarus from the dead, he does it not to manifest his power, but to show the dimensions of his relationship with the Father. He says, "Father, I thank you because you have heard me. I know that you hear me always but I have said this on account of the people standing by that they may believe you sent me" (John

11:41). He calls on the Father and the Father answers. Now he can act. In front of that tomb that holds a man four days dead, he cries out in a loud voice, "Lazarus! Come out!" The gospel tells us what happens next. "The dead man came out, his hands and feet bound in bandages, and his face wrapped with a cloth." Jesus said to those around him, 'Unbind him, and let him go.'"

Setting the Captured Free

Now we can see our task. It is God who raises up the dead. Our work is the unbinding and the letting go. If we let God be God, we find ourselves co-operating with him. We cannot overcome sin, or its first fruits: death. Only God can do that. But we can do our part of the relationship and allow those who have been set free to live freely. Too often we are unwilling to unbind and set free, because we cannot believe that new life is given to a situation or to people. Our lack of faith in the power of God's love stops us from seeing what is right in front of us. But if we accept the power of the relationship that Christ has with the Father, and that he offers to each of us, we can see as he sees, and then do our part. As Jesus says elsewhere in John's gospel, "Receive the Holy Spirit. If you forgive the sins of any, they are forgiven. If you retain the sins of any, they are retained" (John 20:23). It is only when we share in the relationship that Jesus has with the Father – that is, share their Holy Spirit – that we can unbind and forgive. That is liberation and life.

Questions for Prayer and Reflection

1. When you entered this contemplation, what happened to you? Where did you find yourself? What was your relationship to Jesus? to Mary and Martha? How did you deal with Lazarus?
2. When have you been in a dire situation beyond your control and had to wait for God to act? How did you wait? How did you relate to God at that time? What happened?
3. Are you in such a situation now? How are you relating to God?
4. When you look at your culture and the world, your family, you partner, your relationships, and yourself, where do you find God bringing the dead to life? How do you co-operate with that?
5. Do you ever, like Jesus did, wait on the Father's moment to act, even though you could do something about a situation that needs remedying? How did you discern what to do and when, or not do it? What was your prayer then?
6. When have you been liberated from a situation you considered hopeless?
7. When have you liberated others from situations they found hopeless?
8. When have you experienced your sins being forgiven so that you felt like a new person?
9. When have you forgiven someone in such a way that that person came "alive" again?

18th Exercise: Palm Sunday

(Matthew 21:1-17)

Scripture verse

> The true light that enlightens everyone was coming into the world; he was in the world, and the world was made through him, yet the world knew him not. He came to his own home and his own people received him not. (John 1:9-11).

From the Spiritual Exercises

> We must carefully observe the whole course of our thoughts. If the beginning and middle and end of the course of thoughts are wholly good and directed to what is entirely right, it is a sign that they are from the good spirit. But the course of thoughts suggested to us may terminate in something evil, or distracting, or less good than the soul had formerly proposed to do. Again it may end in what weakens the soul, or disquiets it; or by destroying the peace, tranquillity, and quiet which it had before, it may cause disturbance to the soul. These things are a clear sign that the thoughts are proceeding from the evil spirit, the enemy of our progress and eternal salvation.
> (Sp. Ex. #333)

Grace to be prayed for

> This is to ask for what I desire. Here it will be to ask for an intimate knowledge of our Lord, who has become man for me, that I may love Him more and follow Him more closely.
> (Sp. Ex. #104)

A Servant King

Whom do you look for when you look for God? What do you see when you look at death? This final exercise of the Second Week asks both of these questions. Underlying the contemplation of Christ entering Jerusalem and being treated as a king and a secular saviour is the difference between what the world calls redemption and what God offers. The Second Week of the Exercises begins with a meditation on "The Kingdom." There we are asked to reflect on a king, chosen by God, who invites us to live under his standard. By the time we have journeyed through this Second Week, we discover what that means for us: to be poor with Christ in his poverty, humble with Christ in his total dependence on the Father, to labour with Christ as he labours to build a community of life and love.

But what the crowd wants when it gathers palms and celebrates Christ's entry into Jerusalem is a hero who will right their every wrong, a liberator who will overthrow the tyranny of the Roman imperial power and its brutalities, a magician who will cure their every ill, a religious preacher who will offer a way of life free of stultifying legalism and hypocrisy. When, in their dreadful need, they see Jesus – who raised the dead; cured the sick; challenged the religious leaders; consorted with the poor, the dispossessed and the outcast; fed a multitude from the little they could offer – and when they heard his preaching and his claims to be the chosen one of God, they see this son of Mary as the answer to their dream of a messiah. A new, just world order, so long promised by prophets and so long the passionate and desperate dream of humankind, was to be fulfilled in their time and in their world.

They take off their cloaks, strip the palm trees of their leaves and celebrate the entrance of Christ into Jerusalem, the holy city, so long despoiled by corruption at every level. Now is the time of transformation. And it does become a time of transformation. The Christ is the Messiah, the warrior saviour of God – but as God sees and enacts this, not as the crowd desires it.

Even here, even now, we need constantly to ask ourselves: Who is God for me? How does God act in our world? Is that God the one we want? Is the God of our needs the same as the God who reveals himself in our prayer and in our lives? Which God do we commit ourselves to follow and to be intimate with?

A New Human

When we look at the Scriptures, we see an interesting development in the way Christ presents himself. In the beginning, he heals the sick, cures ills, raises the dead, transforms water into wine, feeds the multitudes with almost no food, performs miracles, preaches with power. But when Peter acknowledges him to be more than a miracle worker and more than one of the earlier prophets come back from the dead – when Peter declares him to be the Messiah, the Special One of God – Jesus begins to present himself differently and to talk about his suffering and death.

Peter tells him that this is not how a god behaves. Christ rebukes Peter, saying he speaks as a human who knows nothing of how the true God acts. But after Peter's declaration, Jesus performs fewer miracles, and when he raises Lazarus, he does so in a way that informs the witnesses that the significant point of his ministry is to reveal who the Father is and how the Father operates. His kingship, though it is *in* this world, and is firmly concerned with the way the world operates, is not *of* this world. Christ does not act as the world wants him to act. His behaviour always manifests his relationship with the Father. So, even though he enters Jerusalem with all the ritual allusions of a worldly liberator, he understands those signs differently. He is entering the contest where the powers of the world are overthrown: he becomes the prototype for the new human who can be so intimate with God, and who can allow God to be so intimate with us, that the values of this world are no longer the most important.

Facing Death

The world's values revolve around coping with death. Death ultimately devalues the world. On the one hand, people flee from death by maintaining the ego and subscribing to forms of ambition. Such people give the world an importance it cannot maintain. They become overinvolved in this world and overcommitted to the values it manifests. On the other hand, there are people who, confronted with death's reality, despair about the world, which radically limits their scope in the world. They refuse to become involved.

Even if we accept the reality of death and the absurdity it casts on the human project from a purely natural perspective, we are left with a hollow stoicism or the angst of existential absurdity. The non-spiritual death provides the outer limit of the human condition.

Jesus entering Jerusalem faces his death. He realizes that it will be horrible, shameful, and painful, and he wonders if he will break under it. The test for him, as it was in the temptations in the desert, is to see if he will abandon his relationship with the Father and his trust in that relationship. But as he enters Jerusalem, he sees death as a door through which he must go to meet the Father. For him, death is not an ending – it is a step on the path of his return to the Father. He will enter into death. He will wait for his Father to rescue him in whatever way the Father sees best.

We, too, will die. In fact, each of us is dying at this moment. We can try to avoid thinking about it by hurling ourselves into the world, or we can become so obsessed by it that we are useless in this world. But we have another choice. We can see it as Jesus sees it. We do not know the circumstances of our end, but we know that we can face that end: not as an end in itself, but as a new beginning. How we live shapes how we die, for we die as we live. Like Jesus, we can live in relationship with the Father; like Jesus, we can die maintaining that relationship.

Questions for Prayer and Reflection

1. Out of what self-image do you live? How is this manifest in what you do each day?
2. Do you feel confident enough of your relationship with the Father to trust your life with him? How could this be a foolish question? Why is this not a foolish question?
3. How does the Father trust you? How do you know this? Is this any different from any other relationship of trust you have?
4. What do you need to do to grow in trust?
5. In a conversation with the Father, ask what he needs to grow in trust of you. What does he say?
6. How do you face your death? How does this shape the way you live?
7. How have you dealt with the imminent death of someone close to you?
8. In your prayer, how do you deal with what Christ is doing? Where are you in relation to Christ in this?

19th Exercise: Overview of the Second Week

Scripture verse

Set me as a seal on your heart,
As a seal on your arm;
For stern as death is love,
Relentless as the nether world is devotion;
Its flames are a blazing fire.
Deep waters cannot quench love,
Nor floods sweep it away.
Were one to offer all one owns to purchase love,
Such a person would be roundly mocked.

(Song of Songs 8:6-7)

From the Spiritual Exercises

Let him desire and seek nothing except the greater praise and glory of God our Lord as the aim of all he does. For everyone must keep in mind that in all that concerns the spiritual life his progress will be in proportion to his surrender of his self-love and of his own will and interests. (Sp. Ex. #189)

Grace to be prayed for

This is to ask for what I desire. Here it will be to ask for an intimate knowledge of our Lord, who has become man for me, that I may love Him more and follow Him more closely.

(Sp. Ex. #104)

The Journey So Far

If the First Week of the Exercises is falling in love, the Second Week is the engagement period. What distinguishes this Week is the growing intimacy between God and ourselves as lovers. The grace we ask for is "an intimate knowledge of our Lord who has become human for me, that I may love Him more and follow Him more closely." In this intimacy, God reveals himself through the Christ, and the Christ reveals his secret self, his relationship with the Father. He invites us to share that relationship; through that union we discover what it means to love him and to follow him out of love for him.

The First Week of the Exercises begins within a fallen creation ruined by the malice of evil, but as we journey through it we discover a path to love that allows us to live in this world in a liberated way. The Second Week invites us deeper into that love, to put on the perspective of God and to see the world as capable of redemption. It further invites us to unite ourselves with God in working for that redemption. In this we not only enter God's world, but we allow God to enter into our world, for it is in our world that this redemption takes place.

To work concretely towards that redemption we need to know ourselves, as well as Jesus; we need to know how Jesus comes to us as well as how the enemies of our human nature lure us away. The easiest way of reflecting on this is to see how we react when we are vulnerable.

With Christ we can accept our vulnerability and the social shame that comes along with living in such an exposed way. This leads to the humility we identify with in Christ. Living from this stance creates community. Or we can flee from our vulnerability into forms of social approval that reinforce the walls around our ego. Then we remained trapped in narcissism. To live freely in our vulnerability, we need the humility to ask God not only for help to recognize the pattern of our disorders and to resist them, but also for the grace to love and follow Jesus intimately in our daily life.

To do this we contemplate the life of Christ and the way that Christ's life operates in the world. We see what it is to have love enter our world in a vulnerable way and watch it grow to be mature and responsible. We see that this life operates not out of self-interest but out of an authenticity that constantly calls it beyond itself to risk in the world, trusting God's mercy to protect and sustain it in its needs and relationships. We see this love building relationships and trust; we see it challenging the forces of disorder that tend to deny or subvert the witness of God's love. As this Second Week draws to a close, we see this love, of which we are now a part, walking steadfastly into the face of a death arranged by those forces of disorder, eyes and heart fixed firmly on the love of the Father, whom it trusts to redeem it from death.

When we reflect on this Second Week, we review the way we have journeyed to the place we are at now. We can use our journal to see the path we have taken.

Walking to the Beloved

We look to see how the freedom we felt at the beginning of this Week became focused and mature and grounded in our life. We see if the decisions made to follow Christ more concretely in this world really allow us to do that. We can determine this by noting, as we continued to pray and reflect on Christ's life, whether we are closer to him or farther away. Whether we are making a decision or not, upon reflection we may see if we are rooted in our daily life in a way that allows us to face uncertainty more calmly and creatively. Are we enjoying life more, celebrating what is good, and facing more responsibly the things we find destructive or debilitating?

If we find ourselves rooted in the Father's love, we can continue our journey with Christ and be with him in his suffering and death – the time of the naked and intimate embrace of God and the world. It is a time of God's embracing us and our embracing God, as Jesus stretches out his hands on the cross to embrace both us and his Father.

The Embrace

Imagine someone running to God with arms full of gifts to give him, and God running to that person with arms full of the gifts he, too, wants to bestow. They meet, but they cannot embrace because their arms are full. If God puts down his gifts to embrace the beloved, God is seen as naked and vulnerable. This is not a God of power and might, but one who is empty, humble, despised by the world. Often this is not the God we want to follow or get close to or even recognize. We turn away.

Instead of God putting down his gifts, imagine that we put down our gifts to embrace God. Then we see ourselves in our abject nakedness, with our deceptions and fears, our selfishness and our disordered passions, and we turn away, ashamed, from that embrace.

The embrace can only happen if God puts down his gifts and we put down our gifts. We must both have empty arms. In that emptiness is the intimacy of the lover with the beloved. The embrace is possible only if we experience deeply the commitment the Father has for us, and we trust and lean into what is offered in love. In the Third Week, we will enter that loving embrace.

Questions for Prayer and Reflection

1. As you review this whole phase, what was your most life-giving moment? As you reflect on it, what does it mean in your life's path?
2. What was your most desolate moment? What does it signify to you?
3. How does the pattern of riches, leading to honour and then pride, operate in your life?
4. How does the pattern of poverty, leading to social dismissal and then to humility, operate in your life?
5. What things would you like to do with your life, if you were free to do them? Would those things make you a better person and this world a better place to live in? What would be the cost of doing those things?
6. How do you share life with those you care about? How do you let them share life with you?
7. How do you deal with death in your life, in your world? How do you deal with the forces of death around you?
8. How do you celebrate life in the midst of a busy and chaotic world?
9. How do you find your rootedness? How do you maintain your relationship to that rootedness so it can support you in your daily life?

Part 3

The Third Week: A Passionate Love

1st Exercise: Preparation for the Third Week

Scripture verse

> O Lord my God in you do I take refuge;
> Save me from all my pursuers, and deliver me,
> Lest like a lion they rend me,
> Dragging me away with none to rescue.
>
> (Psalm 7:1-2)

From the Spiritual Exercises

> Consider how the Divinity hides itself; for example, it could destroy its enemies and does not do so, but leaves the most sacred humanity to suffer so cruelly. (Sp. Ex. #196)

Grace to be prayed for

> This is to ask for what I desire. Here it will be to ask for sorrow, compassion, and shame because the Lord is going to His suffering for my sins. (Sp. Ex. #193)

Sharing the Beloved's Pain

In the Third Week we follow Christ from the Last Supper to his entombment. We pray for the grace to be as present as possible to him as he journeys through loneliness, pain, humiliation, and death to the Father. It is a huge grace to be simply present to another's suffering without running away, falling back into ourselves, or trying to remedy the situation. The Christ has chosen to walk to the Father. The circumstances of his life and times have conspired to make this part of his journey as destructive as humanly possible. Yet, in the face of that horror, he does not turn away. We ask for the grace to be with him as we would be with a loved one who is betrayed by friends, wrongfully accused by the religious and political authorities, mocked and tortured by their underlings, and then shamefully left to die on a cross. In being present to him as he endures all of this, we share his pain and sorrow.

It is not our pain and sorrow we hold, but his. This phase of the journey is not about us – it is about going out of ourselves in compassion to embrace the beloved in his time of greatest need.

What is awe-full about the drama of the Third Week is the destruction of human good and of the best about human nature – by sin, as manifested in personal, social, and cultural relationships. Sin moves to make life meaningless. We need to walk through those deserts of meaninglessness to discover that there is an indestructible base to human nature: God's love for each one of us. This is the most difficult human journey we can make, but we know it is possible because Jesus has made it, as a human being, before us. In making this journey, he breaks the tyranny of the fear of death, and destroys the fatal human illusion that insists we are determined fully by our social conditions and even by the stories we tell ourselves. He shows that, even when everything is stripped away and we remain as naked desire, even beyond emotion, that desire leans into the Love who creates it, sustains it, and now redeems it. This love does not ignore any of the brutal realities of sin or reduce its consequences. Rather, it demonstrates a love that is stronger than any evil, a light that refuses to be put out by any darkness, a compassion that will not turn aside from any horror. This loves manifests the intimacy out of which it springs.

Entering Mystery

When we enter into situations that reflect this constant reality, we are carried beyond ourselves into silence and stillness. Here we enter a mystery that is so personal and so beyond our own imagining that we feel we have entered a sacred space. We sense our unworthiness and finitude, which manifests in the graces of shame and confusion that Ignatius asks us to pray for at this time. This is not breast-beating or a guilt trip that subtly affirms the ego. It is simply the mode of felt experience of finitude in the presence of the holy.

For St. Ignatius, spirituality is very practical. He asks what we ought to do and suffer for Christ now that we have become intimates with him. We are invited to share in the work and the path of the beloved in the concrete circumstances of our lives. This is not a form of masochism or some contract of repayment. Here we might want to consider how Moses, after encountering God in the burning bush (Exodus 3:1-12), is invited to share in God's work of liberation. We can only respond to that invitation if we ourselves are free, for we cannot give others what we do not have ourselves. Intimacy with the divine makes us free; it is that freedom we see when we follow Jesus as he freely chooses to hand himself over to the Father's will, even as the powers of this world capture and torture him. In these prayer periods, we can exercise our freedom by being as present as we can to that witness of freedom. It leads to resurrection, a life that encompasses and transcends the powers of this world.

Questions for Prayer and Reflection

1. Have you ever been present to the dying of someone you loved? How did you feel? What stages of being present did you go through?
2. How was God present to you at that time? How were the people who are close to you present? How were you present to yourself?
3. How did you survive that experience? How has it shaped the rest of your life?
4. When you consider the significant people of your time, or in your life, who have struggled for justice, freedom, human rights, or for a more human and loving life, how does your spirit react? Stay with that feeling and see what it brings to you.
5. How do you enter the quiet heroism of daily living and the quiet martyrdoms it calls forth?

6. When have you had an experience when your circumstances caused you to behave in ways that took you out of yourself? As you re-enter that experience, now in a more self-conscious and prayerful manner, what does it tell you about yourself? What does it tell you about the forces around you? What does it tell you about your God?
7. Sit with this reflection. What parts move you particularly? Go back to each of these moments and stay with them. What else can you find there? What is revealed to you?

2nd Exercise: The Last Supper

(Matthew 26:20-30; John 13:1-30)

Scripture verse

> While we were still helpless, at the right time Christ died for the ungodly. Why, one will hardly die for a righteous person – though perhaps for a good person one will dare even to die. But God shows his love for us in that while we were yet sinners Christ died for us. (Romans 5:6-8)

From the Spiritual Exercises

> Consider what Christ our Lord suffers in His human nature. (Sp. Ex. #195)

Grace to be prayed for

> This is to ask for what I desire. Here it will be to ask for sorrow, compassion, and shame because the Lord is going to His suffering for my sins. (Sp. Ex. #193)

Celebrating Freedom

In Western culture, our ideas of the Last Supper are strongly coloured by religious paintings of the event and by the piety that surrounds the eucharistic liturgies that derive from it. From these we have received such a formal notion of that meal that we have lost sight of its profoundly passionate celebration of life. The meal celebrates Passover, when the Israelite people gained their freedom from their oppressors, the Egyptians, and started their long journey through the desert to form a religious identity. At that meal, families and friends gather to remember and retell that story, to celebrate God's particular and practical concern for them. That gathering celebrates who they are – God's chosen – and celebrates their intimate relationship with God, which is manifest in what that God has done for them.

In the Passover meal that Christ shared with his friends, he celebrates what it means to be God's chosen: to bear witness to God's mercy, to hope even when there is no cause for optimism, to serve even the self-interested, to give over one's very life to make sure that others receive life. In living this way, Christ takes up the meaning of the Jewish Passover and transforms it into something that reveals more of God's intimacy with us. In doing so he reveals to us at a deeper level who we really are and what we are capable of.

Jesus does not deny the past. As a Jewish man, and a rabbi, he has a profound sense of his religious history. But he does not understand himself totally in terms of the past, or the texts of the past. He understands himself most fully in terms of his relationship with his Father. He has a personal relationship with God. The Lord becomes Abba, and Jesus is willing to share that relationship with us. The God who saves the Israelites becomes the one who saves each one of us, and all of us.

What Jesus does at the Passover meal is what every one of us does at our family celebrations. We remember the past with the ones who share life with us, and each year we bring something new to that gathering. We bring what has happened to each of us, and we tend to discuss those happenings in that ritual context so they become part of that occasion.

The ritual gathering on that particular evening becomes more than the celebration of surviving another year under Roman occupation, more than the revival of the hope of yet another liberation from foreign oppression. For Christ, it allows the entry into a new dispensation that offers us freedom in the world, but not the freedom of worldly standards and methods. With the meal, he gives a way of being united with God that is more than just memory and ritual. He makes the bread and the wine of that Passover meal his body and blood. He shares that with his companions. He ensures that his essence remains with those with whom he shares his life and mission. We become what we eat. We become partakers of the same relationship that he has with the Father. This relationship gives a peace the world cannot give, and a rootedness that transcends this world's limitations.

In that rootedness lie freedom and focus. When we love someone, we open ourselves to that person. We give our very selves over to the beloved. We become the beloved, and the beloved, in accepting our gift, becomes us. In Jesus' founding of this new ritual using the elements of the Passover meal, our unity with God is established in a way that is as real and as physical as our own bodies.

The Gift of Mercy

Christ accomplishes this under the most trying circumstances. The people he had gathered around him, with whom he had worked and had trained, with whom he had celebrated life, and to whom he had revealed all that was given to him to reveal, had not been converted. He is intimate to them. He has revealed who he is to them. They have not been intimate with him simply because they do not know themselves the way he knows them. One would betray him; the rest would abandon him in his hard times. Yet he sees past how they act to what they are capable of. He sees, knows, and loves them in ways they do not yet see and know and love themselves. So what he offers to them, he offers in hope. He hopes that what he is doing will make them aware of their deepest identity and that they will live out of that deepest identity. Then, through their lives, they would be able to witness God's love for the world. He knows that, even after being with him for three years, his followers are riddled with self-interest and ambition. They do not yet understand that love is an attentive and disinterested service in the world.

So he serves them. At that Last Supper he washes their feet. Normally this was the role of a servant for guests who had just arrived with dusty feet, or a sign of hospitality for a dignitary. This is humble service, never performed by the master of the house. While Christ humbles himself, the disciples are concerned with prestige and with who will be the first in Christ's new kingdom. They do not understand this kingdom in terms of loving service to the Father and to each other. They can't comprehend that Christ's whole life was one of service, of returning a fallen and dismayed world to its true identity. So, even with his heart breaking and with the awareness of what is coming next, Jesus performs an act that shows them how to act: he washes their feet. This is not the posturing of honour and pride, nor is it the abjection that comes from a corrupt self-image and false humility. It is the response to a question: How do we celebrate our neighbour?

Offered to All

How do we act in this world to bring it life, and to share that life? What do we do to create and maintain the common good? Jesus' answer is humble service. Peter cannot understand or accept this humility. He refuses to have his feet washed until Jesus replies that, unless he allows his feet to be washed, he cannot know whom he follows, and thus cannot be one with him. It takes humility to offer a gift; it also takes humility to receive a gift, accept it, open it, and live it. It is this gift of transforming life that Jesus offers and Peter finally accepts. This is the gift the mercy of God offers to all.

But in the story of the Last Supper, one person refuses that gift and that mercy. Judas leaves the community Christ is establishing and goes to betray him. The gospels tell us that Judas Iscariot kept the community's money and stole from it. In Ignatian terms, from the Two Standards, he chose riches rather than poverty. Scholars have suggested that the relationship between Jesus and Judas fractured because of Judas's ideology. He may have been a zealot who wanted Jesus to use his powers to overturn the political oppression and social corruption of the day. He understood the Messianic rule in secular terms. He was unwilling to follow Jesus' trust in the Father to bring about that new creation. He preferred Jesus to follow him. When it became clear to Judas that Jesus' way was not what Judas wanted, his bitter disappointment led to his rejection of Jesus. We may wonder why Jesus tolerated Judas in the first place, We may wonder about his skills of discerning his disciples. We may even wonder about how this manifests today. But Jesus' position is that no one is to be lost. He offers himself to all without reserve. When we look at the other apostles, we discover that they are equally venal and self-serving. We may even find ourselves among them.

What Christ offers to his companions at the Last Supper, he also offers to us. We may wonder at his choice. But he knows us better than we know ourselves. He knows how fickle we are; but he also knows that we are capable of being one with him, following him, and sharing his life, joyfully and simply. He knows we are capable of love.

Questions for Prayer and Reflection

1. What are your moments of deepest meaning when you reflect on the Last Supper in one of the gospels (e.g., John 13:1-30)? Why do those moments touch you in this way? How do they reflect on your life's journey?
2. Think of an incident where someone you know (e.g., a family member) gave his or her life so that others might have a better life. How did that sacrifice affect your life?
3. When have you sacrificed something for someone you love? For someone you didn't know? For someone who betrayed you afterwards?
4. When has someone hoped in you even when you did not hope in yourself? How do you think that changed your life?
5. How do you feel at seasonal family celebrations? How do you contribute to these gatherings? In what ways do they bring the clan together? If there are tensions, where do these come from? How do you live with them during the gathering?
6. When you contemplate the Last Supper, where are you in the action? Are you an onlooker, one of the disciples, Peter, Jesus, Judas? Did you get your feet washed? What stories were told at this gathering?
7. Have you ever been offered a gift you could not pay back? How do you deal with gratitude?
8. Think of some times when your humility brought you a great deal of freedom. What happened?
9. Think of a situation that did not go according to what you had planned or hoped. How did you discern what to do next?
10. Think of a time when you betrayed yourself or someone else. How did you find forgiveness?
11. What happens if you do not find forgiveness? Can you allow yourself to be held in God's mercy even then?

3rd Exercise: The Agony in the Garden

(Matthew 26:30-46; Mark 14:32-44)

Scripture verse

> Abba, Father, all things are possible to you; remove this cup from me; yet not what I will but what you will.
>
> (Mark 14:36)

From the Spiritual Exercises

> Take, Lord, and receive all my liberty, my memory, my understanding, and my entire will, all that I have and possess. You have given all to me. To You, O Lord, I return it. All is Yours, dispose of it wholly according to Your will. Give me Your love and Your grace, for this is sufficient for me.
>
> (Sp. Ex. #234)

Grace to be prayed for

> This is to ask for what I desire. Here it will be to ask for sorrow, compassion, and shame because the Lord is going to His suffering for my sins. (Sp. Ex. #193)

Freedom and Liberty

As we saw earlier, there is a difference between freedom and liberty. When we are free, we can make choices that affect our lives, even though we might not be at liberty. This is because we are connected to the source of our life. On the other hand, we might have liberty but not be free: even though we are able to move around, we might be trapped in compulsions and oppressive systems. Often we confuse license, liberty, and freedom. License is using our prerogatives to behave in selfish ways; liberty is the right given to us to behave according to social norms; freedom is living out of our deepest desire as relationship with God. When Christ leaves with his remaining companions after the Last Supper and goes to the Mount of Olives, he experiences his last moments of liberty and the agonizing tension between freedom and liberty.

If he keeps his liberty, he must give up his freedom, his union with the Father, which allows him to be indifferent to the things of this world. If he keeps his liberty, he could escape those coming to capture and kill him, but then he would no longer be true to his deepest sense of identity. If he keeps his freedom, on the other hand, he will be captured and killed. The tension is agony for him: he prays for the strength to be true to himself and to the God he loves. The choice is between security and identity: he has reached the intensely emotional stage where he has to make an existential choice. In handing over his life to the Father, he knows that he is handing his body over to torture and death.

Struck by Terror

We, too, are faced with moments of radical choice in which we are asked to abandon familiar and established ways of doing things and to strike out on our own. Like Christ, we find that our friends and companions are not with us. They might like us and be generally sympathetic to us, but ultimately we are alone. Even when we turn to God in prayer, we find emptiness and an absence of consolation. We are struck by terror.

This terror undermines our courage, our connectedness with ourselves and with others; it erodes our self-confidence, and we find ourselves in a no man's land where our very sense of identity erodes. What are we to do in that situation? Like Christ, we must abandon ourselves to divine providence. We wait. We pray desperately in that darkness. We hand over our lives to the forces beyond our control. We act with integrity, being kind when we can and being patient when we must. We accept that suffering as it is received, whether through the indifference of our friends or through the realization that, in our present state, we have fallen through the bombed-out constructions of the world and its illusions of security. There is no comfort there. We go through the motions of living. As the psalmist says, "O my God, I cry by day, but you do not answer and by night, but find no rest" (Psalm 22:3).

Christ enters this intensely human and dark space at Gethsemane. All through Jerusalem, families and friends are celebrating Passover; he has finished his. Oppressed by what awaits him, he goes to one of his favourite places to pray with his close friends. The place offers no comfort; his friends grow tired and fall asleep. Even Peter, who promises to remain with him and who vows never to betray him, cannot stay awake. Jesus is alone. He prays to his Father, in the intimacy of this relationship, that the upcoming trial be taken from him, but affirms that he wants to do the will of that mysterious one he calls "Abba." As he prays, he comes to the understanding that if redemption is to be achieved, then he must go through with what lies ahead.

Leaning into the Darkness

He embraces his Father's will, and in this embrace his prayer moves from seeking an escape from suffering to accepting that suffering. In that acceptance he moves from being resigned to Divine Providence to actively participating in that providence. Within this movement, we do not see the Father's presence. Christ receives no assurances that things will turn out right. Throughout his life, Christ has always actively participated in the workings of the divine providence of the Father. To reach that level of co-operation, he has learned to wait on the Father. His waiting here in this pain is not hopeless. He leans into the darkness, painful though it is to say yes to what will happen, because he trusts the Father. His "yes" is more than a passive acquiescence to fate. Instead, it says, "I will maintain that integrity that has been my life path." That integrity has been manifested in his three years of public ministry. It has been a constant and loving dependence on the Father's mercy. It will be maintained now, even in the face of God's silence.

Jesus arrives at this hard-earned moment and returns to his companions to find that Judas and a band of soldiers have come to arrest him. The public drama of his passion is about to begin. His liberty is taken away and he is prey to the whole range of human evil, from malicious brutality of his captors to the cowardice of political authority. In the presence of all these, he maintains his freedom, his relationship to the Father.

Questions for Prayer and Reflection

1. When you read and prayed the scripture passages, were you able to stay with Jesus? What kind of resistances came up? What do they suggest to you?
2. When you spent time with the above reflection on Christ in the garden, what aspects struck you? Did they cause any aspect of your life to rise to your awareness? What was significant about those aspects? How do you deal with them? Can you bring them now to God and stay with those moments? What happens when you do that?
3. How do you live your freedom? What would you consider to be areas of freedom in your life? What would be areas of unfreedom? How do they manifest themselves in terms of this prayer exercise?
4. Recall times when you risked your life in some moment of self-transcendence even though you knew that it would be painful. Is there a common pattern to those moments? What does that pattern tell you about your relationship to God?
5. What areas of your life or your world do you despair over? Does that despair make you frozen or resigned? How can you start to move within that despair? Can you move from resignation, to passive acceptance, to active acceptance? Can you imagine that movement? What does it do to your sense of rootedness?
6. When have you been present to others as they made critical decisions about their lives? How did you find them? How did you find yourselves with them?
7. After reflecting on and praying through these questions, what sense do you have of yourself? Can you accept that sense of self?

4th Exercise: The Betrayal

(Matthew 26:47-58; Luke 22:47-57; Mark 14:44-54, 66-68)

Scripture verse

> If we say we have no sin we deceive ourselves and the truth is not in us. If we confess our sins, he is faithful and just, and will forgive our sins, and cleanse us from all unrighteousness.
> (1 John 1:8-9)

From the Spiritual Exercises

> We must carefully observe the whole course of our thoughts. If the beginning and middle and end of the course of thoughts are wholly good and directed to what is entirely right, it is a sign that they are from the good angel. But the course of thoughts suggested to us may terminate in something evil, or distracting, or less good than the soul had formally proposed to do. Again, it may end in what weakens the soul, or disquiets it; or by destroying the peace, tranquillity, and quiet which it had before, it may cause disturbance to the soul. These things are a clear sign that the thoughts are proceeding from the evil spirit, the enemy of our progress and eternal salvation. (Sp. Ex. #333)

Grace to be prayed for

> This is to ask for what I desire. Here it will be to ask for sorrow, compassion, and shame because the Lord is going to His suffering for my sins. (Sp. Ex. #193)

Intimate Acts of Violence

After the intense inner journey to freedom in the Garden, Jesus is taken captive by the temple guards. When Judas identifies him with a kiss, Jesus is seized. Someone tries to defend him by striking out at the high priest's servant. In the ensuing conflict, a young man runs off naked. The guards bring Jesus to the courtyard of the high priest where, as Jesus waits, he hears Peter deny him three times.

The sequence revolves around the shame of betrayal and of Jesus' response to that betrayal.

Betrayal is an intimate act of violence. The integrity of the person betrayed is shattered: the betrayer has entered a personal sacred space through trust and has violated it. Betrayal destroys the bonds of human relationships and undermines those connections that make us who we are. The betrayals Jesus endures here eat away at his confidence in human nature to maintain the sense of community he strove to witness to. He sees clearly, as the prophet Jeremiah does, that there is nothing so devious and desperately corrupt as the human heart (Jeremiah 17:9). But even here he holds on to what the Father sees of the human heart, rather than what he is experiencing.

The Father sees the human heart as lovable and loving. He sees it in the human heart that is Jesus'.

It is this Jesus whom Judas identifies with a kiss to the crowd arriving with clubs and swords to seize him. Judas's despair has turned to malice, and his kiss reveals the opposite of what it symbolizes. It is a lie. Lies destroy relationships – it is no wonder that Satan is called the prince of lies. He stands for the destruction of community, as the Christ stands for the creation of community. Judas's kiss betrays the spirit of community. Yet Jesus does not react by rejecting Judas. He still calls him "Friend." What Jesus sees in Judas, Judas cannot see in himself. It is because he is so caught in this false self-image that he later destroys himself. He cannot live with what he has done. He cannot conceive of a love that can forgive him. God's mercy asks us to live out of God's image of us. It says that no matter what we have done, we are forgiven. We need to learn to accept that forgiveness. Here we can do that by being as present as we can to Christ as he manifests the extent of that forgiveness. His fidelity to the Father and to us, even in his suffering and death, shows that we will not be abandoned. We are asked to dare to believe this and to live out of that belief. It is the path to liberation.

Often we think, and sometimes it is true, that we need to fight for what is right, and that those acts of resistance bring liberation. But here, the person who defends Jesus by cutting off the servant's ear is using violence in reaction to violence. Jesus has accepted his path; the violence enacted here tries to stop Jesus from walking his path.

As Ecclesiastes says, there is "a time for war and a time for peace" (Ecclesiastes 3:8). How can we know the right thing to do at a particular time? That knowledge comes from doing as Christ does. His face is turned steadfastly towards the Father. In our path to intimacy, as we face what Jesus faces, we can also face who Jesus faces. It is the Father. Here, at his arrest, Jesus does not resist his capture. The one who tries to defend him is not one with Jesus. This is another type of betrayal, no less significant than Judas'. As with Judas, such behaviour claims to know the best way for God to act. Once again, self-will displaces obedience to God's will.

If we are making a discernment at this time, we must see if our choice allows us to be present to Jesus as he is, rather than attempting to conscript him to our cause. If the latter is true, we will find ourselves alienated from Jesus in the prayer. We will either be trapped in a self-righteousness that brings desolation, or we will be exposed the way the young man in the story is exposed.

Naked to My Enemies

Mark's gospel tells us this story: "A young man followed him, with nothing but a linen cloth about his body; and they seized him, but he left the linen cloth and ran away naked" (Mark 14:51-52). Had the young man allowed himself to be seized, he would not have been thus exposed, but he chose his own security and his own shame rather than accompany Jesus. It may be a very short story, but it contains the same dynamics as that of Cardinal Wolsey. Wolsey sacrificed his integrity and his vocation to serve his king, Henry the Eighth (1485–1547), a contemporary of Ignatius and the early Jesuits. After Wolsey had served Henry's worldly purposes, Henry had him deposed for high treason. Wolsey is reported to have said, "Had I served my God with half the zeal I had served my king, He would not have left me thus naked to mine enemies." This betrayal occurred, Wolsey realized, because the values he held did not arise from a living, passionate, and intimate relationship with God.

The Long Last Night

When Jesus is taken, he is carried to the high priest. There, many false witnesses testify against him, but since they do not agree among themselves, the high priest asks Jesus directly if he is equal to God. Saying yes would convict him of blasphemy under Jewish law, since no one was the equal of God. The punishment for such blasphemy was death. Knowing the law, Jesus refuses to betray his relationship with the Father. He is true to that intimacy even though he is humiliated by being spat upon and beaten up by those in the high priest's house.

Outside in the courtyard, though, is one who had followed him so far. It is Peter, with whom Jesus had an especially close relationship. It was Peter whom he had appointed as his right-hand man; Peter who first recognized him as the Messiah; Peter who saw his transfiguration; Peter who was rescued walking on the water. That same Peter had said he would never betray Jesus, no matter what. Yet, when those in the courtyard ask whether he is a follower of Jesus, he denies this relationship three times. At the third time, when a cock crowed twice, Peter remembered that Jesus had said to him, "Before the cock crows twice, you will deny me three times" (Mark 14:72). He breaks down and weeps. He realizes that despite his special intimacy with the Christ, he is no different from the others who abandoned Jesus.. He betrays himself in his denial of Christ. His self-image cannot withstand the pressures of the social situation. It is not that he does not know and love Jesus. He does. But here he is a coward. Up to this point, Peter has been brash, impetuous, charismatic. But he lacks courage, a heart bonded to Jesus' heart. As Ignatius is to point out later, love is demonstrated more in deeds rather than words. Where we put our lives and our bodies shows what we value.

The Passover meal was celebrated at sundown. Morning has not yet broken. Jesus waits. He has waited for the betrayer to arrive; he waits for the trial and the verdict of the high priest; he waits for his Father. He waits for the next move. In the midst of this waiting, he is focused, not knowing exactly what will come next, but knowing that, when all is being taken away from him and his mission is in ruins, he is still committed to the Father.

Questions for Prayer and Reflection

1. As you prayed the scripture passages, which part of the contemplation struck you the most? Where were you in the action? What does this suggest to you?
2. When you read the above reflection, what moved you the most? How does that aspect connect to your life and your path? Does it bring back memories? If you go back to those memories with Christ as your companion, what happens?
3. When have you felt betrayed? How did you cope with it? How do you cope with it now?
4. When have you betrayed another person, an ideal, or the way you saw yourself? How did you experience forgiveness? How do you live with those areas where you have not experienced forgiveness? What can you do now about those situations?
5. Do you experience tension in your life between your religion and your spirituality? If so, how does it express itself?
6. How are you rooted in these prayer periods? How does it feel?
7. How are you distracted in these prayer periods? How can you dispose yourself to be rooted?
8. Sometimes the temptation is to try to persuade Jesus not to walk the path he has accepted. Have you experienced this temptation? How does it manifest itself in your life?
9. What happens to you when you stay, simply, with Christ?
10. What are your conversations with Mary, Jesus, or the Father like at the end of these prayer periods?

5th Exercise: Jesus Before Pilate

Scripture verse

> [Pilate said to Jesus] "Do you not know that I have the power to release you, and power to crucify you?" Jesus answered, "You have no power over me unless it had been given to you from above." (John 19:10-11)

From the Spiritual Exercises

> Consider all blessings and gifts as descending from above. Thus, my limited power comes from the supreme and infinite power above. (Sp. Ex. #237)

Grace to be prayed for

> This is to ask for what I desire. Here it will be to ask for sorrow, compassion, and shame because the Lord is going to His suffering for my sins. (Sp. Ex. #193)

Politics and Religion

In the previous contemplations, we saw Jesus betrayed by his companions and by the corruption of some religious authorities. The destructiveness found in venal religious figures is one of the shocking realities of human history. It has set people against people; thrown countries into civil war; divided families; alienated individuals from their deepest selves; exploited to justify the pillaging of the earth; and even separated people from the merciful love of God. Yet religious institutions have not disappeared from the face of the earth. We are created to be spiritual, but we need religion to incarnate that spirit. And so we struggle with the institutionalization of the spirit, which gives it expression, but which at times seeks to repress it for institutional reasons. That spirit is not to be denied; it blows where it will. Jesus embodies that spirit as the manifestation of God in the world. It led him to a profound appreciation of the law, which he does not deny but transcends in his own person and in the living community to whom he gives it. For him the fullness of the law is summed up in two basic principles: the total, shameless, passionate love of God, and the love of one's neighbour as oneself. We belong to each other; in that belonging we are the community of the Christ longing for the Father.

The political world embodies the rules for belonging, just as the religious world embodies the rules for the spirit. The religious leaders turn Jesus over to the political powers not because they respect them, but because they do not have the authority to put anyone to death. Because Jesus has shown with his life their lack of spirit, they claim he does not belong and is to be treated like an outcast. But their malice goes even further than a tribal or cultic expulsion of a heretic. He must be eradicated in such a way that will leave no doubt in people's minds that a spirit like his will never be tolerated – by the public humiliation and the torture of dying on a cross. For this, they needed the collusion of the Roman authority, who alone had the right to execute criminals.

Jesus is taken to Pilate, the Roman governor of the province. The religious authorities must decide how to use the Roman law to accomplish their goal. The charge they bring before Pilate is this: "We have found this man perverting our nation and forbidding us to give tribute to Caesar, and saying that he himself is Christ a king" (Luke 23:2). Under Roman law there was one emperor, Caesar. All the lands under Caesar paid taxes or tribute. The accusation against Jesus, then, is that of treason; the penalty for treason is death by crucifixion. Jesus does not reply to the charges.

It is the way of a soiled world to rationalize its needs. Against those forces, innocence and truth are crushed. Perhaps it is naive to expect more than the politically expedient in corrupt and duplicitous social systems. Pilate chooses pragmatically. Even though he can find no fault with Jesus from the charges brought against him, and even though he judges that "nothing deserving death has been done by him" (Luke 23:9), he is trapped by the insistent demands of the chief priests, the rulers, and the people, and hands Jesus over to his death. The horror of what he has done is compounded by the fact that, instead of releasing Jesus, he is forced to release Barabbas, a man "who had been thrown into prison for murder and insurrection" (Luke 23:25). It may be a scriptural irony that the name "Barabbas" translates as "son of the Father." Jesus also calls himself the "Son of the Father," yet his world will accept only a murderer and a rebel by that name.

Victim and Oppressor

In our own world, we have seen the innocent brutalized and crushed by political and religious forces that seek only their own ends, not caring who is destroyed in the process. Many starve in a world that can feed all; many have no voice or power in their own country; many commit violence after being swayed by the lies of their leaders; many have souls that are deformed by generations of hate; many disappear, unnoticed. This is the fate of the victim. But every single one of these is a member of the human family, a community that extends across time and place. Each one has been uniquely named a child and the beloved of God, just as Christ was. In Christ, each has an identity. Even though the world has denied or ignored or subverted this identity, in the suffering of Christ, each is carried to the Father. Our own lives and identities are carried there, too. What Christ suffers, we suffer; what anyone suffers, we suffer, too. We are all one.

We are all one with the oppressor, also, for the oppressor is a victim, too. In denying part of his or her humanity to maintain a position of privilege, the oppressor lives a crippled, wounded life. In fact, it is because of one's hurts that one hurts others. The malice of the chief priests of Christ's day; the self-destructive hate of the Roman soldiers; the animal passions of the crowd; the confusion of Pilate; the circus curiosity of Herod; the self-absorption of Judas – these are all forms of hell. Christ walks through those hells without losing his integrity, even though he is battered and scarred by these encounters. He does not engage those powers at the level on which they operate. He maintains his silence in the face of lies and his humanity in the face of inhumanity. He keeps his focus on the Father, even as he is treated as an object.

It is often hard for us to see how we damage ourselves and others – such awareness is usually too painful to bear. When we hurt others, we tend to rationalize our actions so we can live with ourselves. When we are present to Jesus in his suffering, we face the suffering of the world as both victim and oppressor. But we are also liberated from the passivity of the victim and from the aggression of the perpetrator. We start seeing things as they are. With the integrity of Christ, we behold a world in pain, needing to be redeemed. We also see the work of redemption lies in embracing suffering with a love that comes from the Father and returns to the Father.

Questions for Prayer and Reflection

1. As you contemplate Christ's journey from the house of Annas to the House of Caiaphas, and from there to Pilate, then to Herod and back to Pilate, what strikes you as most compelling? As you stay with those moments, what is revealed to you?
2. What stops you from being seduced by moral disgust? How does that affect your relationship with modern religious institutions? How does that affect your understanding and involvement in the political world around you?
3. Where do you find the face and the person of Christ in the world today? How does that presence engage you?
4. In what ways are you a victim? In what ways does the role of victim rob you of your integrity? How do you cope with that? What happens when you pray about your sense of being a victim?
5. In what ways do you identify with the powers of the world? How does this manifest itself in your daily life, in the choices you make, in the values you adopt? How do you justify that perspective? How do you feel moved when you realize your depth of complicity in that world?
6. How do you find your integrity? How do you maintain it? What are the costs? What is its value?
7. In your prayer, what emerges in your conversations with the Father and with Jesus?
8. Who, in the world today, is Jesus for you? How?
9. Who, in the world today, are you Jesus for? How?

6th Exercise: Jesus Tortured

(Matthew 27:24-31; Mark 15:15-20)

Scripture verse

Jesus said to his disciples, "I say to you that listen, Love your enemies, do good to those who hate you, bless those who curse you, pray for those who abuse you. If anyone strikes you on the cheek, offer the other also; and from anyone who takes away your coat, do not withhold even your shirt. Give to everyone who begs from you; and if anyone takes away your goods, do not ask for them again. Do to others as you would have them do to you." (Luke 6:27-31)

From the Spiritual Exercises

How much more worthy of consideration is Christ our Lord, the Eternal King, before whom is assembled the whole world. To all His summons goes forth, and to each one in particular He addresses the words: "It is my will to conquer the whole world and all my enemies, and thus to enter into the glory of my Father. Therefore, those who wish to join me in this enterprise must be willing to labour with me, that by following me in suffering, they may follow me in glory. (Sp. Ex. #95)

Grace to be prayed for

This is to ask for what I desire. Here it will be to ask for sorrow, compassion, and shame because the Lord is going to His suffering for my sins. (Sp. Ex. #193)

Denying the Human Bond

After Pilate has declared Jesus innocent, he gives into the demands of the mob, which has been incited by the priests. He orders Jesus to be scourged and crucified, but absolves himself of any responsibility. Scourging so weakens a man that he dies more quickly when crucified. It says something about the horror of the world when its compassion must manifest itself in such brutal ways.

In our world, the free gift of our bodies to another is an act of love. The taking of our unwilling bodies by another is an act of constraint. In the latter case, our liberty is significantly compromised and we are subject to another. Torture goes even further. It radically denies the person any right as a human being or human animal. Its power is in removing those rights in as painful a manner as possible. It says to that person, "You are not equal to other human beings; you have no control over your life, your body, or your mind. You are nothing except what the torture creates you to be. You are nothing except in how the torture chooses to humiliate and destroy you." Torture radically denies the bond that connects human to human. For the tortured, isolation focuses their awareness on the violent and brutal pain over which they have no control but which becomes the centre of their identity. They are aware only of their pain.

The Violence of Power

Scourging in Roman times involved stripping the victim naked and lashing the body with a whip made of leather thongs, the tips of which were dipped in lead. Its range covered the whole body. It could remove skin from muscle and muscle from bone, desex the person, smash nerve endings, separate tendons, and even cause toxic shock and death. This was the Roman act of "kindness" to those condemned to be crucified. Jesus received this treatment by the Roman soldiers. Scripture is discreet and succinct on this subject, saying merely that Pilate, "having scourged Jesus, delivered him to be crucified" (Matthew 27:26). When we contemplate this sequence, we are not asked to be voyeurs to this spectacle. Rather, we ask for the grace to be present to Jesus in his agony and to the pain, shame, and confusion we experience as we bear witness to the cruelty of the world and to Christ's love for the world. He loves the world and he endures its testing of that love.

That testing includes the gratuitous humiliations the Roman soldiers inflict upon him after the scourging. The Romans regarded everyone else as inferior, and so many of the soldiers sent to the provinces to guard the borders, to maintain Roman law and peace, and to be the symbol of Roman power and might were arrogant and dismissive of those they subjugated. For them, Jesus was just another nonentity from a treacherous mass of tribal conflicts. After he is scourged, the whole battalion of some 500 men gather. They show him what they think of the Jews and of the one who was said to be the king of the Jews. Instead of an honourable crown of laurel leaves, a wreath of thorns was woven and jammed onto his head; instead of the sceptre of royalty he is given a reed; he is stripped and a scarlet robe, signifying nobility, is draped over him. "And kneeling before him they mocked him, saying, 'Hail, King of the Jews!' And they spat upon him and took the reed and struck him on the head" (Matthew 27:29-30).

Here is someone without power, innocent, woefully accused, and sentenced to death. Now, just after being badly beaten, he is treated as an object of derision and contempt. What are we to make of this act? We may think of the way power abuses the powerless; we may consider how vulnerability brings out the aggression of the insecure; we may even be horrified at humanity's inhumanity to other humans. We could even consider how such things happen today, in foreign places and close to home. We may be filled with a sense of moral disgust and a sense of helplessness. We grieve.

The Mystery of Evil and Suffering

But we are asked to be present to Jesus at a deeper level. He does not curse his tormentors. He does not fall back into a self-enclosed world. He remains open to the mystery as it unfolds – even in the grimmest horror and existential darkness. For him, as for us now, there is the mystery of suffering and evil; the mystery of the Father's presence in that suffering and evil; the mystery of Divine Providence; the mystery of our own path. Finally, there is the mystery of ourselves as we walk that path and ask, Who am I? Why is this happening to me? How can I endure it?

Christ endures it by taking it one moment at a time; we can endure it by being there for him and with him as he journeys to the cross and moves through the darkness to meet his Father.

Questions for Prayer and Reflection

1. How are you doing in these contemplations? Can you stay with Jesus? What temptations take you away from being present to him?
2. Where do you find Christ suffering and tortured in the world today? How does that affect you?
3. How are you present to the world of suffering and duplicity that you see in the newspapers and on television?
4. What happens when you become numb to the pain of the world? How does this affect your daily life?
5. How can you be attentive to the world's pain and your own without being destroyed by it?
6. In the above reflection, what points moved you most? What does that say to you? What happens when you go back to those points and remain quietly and prayerfully with them?
7. Where does that prayer carry you?
8. What happens in your conversations with the Father, with Jesus, or with Mary at the end of your prayer? What questions arise? How are they answered? Do any of them ask you any questions? What do you say?

7th Exercise: The Path to the Cross

(Luke 23:26-31; Mark 15:21)

Scripture verse

"Do not ask me to abandon or forsake you! For wherever you go I will go, wherever you lodge I will lodge, your people shall be my people, and your God my God. Wherever you die I will die, and there be buried." (Ruth 1:15-17)

From the Spiritual Exercises

I will beg God our Lord for grace that all my intentions, actions, and operations may be directed purely to the praise and service of His Divine Majesty. (Sp. Ex. #46)

Grace to be prayed for

This is to ask for what I desire. Here it will be to ask for sorrow, compassion, and shame because the Lord is going to His suffering for my sins. (Sp. Ex. #193)

Crushed by Suffering

The distance from where the Roman soldiers mocked and spat upon Jesus to where he would be crucified is a little less than a kilometre. He is too weak from the beatings to walk that distance carrying the crossbeam to which his hands would be nailed. The Roman soldiers force a man from the crowd to carry the wooden post. (Roman law allowed any Roman soldier in the line of duty to conscript a bystander to carry his gear for a mile.) Stumbling to his Calvary, Jesus meets the pious women of Jerusalem who would weep and lament for the prisoners going to their death along this route. He tells them not to grieve for him, but rather for what the Romans will do to them and their children when those same Roman armies destroy Jerusalem in the not too distant future. As Simon of Cyrene, the conscripted bystander, reaches out to help him in his suffering, Jesus reaches out in that same suffering to comfort the grieving women.

It would be comforting for us to see Jesus in this state as a strong, heroic figure, but he is not. He is a man so crushed by suffering that he arouses pity in those who see him. In his dire poverty he accepts help from others, but he still gives something to the women grieving him. There is a bleak simplicity and an abject nakedness in this pilgrim figure stripped of almost all humanity on his way to his death. We can see this figure in the dispossessed of the world: the starving mother crossing the drought plains of Ethiopia holding a pot-bellied baby too weak to brush the flies from its eyes; the silent stare of a street person in a prosperous Western city looking in what seems like madness beyond the forms of this world; and, if we are honest, in our own poverty of spirit, the figure of the pilgrim beggar who finds in every act of human outrage its own suffering. But whether we can see this or not, we all journey through a life we cannot control towards a death over which we have no control. We are powerless. We take what we have been given, and we offer what we have. Jesus, on his way to his death, does the same.

Transformed by the Encounter with Suffering

He accepts Simon of Cyrene's carrying his cross. Simon, a Jew, had come to Jerusalem to celebrate the Passover and the Feast of the Unleavened Bread, as was required by law for all Judean males. He would have had no desire to carry the cross of a criminal: in doing so he would have become ceremonially unclean and thus unfit to eat the Passover meal. To be drafted to do this by Roman force was, for him, not only demeaning, it broke the ethical taboos of his religion. Although his act is not one of gratuitous kindness, it has interesting results. Simon's family is mentioned later in the Scriptures as being Christian and helping Paul in his works. The power of his act of humiliation changes the path of his life. It carries him beyond the safe, established confines of his religion to an encounter with a broken man. But instead of being destroyed by that encounter, Simon is transformed. He becomes part of the living force of redemption.

When people go to impoverished countries to help out for awhile, their values are often radically transformed. They encounter the poor in all their misery and ingenuity, and they discover, oddly enough, that that encounter gives their own lives meaning and direction. The same thing happens when we deal with another's poverty and handicap. We might initially experience feelings of distaste and revulsion, but our perceptions change when we discover a common humanity and admit that we do not need to live the life of indifference we had lived before. We may go even further and discover, through another's poverty and suffering, our own poverty and suffering. In touching that intimate and delicate place in ourselves, we become more attuned to the world's pain and suffering, and begin to speak in a language of the heart that is compassion and simple, practical love. If, in our contemplation, we enter into Simon of Cyrene's world and life, we unearth the transformation occurring in ourselves.

Witness as an Act of Resistance

As such, we can reach out to others in our suffering as Christ reaches out to the grieving women on his path that day. In grief, we can be trapped by the pain of our lives. Those women are not there as paid mourners. They are there because, like marginalized women anywhere, they see the cruel fate brutally meted out to their sons and daughters, their husbands and families. Their act of resistance is to witness and to mourn. They line the route and offer what comfort they can. In response, Jesus offers what he can. He tells them the truth of their lives, saying, "Weep for yourselves and for your children .... For if they do this when the wood is green what will happen when the wood is dry?" (Luke 23:28-31). If the living presence of Divine Mercy in the world is treated this way, what will happen after it is killed? Historically, before the century was over, Jerusalem was sacked and the Jews were driven from the city. But Jesus' lament cuts across time and place. He is the fullest manifestation of the Father's love, and the world in its malice and blindness treats him like a despised criminal. How will the world treat those who come after as his representatives? How will the world treat itself and any who fall under its dominion?

We who live in these times know the answer. But in the face of that death, we, like Jesus, can attest with our lives to the love that is beyond death. We live in this world, but we do not have to live by the values of this world. The mystery that calls Jesus beyond death calls us also.

Questions for Prayer and Reflection

1. In the prayer, what moved you most? How? Return to that moment and stay there to see if there is anything else there for you. When you speak to God about this moment, what is revealed to you?
2. In the prayer, what repelled you the most? Where did you feel the driest, or the most alienated, or the least like praying? Why? Return to that moment and stay there for some time to see if there is something there for you. When you speak to God about this moment, what comes to you?
3. Have you ever been compelled to do something for someone else that changed your life for the better? What aspects of your life are like Simon of Cyrene's?
4. In our world today, we are called to witness to violence and the destruction of innocence without turning away from that destruction. How do we witness to that in ways that maintain our integrity?
5. In your conversations with God, or with Mary, what strikes you?
6. In the contemplations, where do you find yourself – as an onlooker, a participant in the action, or one of the main figures? What does this say to you?
7. Do the prayer or your reflections trigger memories in you? What is the relationship between the prayer and those memories?

8th Exercise: The Crucifixion of Jesus

(Mark 15:22-40; Matthew 27:33-55; Luke 23:32-49; John 19:17-37)

Scripture verse

We know that all of creation groans and is in agony even until now; and not only creation but we ourselves, who have the first fruits of the Spirit, groan inwardly as we await the redemption of our bodies. For in this hope we are saved. But hope is not hope if its object is seen; how is it possible to hope for what one sees? And hoping for what we cannot see means awaiting it with patient endurance. The Spirit too helps us in our weakness for we do not know how to pray as we ought; but the Spirit himself intercedes for us with groanings too deep for words. (Romans 8:22-26)

From the Spiritual Exercises

We must make ourselves indifferent to all created things, as far as we are allowed free choice and are not under any prohibition. Consequently, as far as we are concerned, we should not prefer health to sickness, riches to poverty, honour to dishonour, a long life to a short life. The same holds for all other things. (Sp. Ex. #23)

Grace to be prayed for

This is to ask for what I desire. Here it will be to ask for sorrow, compassion, and shame because the Lord is going to His suffering for my sins. (Sp. Ex. #193)

Witnessing a Death

In a crucifixion, the arms and feet are nailed in such a way that when the body is upright, the shoulders become dislocated. The result is agony, as those limbs are asked to bear the weight of the body. If one relaxes, one suffocates, and so one thrusts against the cross for breath. But this pushes against the nails and that pain becomes unbearable. The gospel writers are aware of the medical effects of such a torture, which was commonplace in their time. Their accounts contain the discretion of the lover who is aware of, but unwilling to depict, the beloved's final anguish. What they hold in their hearts of an experience that goes beyond words, we too can hold in our hearts as we contemplate those final hours of Christ on the day before the Jewish sabbath began.

Yet we are given something in the scriptural descriptions of Christ's dying on the cross. For Mark, the crucifixion plunges us into the profoundest depths of human misery and abandonment. Matthew gives us Jesus as the new Moses, whose suffering allows us to become intimates with the Father without the intermediary of temple religion. Luke presents the Messiah who remains as a healer and reconciler even in the midst of his anguish. John shows us a Christ who, even on the cross, is in full command of his destiny. The central questions for us, though, are these: How are we present to Christ on the cross? What Christ is given to us in our contemplation at this time?

Throughout the Exercises, St. Ignatius presents us with a Christ who enters his poverty to be completely disposed to the Father's will. He witnesses with his life to his trust in the Father's compassionate mercy for all, even in the face of his suffering and death. The Exercises present an encounter with Jesus that is in accordance with the different facets of the crucified Christ of the gospels. We are asked to be present as fully as possible to that Christ.

Those passages leave out many painful things, even though the gospels are written from the perspective of the resurrection. None describe the actual crucifixion and, like the contemplation of the hidden life, we depend on what we need from it to be given in prayer. But we do know that Jesus' scourged and bleeding body was stripped naked and nailed to the cross, which was then lifted and fixed in a hole in the ground. Medical evidence says that a crucified person would slowly drown as the exhausted body slumped and the lungs filled with water. And so the victim dies.

Living Our Own Deaths

But we are here not only to witness to a death, although there is a death. We are here to be present to the way Jesus lives his dying, trusting in a life beyond death. He is stripped and soldiers gamble for his blood-stained clothes. As he hangs there, struggling between the pain of dislocated joints and shattered nerve endings pushing against the nails, trying to breathe, he remains faithful to the Father. This is a level of intimacy that goes beyond emotional bonding. He prays for those who crucified him; he pardons the thief; he gives his mother a home; with his dying breath he hands his spirit over to the Father. All this occurs amidst his growing pain and exhaustion.

It is not as if he forgets himself. He thirsts, and he acknowledges his sense of abandonment. He is besieged by temptation and cries out, in the words of the psalmist, "My God, my God, why have you forsaken me?" (Psalm 69:21). Even though he feels forsaken by the Father, he dies as he has lived, faithful to that relationship. On the cross, Christ waits on the Father as he has waited on him all his life. In that waiting he is stripped of any felt sense of his relationship with the Father.

We contemplate this dying, knowing how the story continues. We know that at his death there are signs that he does indeed witness to the Father's love for the world. The unbelieving Roman centurion who is stationed at the cross acknowledges, "Truly, this man is the Son of God" (Mark 15:39). Death is overthrown, for as Matthew tells us, "Tombs were opened, and many bodies of the saints who had fallen asleep were raised, and coming out of the tombs after his resurrection they went into the holy city and appeared to many" (Matthew 27:52-53).

But Christ, in his humanity, does not – cannot – live his resurrection before his death. He can only live his death until, at the Father's dispensation, he is raised. He endures the fullness of his death, just as each of us must live out our death – we cannot avoid it. We can know and believe the Father's mercy for each one of us, for we experienced it as we did the Exercises of the First Week. But we do not know, until we experience it, the Father's mercy for us in our dying. Like Christ, we lean into that mercy and that mystery. Doing so allows us to put death in perspective, but it does not allow us to dismiss death. We all must die.

In contemplating Christ's death, we are not asked to die his death, or to take him down from the cross. We are asked only to be as fully present as possible to his dying, and to our own dying, as he was to his. We can do both because his dying reveals to us something we, even now, find it almost impossible to believe: that God manifests his love by enduring, without cursing or damning us, a shameful and agonizing death for us even as we reject him and his mercy. He does this not to make us feel guilty or duty bound to follow him. On the contrary, it is to assure us we are free and can live that freedom in the face of the trials, illusions, and punishments of this world. When we contemplate the death of Christ, we live the deaths of our own lives and of our world in hope of the resurrection.

Questions for Prayer and Reflection

Note: When we contemplate Christ's crucifixion, anything can happen. We must be careful not to manipulate ourselves to feel or experience one thing or another. All we are asked to do is to be present. Sometimes our emotions go deeper than our feelings, and we feel nothing. Sometimes we are carried by our prayer into moments of deep feeling. We need only to be truthful to what happens in the prayer.

1. How did the prayer go? What stood out for you as you entered the scene of the crucifixion?
2. Where were you in the action of the contemplation? Why is this significant?
3. How do you live your life in the face of your own oncoming death? How would you like to live your life when you face this fact?
4. How does God's mercy shape the way you live with yourself and with others?
5. As Christ continually suffers in every act of injustice, every broken relationship, every illusion maintained, any beauty despoiled, every act of violence, how is the mercy of the Father brought to that situation for you?
6. What do you do when the Father does not seem to care?
7. How do you pray in the face of pain and suffering?
8. Call to mind times when you were in situations that were destructive of the life you needed. How did you maintain your integrity at those times? How were you rescued?
9. What does the cross of Christ truly mean in your life?
10. How is that cross misrepresented and misused in this world? How does this trap people?

9th Exercise: Christ is Laid in the Tomb

(Matthew 27:55-61; Mark 15:42-47; Luke 23:50-56; John 19:38-42)

Scripture verses

Wretch that I am! Who will deliver me from this body under the power of death? All praise to God through Jesus Christ our Lord .... (Rom 7:24-25)

Death no longer has dominion over him. (Rom 6:9)

From the Spiritual Exercises

The more the soul is in solitude and seclusion, the more fit it renders itself to approach and be united with its Creator and Lord; and the more closely it is united with Him, the more it disposes itself to receive graces and gifts from the infinite goodness of its God. (Sp. Ex. #20)

Grace to be prayed for

This is to ask for what I desire. Here it will be to ask for sorrow, compassion, and shame because the Lord is going to His suffering for my sins. (Sp. Ex. #193)

The Ruins of a Life

We are told some of those who followed Jesus witnessed his death. After he died, one of his disciples asked Pilate for the body, and it was taken down. His followers wrapped it with spices and laid it in a nearby tomb. In this contemplation, we are asked to be present to this sequence of events.

When we see someone suffering in agony, it comes as a relief to us when that person dies. We think, well, at least now it is over and we can get to the business of the funeral. This gives us something to do. We get a break from the dreadful burden of waiting and from the painful awareness of our limited abilities to control our own or anyone else's living and dying.

In their waiting by the cross, those who followed Jesus – as family, friend, and disciple – enter into his anguish and grief. Since our lives are all woven together in a common fabric of relationships, the cruelty inflicted on someone who is part of our life traumatizes us. A sense of disbelief eats away at what has become familiar, and we are forced to chart a course through the unknown. We may struggle against the strangeness that envelops us, and experience a profound desolation for what is lost. We become strangers to ourselves. As we wait with those waiting by the cross, we mourn the loss of hopes, ideals, and dreams. We had cherished the possibility that God's mercy would touch human hearts, and that the works of the one we followed would bring about that intimate sense of belonging and community where all could find a home.

Instead, we wait for a tortured man to die, a man who has touched our hearts and imaginations and lives. Here hangs someone with whom we were willing to risk our lives. He dies calling out to the Father. In our pain as his lovers, we cannot even begin to imagine the pain of the one who called him "Son" and "Beloved." What can we do now? The big schemes of a transformed world are in ruins. The ache in our hearts, which we finally acknowledged because it seemed something could now be done about it, is again rawly exposed to the absurdity of the world.

An Act of Mercy

That pain, outrage, and despair made Joseph of Arimathea bold. He asked Pilate for the body. Once Pilate had ascertained that the Christ was dead, he gave the body to Joseph. Maybe this is the work of good people in the world, to bury the dead so that they may not be further desecrated. It is a small and manageable good, and may be all that is possible today. The charitable act of burying the dead is a profoundly human concern that echoes through the ages and stories of diverse cultures. We find it in the biblical story of Tobias's father and in the Greek drama *Antigone*, where a young girl follows her heart and attempts to bury her dishonoured brother even though that ritual act has been forbidden on pain of death. Sophocles reveals the capability of the human heart to harbour such malice that even a work of mercy might be regarded as a crime. We find it in stories of indignities suffered by the dead to show their persecutor's power, and in Christ's mockery on the cross in the crucifixion. Joseph of Arimathea's action restores some dignity to Christ's body.

This is an act of love and relief, though bitterly anguished, to touch the corpse of someone we love. It is the body and yet it is not the body. And in the case of Jesus, it is a body transformed. Cold, bloody, broken, the smell of terror and human waste. In the gathering dark, his followers can perform only the bare necessities: with no time to prepare the body properly, they bind it with linen cloth and spices, and lay it in the tomb.

Keeping Vigil

In our contemplation, we are asked to keep vigil by that tomb. We are asked to continue to be present as fully as possible. And so we wait. We do not know what will happen or how it will happen for us. We cannot create resurrection for ourselves. It is a gift, and it depends on the dispensation of the Father. We cannot will Christ's resurrection. We can fantasize about what it might be like, and imagine it happening, but such stories come from ourselves. The resurrection, when it happens, comes from beyond ourselves.

As we wait, let us reflect on how we first got to know Jesus in this retreat. Let us reflect on how we became intimates of Jesus. Let us remember our good times and our bad times together. Let us ponder on those things that did not make sense at the time.

Even if we run out of things to think about, this does not mean that the prayer is finished. We need to wait in that empty space when first the mind goes blank, and then the heart settles into the silence of the pain and sinks deeper and deeper – past feeling, even past emotion – into that presence that holds us and all things into being.

Questions for Prayer and Reflection

1. What happened to you as you waited for Christ to die?
2. How did you deal with his death?
3. Were you able to be merciful to the body? to the others around you?
4. How did you wait at the tomb in prayer? in silence? just waiting? What came up during those times? What happened when you brought this to your conversation with God, the Christ, or Mary?
5. How do you behave at the funerals of those you have known? How was the prayer the same as, or different from, those times?
6. When has something or someone precious been taken from you? How did you cope? If you re-enter those moments now in your prayer, can you see in them the death of Christ for you? What happens when you do so?
7. What are the dead in your life now that you keep watch over? Can you allow yourself reverently to bury them? To offer them back to the mystery Jesus calls "Father"? What happens when you allow yourself to do this?
8. If, in a separate prayer period, you were to go over the events of this Third Week – from the Last Supper to the Waiting at the Tomb, as you have experienced them in prayer – what strikes you as most significant? Why? How does this affect you?
9. Is there any unfinished business to this Week, or to your prayer at this time, or to your life as you see it now, that you would like to pray about?
10. Can you speak to the mystery called "Father" about those things? What happens when you do?

10th Exercise: The Descent into Hell – The Interlude Between the Burial and the Resurrection

Scripture verse

> Now the Lord is the Spirit, and where the Spirit of the Lord is, there is freedom. (2 Corinthians 3:17)

From the Spiritual Exercises

> It will be very profitable for the one who is to go through the Exercises to enter upon them with magnanimity and generosity toward his Creator and Lord, and to offer Him his entire will and liberty, that His Divine Majesty may dispose of him and all he possesses according to His most holy will.
> (Sp. Ex. #5)

Grace to be prayed for

> This is to ask for what I desire. Here it will be to ask for sorrow, compassion, and shame because the Lord is going to His suffering for my sins. (Sp. Ex. #193)

Intimate Healing

In the next stage on our spiritual journey, we will move onto Christ's resurrection. In the first contemplation to the Fourth Week, which deals with the resurrection and living that resurrection in our daily lives, St. Ignatius makes this interesting observation: "This is the history. Here it is how after Christ expired on the cross his body remained separated from the soul, but always united with the divinity. His soul, likewise united with the divinity, descended into hell. There he sets free the souls of the just" (#219).

The work of the Christ extends through all states of being. In Ignatius's iconography, that work extends to those who, through no fault of their own, are trapped in situations where they cannot express or receive love. What they experience is very similar to what Christ experienced on the cross: a sense of innocence violated and forsaken, of peace frustrated, of goodness tormented, of wholeness broken, of longing unfulfilled, of blessedness misinterpreted. What they experience is their radical helplessness. All they can do is wait, as Christ waited on the cross.

We experience much the same thing today, and during our vigil outside Jesus' tomb. But the divine mission of God is not constrained by bodily limitations. That spirit of compassionate love desires to liberate all from whatever limits their freedom to live fully. It enters our places of imprisonment to bring us to a spiritual freedom from oppression. When we are present at the tomb in a state of unknowing, something is happening to us at levels below our bodily consciousness. We are being liberated. This is the continuing work of intimacy. It loves what is lost into life. This is a deep, hidden work. Its effects rise slowly to awareness.

Radical Transformation

Just as the Father reaches into death and brings the Son to resurrection, so the Son reaches into the most broken and desolate places of existence to witness with his spirit the depth of the compassionate mercy of his Father. That transformation is one of spirit, of heart, of imagination, of desire, of perception. The spirit is transformed because we experience in the midst of our despair a hope that refuses to give us up. It encourages us to believe that we are redeemable and that, even as we wait by the tombs of our lives and hopes, we are in the process of being redeemed. When we finally dare to allow ourselves to accept that gift, offered freely and simply, we discover our hearts expanding to accept our own suffering and the suffering of others. We find we can hold the world, without despair or depression, but with a sense of wonder. That wonder transforms our imagination. It realizes the world and life do not have to be the way they seem, and we do not have to accept the world in its distortions.

In fact, we discover our heart's desire – that unbroken intimacy with the Father, through Christ – to re-create the world into a home for all. We can do this because we now perceive the possibilities for life inherent in the situations we live through. We are no longer trapped. We see a path through the gloom. We find the energy to follow it, and we walk that path with hope and commitment, and in union with everyone who lives the same felt relationship with the source of life.

The Liberation of the Most Alienated

Christ's descent into the dead and into hell brings to life what he finds there. What rises from the depths, deeper than original sin, is original grace. As that grace emerges into our daily lives, it brings with it the deaths it transforms as it passes through them. We discover that we come from God, we return to God, and the path to God *is* God. This is not to say that there is no suffering on the path. In fact, on this journey we constantly leap into the furnaces of affliction, and are transformed there. Thus we do what the Christ did in bringing us to freedom. The creativity of God transforms evil into good, suffering into joy, isolation into community, imprisonment into freedom, death into resurrection.

In death, Jesus waits on the Father for deliverance. He waits in a love that does not deny death and suffering, but accepts it on the path back to the Father. That waiting is active, not passive; in fact, Christ is most creative when he is on the cross. That dying, death, and entombment draw out into the open all the pain and malice of a betrayed creation. There it encounters the constant love of God, who does not shrink from this horror. In that embrace Jesus dies; in that embrace creation is renewed. In the patience of Christ on the cross we discover the patience of the Father, whose gift is time and the open door in every moment of time to the fullness of life. Christ's descent into hell is a manifestation of that gift. It is the Father's desire that nothing and no one, in no moment of creation, be lost – not even what seems irredeemable, not even what is trapped in hell.

When we enter into this contemplation and spend time in it, we aid in that redemption and we uncover its effects in our lives.

Questions for Prayer and Reflection

1. What were the most moving moments in this contemplation? Return to them, one at a time, and wait for their significance to be expanded in your prayer.
2. Is there a pattern to those moments? What does it suggest? How do you find yourself responding as you become aware of that pattern?
3. Can you, in your prayer, bring Christ to those places in your life and in the world where you experience hell? What happens when you do that?
4. When have you been in situations that were sheer hell for you? How were you liberated? How do you account for that liberation? Return to those moments prayerfully and see how the Christ was present at those times. (You might want to ask at the beginning of that prayer for the presence of Christ to identify itself to you.)
5. What was the most desolate moment in this contemplation? Why do you think this moment stands out? Return to that moment in prayer. Stay there and see what happens.
6. How does this prayer, and its repetitions, help you see what has been going on during the Exercises of this Week?
7. In what ways are you creative? In what ways are you now asked to be creative? Pray for the answers to these questions to be revealed to you.
8. How do your conversations about these prayers with the Father, the Christ, or Mary illuminate your life and your path?

11th Exercise: An Overview of the Third Week

Scripture verse

And he said to me, "You are my servant,
Israel, in whom I will be glorified."
But I said, "I have laboured in vain,
I have spent my strength for nothing and vanity;
yet surely my cause is with the Lord,
and my reward with my God."

And now the Lord says,
who formed me in the womb to be his servant,
to bring Jacob back to him,
and that Israel might be gathered to him,
for I am honoured in the sight of the Lord,
and my God has become my strength –
he says,
"It is too light a thing that you should be my servant
to raise up the tribes of Jacob
and to restore the survivors of Israel;
I will give you as a light to the nations,
that my salvation may reach to the end of the earth."

(Isaiah 49:3-6)

From the Spiritual Exercises

Fifth Point. The fifth, to consider how the Divinity hides Itself, that is, how It could destroy Its enemies and does not do it, and how It leaves the most sacred Humanity to suffer so very cruelly. (Sp. Ex. #196)

Grace to be prayed for

To be found in all things by God.

A Transforming Love

The journey through the passion is a journey into intimacy. The lover enters into the despised places of the beloved's world, where the duplicity of the human heart is exposed. There is nothing hidden there that is not revealed. Here one discovers the depths of human depravity. Here one also discovers the dimensions of a human love present to this self-destructiveness in a way that does not deny the integrity of love. This love understands evil as ignorance. It knows those who commit it do not understand what they do. It sees its violence as the frustration of love so thwarted as to become malice.

It endures the grinding repetition of patterns of sin so ingrained as to distort humanity's nature to be free and joyful. And while it is a journey through the unredeemed places of creation, marked by suffering and hate, death and despair, betrayal and self-recrimination, its journey is also marked by an unwavering passion for life and for the source of all life. Its passage does not take away sin. It takes away the power of sin to stop our movement towards the one who calls us to the fullness of life. In that movement, we see the possibilities of transformation evil cannot see or countenance. Its very movement is its witness to life.

At every moment of our lives we are on a journey. Every moment is a transition. We leave something behind and we accept something new. Passover is not just a Jewish feast, or the roots of the Christian Easter. It is the state of every human's life. We come from God and we ultimately will return to God. Sometimes, like those ancient Israelites, because of our hardness of hearts, we wander in the wastelands until we are purified enough to see the next step home. Christ's life shows us that path home. Our passover happens when we, too, enter into the furnaces of affliction to transform through forgiveness what has been despoiled. We experience and offer such forgiveness when we are not trapped by the past, but offer that past to the future, which embraces us in a hope not seduced by moral disgust. It sees in that past the possibilities of a new creation.

We are still being formed. Sin stops creation and creativity, causing despair. We can be so terrorized by death that we give up living and enter an endless cycle of dehumanizing existence. Then we find life brutal, and we brutalize others in our fallen state. We remain in a state of death.

But passover brings a movement from death to life. We set out on that path to freedom by following Jesus into the darkness where our fears trap us, our blindness causes us to lose the way, our selfishness makes us alone, our greed burdens us, and our self-righteousness condemns us. We discover we are our worst enemy in that darkness.

In the passion of Jesus Christ, all of the enemies of our human nature are depicted. Jesus is caught by these, but he is not trapped by them. His passion for the Father, which arises from his intimacy with the one who calls him "Beloved," carries him through death into the arms of the One who loves him.

Our journey along the path of intimacy, which has opened to us in the Exercises of St. Ignatius, roots us in the one who also calls us "Beloved."

The one who has gone before us shows us the way back to the Father. When we pray the Third Week of the Exercises of St. Ignatius, we contemplate that part of the way of the Christ back to the Father, which leads through his suffering and death. By being present to him there, we discover within ourselves a deeper intimacy with him and with the Father. We discover ourselves to be bonded in the human relationship they have with each other.

In that relationship, we wait at the end of the Third Week for the Father's compassionate love to bring us to resurrection. How or when or what that will be happens in his time. We wait in the midst of death for that certain love to come to us. In that waiting we are not alone. All of creation cries out to be redeemed. We are a part of that creation. Christ is redeeming creation even here and now. We hold onto him as he does this work of redemption. In the depths of the intimacy we have with him, we are changed. That change rises up in and through us as resurrection.

Questions for Prayer and Reflection

1. In what ways have being with Jesus through his sufferings and death changed you?
2. How do you relate to the Father now?
3. How do you understand intimacy from this new perspective?
4. How does entering into Christ's passion and his relationship to the Father carry you beyond feelings?

Part 4

The Fourth Week: A Transforming Love

1st Exercise: Preparation for the Fourth Week

Scripture verse

I am about to create new heavens and a new earth;
The things of the past shall not be remembered
or come to mind.
Instead there shall always be rejoicing and happiness
in which I create;
For I create Jerusalem to be a joy
And its people to be a delight;
I will rejoice in Jerusalem and exult in my people.
No longer shall the sound of weeping be heard there,
Nor the sound of crying. (Isaiah 65:17-19)

From the Spiritual Exercises

Consider the divinity, which seemed to hide itself during the passion, now appearing and manifesting itself so miraculously in the most holy Resurrection in its true and most sacred effects. (Sp. Ex. #223)

Grace to be prayed for

Here it will be to ask for the grace to be glad and rejoice intensely because of the great joy and the glory of Christ Our Lord. (Sp. Ex. #221)

The True Meaning of Joy

This final set of exercises moves through a sequence that ranges from experiencing the resurrection of Christ in the world to living the spirit of that resurrection in this world. This range brings out yet another dimension of the spiritual intimacy we are invited to share with Jesus and the Father. It brings us to the gift of the Spirit and into the life of the Trinity. The outpouring of that life extends towards all of creation. As we perceive this, we discover the effects of the power of God. Everything is charged with energy. We resonate with it. We experience it as joy and we respond to it with gratitude.

The grace we ask for at the beginning of every prayer period is "To be glad and rejoice intensely because of the great joy and glory of Christ our Lord" (#221). Two things should be noted of this grace. First, the focus is on the great joy and glory of Christ. That joy gives us our own joy – not vice versa. Imagine seeing a young child playing, and feeling happy because that child is having fun. Our first experience of the resurrection is like that. That first state of joy carries us out of ourselves; we pray to be happy because we experience Christ's joy and can enter into that joy.

Ignatius also recommends we ask for the grace to be intensely glad and to rejoice intensely. Not only do we need to ask for that grace and expect it, we also need to live as if we have received it. At this time, we avoid all those things that may cause us to lose that grace, and we seek those things that contribute to that state of being.

Joy is often equated with loud celebrations. True joy is not like that. Joy is the felt sense of being rooted in God's love. It is calm and focused and deep. The enemy of our human nature does not want us to be joyful, and so lures us away from it. Unless we counteract that temptation, we start moving from being joyful to being happy, from being happy to being excited, and from being excited to being in a state of pleasure. From there it is easy to slip into giddiness and then to desolation. Pleasure is a delight in the things that stimulate the senses. I can have pleasure in a good meal or in an ice-cream cone on a hot day. Excitement is an intensification of that pleasure, to the extent that it blocks out a sense of calm and of control. Happiness occurs when my desires coincide with the energies around me, and I am affirmed in myself. Joy is acknowledging, in a self-conscious manner, my rootedness in a love and a life that is larger than me and that I know cares for me. In joy, I live out my awareness as the redeemed beloved of the Father; in pleasure, I experience my selfhood solely in a physical way. Joy lies at one end of the continuum of delight; pleasure lies at the other end.

In this Week, as we enter more and more deeply into the resurrection, we want to remain recollected so that we do not lose all the gifts we have been moving towards during our retreat. If we did so, we would be like those people who earn a small fortune working long, hard hours in remote areas, only to lose it in a frenzy of mindless self-indulgence when they return to the world they left behind.

Remaining Recollected

As we remain recollected, we become more united with God. We share the same spirit and the same focus, work, and joy with the Christ as we become his continuing presence in the world. A path leads through this Week of our growing union into the mind and heart of God. We left the previous Week in a state of waiting. That waiting empties us. In that emptiness, we glimpse the risen Christ. As we reflect on these glimpses, learning to believe and accept what we are being given, we enter a state of quiet, focused awareness of the joy present in every moment and in everything. We celebrate that awareness by sharing with whomever we meet what has been given to us. This work is resurrection in the world. We don't proselytize or graciously condescend from a spiritually superior position. Rather, we live out of the joyful sense that we are related to everything and everyone, realizing that dimensions of that relationship remain oppressed or live with illusion.

As we strive to repair those relationships, we find ourselves back in the world of the First Week, but at a deeper and more comprehensive level. Thus the journey starts over again. It is a spiral, a never-ending journey into the unfathomable depths of God's love. In this we are like Mary, the mother of Jesus. She brings Christ into the world. She shares Christ with the world. She suffers with Christ in the world. She experiences his resurrection, and becomes part of the community that is his resurrected presence in the world.

A Meeting with a Mother

And so we start with Mary. Ignatius presents Jesus appearing to Mary as the First Contemplation on the Resurrection of Christ. He writes, "He appeared to the Virgin Mary. Though this is not mentioned explicitly in the Scriptures it must be considered as stated when Scripture says that He appeared to many others" (#299). For Ignatius, the relationship between Jesus and his mother is very special. Without her free and generous consent at the Annunciation, his whole mission as a human would have been frustrated. Ignatius has included her in the conversations he invites those making the Exercises to conduct at the end of their prayer periods. Here he suggests that she is the first person Jesus appears to after he is raised from the dead.

He is, after all, flesh of her flesh, for it is through her that he has become incarnate. Beyond the bonds of parent and child, of Jewish mother and son, lies the deeper connection of resurrected body to its closest kin. She is the closest human being to him and so, for Ignatius, it is only in the nature of love that he should appear to her first.

We are invited, as we are at every contemplation, to be present at that meeting in all of its quiet, deeply personal intimacy, when grief and resignation turn to incredulous wonder, mutual concern, and affirmation. What had been told to her before – that he was to suffer, die, and then rise from the dead – and what she had pondered on and held in faith, now is seen and felt as fact and truth. In these moments of acceptance between Jesus and his mother, and between them and us in prayer, there is only the simple, open conversation of heart to heart.

We have all heard stories of relationships or people lost, or of a life spent dealing with the emptiness, where what was believed to be gone forever returned forever. Such things happen in real life, too. Soldiers lost in battle are held for dead, mourned for, and then turn up again. Families separated by war or other circumstances reunite years later. Reunion is part of the human story.

Here Jesus and Mary experience something similar, except she saw her son tortured and killed. We lived with Mary's grief. Just as her son's life was held as worthless, so too her sacrifices to bring him into the world and to protect him with Joseph had become worthless. Two lives wasted. One was devoted to the other, and that other was forsaken and crucified. We must sit with that welling sense of emotion that comes from places too deep to be named, as love comforts love, and claims love. We must sit with Mary's embrace of Jesus and Jesus' embrace of Mary. We must abide, quietly and passionately, with our embrace of both. We, too, are included in that love and that intimacy.

Questions for Prayer and Reflection

1. Have you ever lost anything and then, against all odds, found it again? Enter into that state of simple joy again. What other memories or incidents does it raise for you? What do you experience as you savour those memories?
2. Where are you in the contemplation when the resurrected Jesus comes to his mother? How did that feel? What were the most moving moments? Why? What did they bring back to life for you? How did they transform the destructiveness of the previous Week?
3. What was your conversation after the prayer with Mary, Jesus, the Father? Where does that conversation lead you to next?
4. What do you do to stay in that quiet joy? What must you do to stay there?
5. What are the forces that try to move you away from that quiet, focused rootedness? Can you acknowledge them without being driven by them?
6. As you sit in that quiet joy, what arises as gift for you?
7. What happens as you stay with that gift? As your staying quietly in that simple space opens that gift, you too are being opened by that gift. How does that feel?
8. Do you experience the gift of being able both to give and to receive as gratitude? Do you have a sense of how gratitude can be a way of life?

2nd Exercise: Christ Appears to Mary Magdalene

(John 20:1-18)

Scripture verse

> Jesus said, "I will not leave you desolate; I will come to you."
> (John 14:18)

From the Spiritual Exercises

> Consider the office of consoler that Christ our Lord exercises and compare it with the way in which friends are wont to console each other, (Sp. Ex. #224)

Grace to be prayed for

> Here it will be to ask for the grace to be glad and rejoice intensely because of the great joy and the glory of Christ Our Lord. (Sp. Ex. #221)

Waiting in Emptiness

It would be wonderful if we could discern a pattern to the resurrection appearances of Christ, but we cannot. They move beyond the limits of our imagination. When we enter the stories themselves, in a contemplative way, we discover they stretch our imagination by constantly surprising us and by inviting us to deeper and unsuspected intimacies with God.

One such story is the first resurrection account in John's gospel. A woman who had been exorcised by Jesus and had become one of his close followers comes to the tomb. Seeing that the stone has been taken away from the entrance, she runs and tells Peter and John. They go to the tomb, see what she has said is true, and return home. She, however, stays there weeping and looking into the empty tomb. As she turns from the tomb, she sees someone she mistakes for the gardener, and asks him where the body has gone. The stranger says her name, "Mary," and she recognizes him as the Christ. She then holds onto him so hard that he says, "Don't hold onto me so hard, but go to the others and tell them, 'I am ascending to my Father and to your Father, to my God and your God.'" She returns to the disciples, tells them what had happened, and repeats his words to her.

Being Found by What We Lost

In this poignant scene of seeking and finding the beloved, of embrace and mission, we find a sequence of events that transforms our own experience of intimacy with Jesus. He has attracted our attention, he has rescued us, we follow him and become part of his life as he becomes part of our life. Then that relationship is destroyed as he is betrayed and killed. In our sorrow we wait by the tomb, but that in itself does not give life. As we linger there, things come to us – images and feelings of consolation – but we cannot name them properly because we are still caught up in the world of death.

It is only when those things strike our sense of identity, which lies deeper than our grief, that we discover what has greeted us. It is the Christ! It is hard to believe – the one we loved and lost returns to us transformed. We fall into the arms of the beloved. But the story does not end there. For that love to be fulfilled, both of us must return to the source of our loving. The path seems to diverge again. Jesus must return to the Father, and we need to create the community that bears his name in its return to the Father. The love we share does not disappear so soon after being found again. There will be a new way of loving – not between individuals and God, but rather in community. The community called Church is the embodied presence of that shared presence of love. As we struggle to understand it, all this might sound like science fiction. But it really isn't. It is simply the nature of love becoming more and more manifest. If we can stay with this state of consolation of being loved, the path to community will unfold. New dimensions of intimacy open to us.

Love does not abandon anyone, and so Jesus in his resurrected state comes back to those he loves. It is significant to note that, in the scripture stories, Jesus does not show himself in his resurrected state to any but those whom he loves and who love him. Those who do not love cannot see love. They always read it as something else. But to those who love and who seek love, love comes. One of the gifts of the resurrection is that it can open us to dimensions of love we did not think possible. Here, in Mary's loving, we experience someone who had thought she had reached the limits of love. She grieved the end of that love by going to the tomb. To her surprise, she finds it open and empty. On our spiritual journey to love, we come to the stage of emptiness and are asked, as in the final contemplation of the Third Week, to wait in that emptiness. When Mary waits, the Christ comes to her.

Waiting in the emptiness, as Christ experienced on the cross, removes all our preconceptions of how love can present itself. So when the Christ appears to Mary, she does not recognize him. She supposes he is a gardener. Christ does not appear in the drama of worldly power with pomp and circumstance and special effects. He does not seek to impress or to terrorize. He appears in a simple, ordinary way. Resurrection comes in simple, ordinary ways. When we are moving through mourning, we notice signs of new life in our ability to appreciate, perhaps even without knowing it, simple, everyday things. As you journey through the day with this contemplation, try to be conscious of the effect in your life of the little things that give you joy.

Named by God

Jesus goes even further in this manifestation with his friend Mary: he calls her by name. In grief we often lose a sense of who we are; we have entered a new territory where everything is strange and we have even become strangers to ourselves. But when we are found by love, we are brought back to ourselves, and to a new sense of ourselves and of life. This is the gift Jesus gives Mary when he acknowledges her and calls her by name. She responds by recognizing him. This is what the gift of love does – it enables us to recognize others for who they really are. To be called by God in love gives us our identity. To respond to that love changes our perspective and our hearts. We see with the eyes of love, and we see God in the commonplace. What before seemed insignificant now becomes worthy of notice and contemplation. When we enter into that state of contemplation, which is not just reserved for prayer periods, we discover God in all things. Here Mary discovers Jesus and embraces him.

We need to remain in that embrace and to allow that healing touch to transform us. When lovers embrace, they open their spirits to each other in mutual vulnerability. That openness has the effect of giving us courage and a sense of connection that remain even when we are physically separated from the beloved. We see this in little children who are loved. They are not fearful and insecure, but are filled with a sense of wonder and creativity. The same thing happens when people fall in love, and when we are touched by resurrection. We fall in love with God again in a whole new way. Like Mary Magdalene, we are tempted to hold onto that love in ways that are appropriate only to a past life. The new life love calls us to fills us with a sense of our true identity, of wonder and of creativity. We find ourselves responding to that love, as Mary did, by wanting to share it with whomever she encounters. That love does not turn us in on ourselves. It turns us to the world and to those who need to know the good news that love is stronger than death, the gift of forgiveness more powerful than any alienation, and that life is more creative than evil. It is this message Mary carries back to the disciples when she tells them she has seen and touched the risen Christ.

Always Going Home

Christ's journey, however, is not over. In sharing his resurrected life, he begins his return to the Father when, in him, all things will be restored to the Father. We become his risen body, on our own spiritual journey to the fullness of life. Christ himself returns to the Father. Love responds to love, is attracted to love, and becomes united to love. He goes before us to assure us of where we, too, are going. He does not only show us death is not the end of life, he also desires us to know life leads to more and fuller life. Death is just a door that opens to the fullness of life. In this contemplation, we are given not only an experience, but a direction and a gift that opens to broader and deeper dimensions of love and intimacy. We must sit and allow that gift to come to us and open us, so that we may open it.

Questions for Prayer and Reflection

1. What gift was given to you in this contemplation? How do you feel about that gift? How do you receive it? How does it change the way you see yourself, others or the world?
2. How do the prayer periods in this contemplation stretch and liberate your imagination?
3. Have you ever mistaken love for something else? How did you find out what it really was?
4. What happens these days when you find a quiet place and dare to let your deepest longings for love rise in prayer? How are they answered?
5. When you look back over your life, what happens to you when you dare to love?
6. Do you feel that sense of daring now? For what?
7. Where does your creativity come from?
8. What causes you to wonder in delight? Do you think of these as manifestations of resurrection? Do you allow yourself the time to savour these moments? What happens when you do?
9. If you were to examine your life, or even the past few days, looking for those moments of wonder, what do you find? What do those moments tell you?
10. In your conversations after the prayer with the Father, Jesus, or Mary – or all three – what comes across or stays with you?

3rd Exercise: Doubting Thomas

(John 20:19-31)

Scripture verse

They said to him, "What must we do, to be doing the works of God?" Jesus answered them, "This is the work of God, that you believe in the one whom he has sent." (John 6:28-29)

From the Spiritual Exercises

Recall to mind the blessing of creation and redemption, and the special favours I have received. (Sp. Ex. #234)

Grace to be prayed for

Here it will be to ask for the grace to be glad and rejoice intensely because of the great joy and the glory of Christ Our Lord. (Sp. Ex. #221)

Fear and Joy

Before the disciples experience the resurrection, they are filled with fear and huddle behind closed doors. In this story, Jesus enters the locked room, wishes them peace, and shows them his pierced hands and side as proof of who he was. Their fear is transformed into joy. In this joy, he breathes the Holy Spirit onto them and missions them to forgive sins. One of the disciples, Thomas, is not there when this happens, and refuses to believe it took place. Eight days later, as they are all gathered again, Jesus reappears. He shows his hands and his side to Thomas, exhorting him to believe. Thomas, transformed by that empirical evidence, believes.

This story opens with Jesus repeating in dramatic fashion the mystery of the Incarnation. In both mysteries, he enters our human world, which is self-enclosed out of fear, and his presence transforms that world. In this resurrection narrative, the disciples are afraid they will be treated as Jesus was by the authorities and the mob. The resurrected Christ does not abandon them in their fear, but enters their little world and wishes them peace. Inasmuch as we become manifestations of the resurrected Christ, we, too, are asked to enter the worlds of fear and self-enclosure and bring a peace that comes from rootedness in the Father's love. That relationship casts out fear. Interestingly, when we do this, we are tested as Christ was tested. We need to show signs we live out of our relationship with the Father before others will believe us. The most effective sign of this is when, in our suffering, we remain faithful and loving.

When the disciples see the risen Christ, he shows them signs that it is truly he. In our prayer these days, when we might have difficulty believing the resurrection can be present in our lives, we need to ask for that grace of having the risen Christ identify himself to us in ways we can believe. In our ill-conceived pride we might wish that we do not need this, but in our experienced poverty, we know we do. This shameless petition of the beloved is our prayer for a particular grace. As in any love relationship, we cannot demand the one we love does what we seek, but we can ask and we can dispose ourselves to receive what we request. The same is true of God. He does not demand that we behave as he wishes, but he asks and disposes himself to receive what we are willing to offer in love.

The Gift of the Spirit

Christ asks, when we accept the proof that he has risen from the dead, we live as he lived and love as he loved. He says, "As the Father has sent me, even so do I send you" (John 20:21). But to do this we need the same spirit as the Christ: a spirit of loving reverence for all, of courage and creativity, of joy and compassion. The spirit embodies Christ's relationship with the Father. Christ gives the disciples that relationship and that spirit when "he breathed on them and said to them, 'Receive the Holy Spirit'" (John 20:22).

This action echoes the creation of humans in the book of Genesis. There "the Lord God formed man of dust from the ground and breathed in to his nostrils the breath of life; and man became a living being" (Genesis 2:7). In the Scriptures, a human is not body and soul – that is a Greek distinction – but dust animated by the Lord God's breath or spirit. This makes humans living beings. When Christ breathes on the disciples, he creates a new being out of the chaos of their creation. When we enter this contemplation, we dispose ourselves for God to breathe on us and make us a new creation. We become transformed. We move from fear to love, from self-doubt to self-acceptance, from confusion to creativity. That new creation makes us more like Christ. We find ourselves filled with his spirit, doing what he has been doing in the world: forgiving sins. In the passage from John we are contemplating, Jesus says, "Receive the Holy Spirit. If you forgive the sins of any they are forgiven; if you retain the sins of any they are retained" (John 20:22-23).

Forgiving Sin

But what does it mean to forgive sins? Maybe it would help if we looked at what sin does. It causes division by setting people against each other and even against themselves. It promotes self-hate and spreads illusions that deceive us about our true nature. It is destructive and does not delight in joy or in celebrating life. It oppresses. To forgive sins, therefore, is to create community and self-acceptance. It is to seek the truth and maintain it. It is to cherish creativity and to celebrate life wherever it may be found. It is to transform chaos into relationships that foster healing and peace. It liberates the imagination and the spirit. It grounds us in that constant and compassionate presence of the mystery we call Father. We see that this is what Christ's coming into our world has done for us: when we experience resurrection, we find our new and transformed selves doing the same thing for the world, and in concrete ways for those we meet.

Until we experience the risen Christ in our lives, we cannot see how this is possible: all we have to inspire us are the exhausted, pragmatic politics of the world and the tragedies that result. We consider it escapist fantasy to believe otherwise, and we think spiritual maturity means accepting the world as it is and accommodating it. We refuse to believe we can experience the risen Christ in our prayer. We refuse to open ourselves to believe – lest we be hurt or disappointed – that the Christ desires to come to those who, in their own small ways, love God.

Personal Proof Beyond Disbelief

This is Thomas's problem. He was not with the original eleven when Christ appeared to them in the closed room. He does not think that what they have told him is possible. Yet, in his mercy, Christ appears to Thomas and to the others once again that very next week in that very same place. He tells Thomas, "Put your finger here, and see my hands; put out your hand and place it in my side; do not be so faithless, but believe" (John 20:21). Jesus does not say, Well, if Thomas does not believe, that is his problem. The Thomas he knows and loves is the Thomas he chose to be his companion. It is this same Thomas who said, when the plots were strong against Jesus, "Let us go up to Jerusalem and die with him." Jesus knows Thomas loves him in his own way. He also knows that Thomas really cannot believe that the Father's love can raise Jesus from the dead, or that Jesus, after all he had been through, including being abandoned by his disciples, would care to return to them if he had indeed been raised from the dead. But Jesus did both things, and here he does one extra thing. He comes back just for Thomas. He gives Thomas the proof he needs to commit himself to the love Jesus offers. And Thomas, in a passionate response, commits himself, crying out, "My Lord and my God!" (John 20:28).

Thomas is like us. When we have been loved beyond our disbelief, we can acknowledge personally and intimately what love is. In this contemplation, we ask for that grace to experience this personal love God has for each of us in ways that move us beyond our disbelief into a new way of seeing and being. It makes us creative, compassionate, and joyful.

Questions for Prayer and Reflection

1. When you entered this contemplation, what were the elements of personal surprise? How did they manifest themselves? How did you respond?
2. How did you experience the risen Christ in this contemplation?
3. What is the relationship between your fear and your lack of belief? Can you see in your history where that fear shaped the way you believe?
4. Where did that fear come from? Can you invite the risen Christ to enter into that fear, or those areas and sources of fear? What happens when you do this in prayer?
5. How do you respond to the experience of the risen Christ in your prayer?
6. What difficulties do you have in forgiving yourself, others, and the world?

7. What happens when you ask that the breath of Christ be blown on those areas? How do you experience that breath?
8. In what ways are you like Thomas? What happens when you contemplate the Thomas incident in these prayer periods? What happens to the Thomas aspects of yourself?
9. In your conversations with God, Jesus, or Mary – or all three – after the prayer, what surfaces that is significant?
10. What is the next step in your growth to spiritual freedom after these prayer periods? What will you do, concretely and practically, to facilitate that next step?

4th Exercise: The Road to Emmaus

(Luke 24)

Scripture verse

Make me know your ways, O Lord;
Teach me your paths.
Lead me in your truth and teach me,
For you are the God of my salvation;
For you I wait all day long.
Be mindful of your mercy, O Lord, and of your
steadfast love,
For they have been of old.
According to your steadfast love remember me,
For your goodness' sake, O Lord.

(Psalm 24:4-7)

From the Spiritual Exercises

This is a cry of wonder accompanied by surging emotion as I pass in review all creatures. How is it that they have permitted me to live and have sustained me in life! (Sp. Ex. #60)

Grace to be prayed for

Here it will be to ask for the grace to be glad and rejoice intensely because of the great joy and the glory of Christ Our Lord. (Sp. Ex. #221)

Moving Beyond Our Fantasies

As we continue to contemplate the resurrection, we find that our joy becomes more integrated into our sense of self. That transformation allows us to become even more open to the mystery that is the journey of our life. We tend to understand this mystery by the story we tell ourselves about our life. Resurrection changes this story. We cannot change it ourselves. In fact, when we try to, we end up with fantasy. There are many kinds of fantasy: simple escapist fantasy, untouched by existential reality, where we can daydream about perpetual youth and riches, or about utopian societies where all are politically equal; modified forms of fantasy, such as a perfect, anxiety-free existence fuelled by the narcotics of drugs, ambition, or social conditioning; and ideological and religious fantasies. In fact, we feed on fantasy. Sometimes we think we are converted, but all we have done is substitute one fantasy for another.

There comes a time when we discover that the fantasies we have lived out of are unable to bear the burden of brute reality. The large systems we might have trusted in and even devoted our lives to maintaining break down. We find ourselves slipping between the gaps of their supposedly impermeable surfaces. We are hurled back into chaos and uncertainty. We suffer from anxiety and a sense of meaninglessness. We hold on to lesser things, knowing their inadequacy, just for the sake of holding on to something. We sometimes guard those things – hobbies, jobs, political affiliations, ethnic partisanship – fiercely and blindly, knowing that without them we would be lost. We even claim that such commitment gives us access to God. One of the fantasies we have is about God and how God operates and is present in the world. When bad things happen, we ask, How can God allow this? Unless we find a suitable answer to that question, we abandon God. That is not a bad thing, surprisingly, because what we are abandoning is not God, but a fantasy of God. Our spiritual drive to seek the true God – our deepest desire – takes over and we begin a spiritual journey that moves beyond our fantasies. We encounter the God who is always coming towards us and walking with us in our pain.

After the celebration of Passover and the Sabbath, two disciples of Jesus are walking to Emmaus, about 20 kilometres outside Jerusalem. They discussed similar fantasies about Jesus. "We had hoped he was the one to redeem Israel" (Luke 24:21). Instead of the political hero they wanted, they got a crucified prophet. In their disillusionment, even when they heard the reports of Jesus' resurrection, they could not grasp its import. For them, it was just anecdotal data. It made no sense in the way they viewed the world.

But something happens to them. On their way back to Emmaus, they encounter the risen Jesus but do not recognize him, because they can see only out of their fantasy. Jesus unravels the material of their fantasy – in their case, the Scriptures – and reinterprets it in light of his relationship to the Father. This allows him to show the path of the Messiah depicted in their sacred writings. He explains that the Christ was destined to suffer and then enter into his glory. When they hear these things, their deepest desire is felt and held, given expression and answered. They move from being despondent to being inflamed in the spirit. As they reflect, "Did not our hearts burn within us while he talked to us on the road, while he opened to us the scriptures?" (Luke 24:32).

Reimagining God

Even though we live in a resurrection context, we, too, need to look at our mistaken expectations of how God should behave. Such expectations cause us to miss the resurrection experience present to us even at this moment; we need to ask to have the Scriptures of our lives, and of our religion, opened to us so we may see who Christ is for us here and now. To help us in this process we might, in this prayerful contemplation, imagine walking with Jesus on the road to Emmaus, and bring to him all the areas in the world and in our lives where we do not see the merciful presence of God. We need him to open our hearts, our minds, and our eyes.

Journeying with God

In the Emmaus story, this is exactly what Christ does. The two disciples so share his spirit that when they arrive at their little town as evening falls, and he appears to be going further on, they ask him to spend the night with them. As he blesses and breaks the bread at supper, they recognize him, and he disappears from their midst. The journey they have made with him changes them – they now share his same spirit. They have become community, manifest in their desire to share their home and their meal with him. Through this sharing, they recognize him in the breaking of the bread – the same act of community that he had enacted at the Last Supper. What they shared was his body. In their new story, the two disciples become the continuing body of Christ on earth.

In their transformation, they do exactly what Christ has done to them. Even though it is night and they are tired, they set out at once for Jerusalem to tell the others what has happened. While they are gathered as community, Christ appears to all of them, "and while they still disbelieved for joy, and wondered, he said to them, 'Have you anything here to eat?' They gave him a piece of broiled fish and he took it and ate before them" (Luke 24:41-43).

The joy the two disciples felt on the road to Emmaus increases as they share their experiences, and in that community Christ comes. His reappearance increases their joy so much, they cannot believe such a thing is possible. To prove he is not a ghost, the Christ eats a piece of fish. When they accept that it is truly him, he missions them to continue his work of reconciling all to each other in the building up of community.

The Path of Joy

As we enter more and more deeply into this contemplation, we discover that the joy we experience opens up to more and deeper joy, and that this deepening joy comes about by the creation of community. In the gospel story, the two disciples encounter the risen Christ and become joyful. To share that joy, they return to the other disciples with the good news. The larger community is missioned to share that joy. That path of joy goes from those two to the rest of the apostles and through these, in mission, to the whole world. That path becomes possible when the disciples accept the reality of a Christ who, through journeying into suffering and death, has risen. He witnesses, with his very life, the reality of a love that is not fantasy. The compassionate mercy of God embraces each and every one of us in an almost unbearable intimacy. If we undertake that journey to Emmaus with our own broken illusions, we experience the growing joy that transforms us, and, through us, transforms the whole world.

Questions for Prayer and Reflection

1. When you were young, did you have fantasies about God? How did you lose those fantasies? What replaced them?
2. This contemplation carries you past the fantasies you might have still held about God. What were those adult fantasies? How did they shape your life and your expectations of life? How does this contemplation and its repetitions move you beyond those fantasies?

3. What were the most significant moments for you in this contemplation? Why?
4. As you walked with the risen Christ through the path of your life, what was explained to you that is helpful for you now?
5. Think of the community of people who are important to you. How do you share life with them? In what way is that a manifestation of the risen Christ?
6. The disciples "disbelieved for joy" when Christ appeared to them. Did that moment in the contemplation trigger memories when you were so joyful you couldn't believe what was happening? What were they?
7. How does this contemplation address the suffering in your life?
8. The contemplations of the Fourth Week invite you to enter into a relationship with the risen Christ and to experience how that intimacy opens up your life. As you reflect on these contemplations, how is your life being opened up?
9. How can you distinguish between fantasy and experiences of the resurrected Christ? How do suffering, forgiveness, community, and an ongoing relationship with the compassionate mystery of the Father help you learn to make that distinction? What happens when you ask the Christ to help you make the distinction? What response do you get?
10. In this contemplation and its repetitions, where were you in relationship to Christ, or to the disciples, or to the apostles back in Jerusalem? Why is that significant for you?
11. What arose from the conversation you had at the end of the prayer periods with the Father, Jesus, or Mary?

5th Exercise: Feed My Sheep

(John 21)

Scripture verse

For God alone my soul waits in silence;
For my hope is from him.
He only is my rock and my salvation,
My fortress; I shall not be shaken.
On God rests my deliverance and my honour;
My mighty rock, my refuge is God.

(Psalm 62:5-7)

From the Spiritual Exercises

I will ponder with great affection how much God our Lord has done for me, and how much He has given me of what He possesses. (Sp. Ex. #234)

Grace to be prayed for

Here it will be to ask for the grace to be glad and rejoice intensely because of the great joy and the glory of Christ Our Lord. (Sp. Ex. #221)

The Mission

Even though Jesus' companions now know he is risen and is present to them, they do not know when and how he will appear to them. This seemingly haphazard way of relating disconcerts them. In retrospect, we see he has breathed on them and given them his mission and spirit: now they need to learn to live out of that mission and spirit. If he remains with them, they will depend on him and not on the spirit, which is his intimate relationship with the Father.

In the last chapter of John's gospel, Peter and the others wait for Jesus. He does not appear. During the night, Peter decides to go fishing, and the rest go along. When morning breaks, they see someone on the shore. He asks them affectionately if they have caught anything; they say no. He suggests casting the net on the other side of the boat: when they do so, they catch an incredible number of fish. John, realizing it is the Lord on the shore, tells Peter, who jumps overboard and swims to the beach. When the rest arrive, they find that Jesus has prepared fish and bread for them on a charcoal fire.

Like the disciples, we cannot predict how and when the risen Christ will appear to us. We realize Jesus has risen from the dead and, in some profound way, he is with us, even though we do not experience him all the time. We cannot compel him to remain with us. Like Mary Magdalene, we want to cling to him, but he says, "Do not cling to me." We are not yet ready, we feel, to strike out on our own, to trust ourselves as he obviously trusts us. But we know we can't just mope. Life must go on. We pick up our lives and our jobs and continue. When we do that, conscious of how inadequate it all is, he comes and offers, within our daily lives, even more than we can imagine. With this we are fed for the next step.

Beyond Friendship to Love

In that next step, Peter and Jesus go walking. Jesus asks Peter, "Do you love me?" He uses the Greek word *agape* (a-ga-pay), which means a self-sacrificing love that gives all of life meaning. Peter replies, "Yes, Lord, you know I love you." But the word John uses for Peter's answer is *philia*, meaning friendship. Jesus responds, "Feed my lambs." Again Jesus asks Peter the same question using the same words, and again Peter replies using the same words. Jesus says, "Tend my sheep." The third time Jesus asks the question "Do you love me?", he uses the word Peter uses: *philia*. It is as if he is saying, are we really friends, then, if not intimates? Peter cries because he knows what he is capable of, and what he is not capable of. He replies, yes, they are friends, and Jesus says, "Feed my sheep." There is a movement in Jesus' questions in terms of Peter's capabilities. The difference between feeding lambs and tending sheep is that lambs are born in enclosures that protect them; sheep are left out in the open. Easily excitable and somewhat stupid, these animals can forage for themselves, but need to be protected from thieves and beasts of prey. That third mission Jesus gives Peter is not only to shepherd but also to nourish Jesus' flock. In accepting and living out this mission, Peter moves from fisherman to shepherd, from being Jesus' friend to sharing his spirit, from *philia* to *agape*. This is his baptism, and it changes his life. In that journey to intimacy, he discovers a love that carries him to a death similar to the Christ's.

In our journey through the resurrection, we are also called to move from being friends of Christ to sharers in his spirit and mission. We discover what it means to die to ourselves, to take up our cross daily, and to follow Jesus' path. Opening the gift of the resurrection does not necessarily make our lives easier, and we may be tempted to stop at any part of the journey. But if we walk make journey, even as we grow in freedom, we find that our liberty is constrained. We become committed to a way of life that demands a practical and spiritual asceticism. We ask ourselves if our daily lives bring us closer to God. This examination calls us to adopt what brings life and to avoid what leads to despair. We realize we are not at liberty to do and act as we please: even though our lives are more our own, they are at the same time less and less so.

Sinking into Selflessness

This rootedness that allows self-transcendence is common in the traditions of the spiritual path we walk. In Buddhism, for instance, Dogen writes, "To study the Way is to study the self, to study the self is to forget the self, to forget the self is to awaken into the ten thousand things." The asceticism of living the resurrection calls for a deep entry into ourselves, to the point where we realize our basic emptiness. Through that emptiness, at their own time, the energies of the resurrection arise. Their rising carries us beyond ourselves into the work of redeeming creation. That work also requires asceticism – the asceticism of self-forgetfulness that promotes joy and community. As the medieval Christian mystic Meister Eckhart points out, "The more deeply we are our true selves, the less self is in us." That is why, on their morning walk after Peter commits himself and receives his mission, Jesus says to him, "Truly, truly, I say to you, when you were young you girded yourself and walked where you would; but when you are old, you will stretch out your hands and another will gird you and carry you where you do not wish to go" (John 21:18). Accepting and opening the gift of the risen Christ carries us beyond ourselves into an afflicted world that cries out to be saved. The cost is no less than everything – even our very lives, as we may imagine them.

Why do it, then? Because heaven is sharing the vision and the work and the ministry of the Father. It is a way of seeing and labouring and being, here in the world, that unites us through space and time with all those forces that unceasingly build up a new creation. In this new creation, God is all in all, and everything and everyone has been healed and transformed by love, celebrating that love in every moment of their lives. This is hard work, yes, and we experience the suffering of a creation being transformed, but we also know the profound and abiding delight that comes from being rooted in love and being creative through that loving.

If we are honest with ourselves, we can see how much we are like Peter in our relationship with Jesus. We would love to be better companions of Christ, but we are aware of our weakness in the face of suffering. We can offer only friendship. Still, Christ sees what we need, and he knows what we can do when we are given what we need. He knows we need the Spirit; when we are given that Spirit, we become his continuing resurrected presence on earth. For now, that is enough.

Questions for Prayer and Reflection

1. How are you living these days with your prayer experiences?
2. How do they shape each other?
3. This contemplation has three parts: the frustrating evening of fishing; the breakfast with Jesus; the missioning of Peter. Which part engaged your attention most? What does that suggest to you? Return to that moment and let it engage you again. What happens?
4. How does this contemplation adjust the way you might have thought about living the resurrection? What questions does it raise for you? How will you deal with those questions?
5. In what ways is the resurrection changing your life? What do you need in order to live those changes in wholesome ways?
6. How do you experience the difference between being a friend of Jesus and a lover of Jesus? What do you need to ask him to do to help you be one with his spirit?

7. The gospel story contains other elements not touched upon here. Do any of them lead you to a closer understanding of yourself and a closer identification with the risen Christ? What does that tell you about yourself and about the way God sees you?
8. Do you think Peter feels guilty during his conversation with Jesus? Do you think Jesus is trying to make him feel guilty? Why is guilt not helpful in loving someone? In what ways does your perception of God make you feel guilty? Do you use guilt to distance yourself from God? How does God respond to you when you are in that state?
9. How does God ask you to feed his lambs and his sheep?
10. How do you feel about being asked to share God's creativity and love?
11. In your conversations at the end of the prayer with the Father, Jesus, or Mary, what do you discuss? What do you hear?
12. Can you stay in the moments of gratitude that this contemplation, and its repetitions, create in you? How?

6th Exercise: The Ascension

(Luke 24:44-52; Acts 1:1-11)

Scripture verse

> Jesus: "I do not pray for these only, but also for those who believe in me through their word, that they may all be one; even as you, Father, are in me, and I in you, that they may also be in us." (John 17:20-1)

From the Spiritual Exercises

> Reflect how God dwells in creatures. (Sp. Ex. #235)

Grace to be prayed for

> Here it will be to ask for the grace to be glad and rejoice intensely because of the great joy and the glory of Christ Our Lord. (Sp. Ex. #221)

Our Mystical Life

We come from God and we return to God. We know this is true, but we do not know exactly how it happens. We live day by day, we have projects and long-term plans, we have a general direction to our lives. Depending on the decisions we make, we can either aid or hinder the community of God's people. Underneath this sense of identity are the larger dynamics of our clan, our society, our culture. These also have projects and orientations, and play themselves out more or less unconsciously in our lives. But pervading all these, rooting and transcending them, are the creating energies of God, present in and working in everything and everyone to bring us to ever fuller and more joyful dimensions of being with God. This will not cease until all becomes all in God.

We start this journey even before we are born, and we continue it even after our bodies have died. In this journey, we imitate the one made by Christ, the Second Person of the Trinity, who became human, died, rose from the dead, and returned to the Father. When we contemplate Christ's return to his Father as we pray on the Ascension, we enter into the dynamics of a mutual love reaching through death to achieve a union of intimacy and creativity big enough to encompass the whole of creation. This is our entry into a life of mysticism that is our true nature. But how do we enter into that mysticism and experience it in our own prayer? First, we participate in the story of the Ascension.

In the story in Acts, Jesus led his disciples to Mount Olivet after proving that he had risen in his body from death and after promising to send them the Holy Spirit. On this mountain he was lifted from their sight. As they gazed into the sky, they noticed two men in white, who informed them that the Christ would return the same way he left in glory.

Claiming Our Deepest Desire

Entering the contemplation, we can experience the joy of the resurrected Christ's return to the Father and the joy of the Father's reception of his Son. This is the moment when Jesus' deepest desire is answered. Resurrection allows us to admit our deepest desire in all of its raw urgency, because we see in the Father's raising Christ from the dead that that desire is answered. We experience the joy of the resurrection when we let ourselves admit that our deepest desire can and will be answered. What does that desire look like? We desire life – life in all its fullness. We desire that all our hurts be healed and all our joys celebrated in ways that even now we cannot imagine. We desire that the terrors of the world be transformed into ecstasy. We desire that broken relationships be healed, that whatever is oppressed be liberated, and that all see and know and love themselves and all others the way the Father sees and knows and loves all. We desire that we become like God, for we are made in God's image and likeness.

In the contemplation of the Ascension, we experience in prayer Jesus' deepest desire being answered, and we enter into the intimacy of that answering. Here the totality of human love embraces and is embraced by divine love. That totality of human love includes our deepest nature, as well as all the manifestations of love we have been offered or have desired. As we enter into this contemplation, we can allow ourselves to experience the love we need to be fulfilled. We can allow ourselves to be immersed and embraced by its delight and its joy of finding its beloved. We can experience something of what the Father and the Son experience at that moment.

Leaning into Love

We can also experience, as in any human parting, the sadness that Jesus' companions felt when they saw him leave. This is not the sadness of a broken relationship – their desire is held by the promise of that further gift of the Spirit Jesus shares with the Father, and by the promise of Jesus' eventual return. We, too, can experience the gift of desire and of anticipation. This is rather like the feelings of a child on Christmas Eve who waits to celebrate Christmas, to receive presents, and to enjoy the gathering of family and friends at Christmas dinner. We can sit with the sense of Jesus' promise, knowing that, even as we have already received more than we expected, what is to be given is more than we can imagine. In that spirit of passionate waiting, we lean into a love that transforms us – body, spirit, and soul. Our bodies in resurrection become as Christ's body did, and so the divine love that embraces us not only liberates our spirit and purifies and redeems our soul, it also reveals to us that our bodies likewise will be glorified, not subject to illness, time, decay, and the laws of nature as we now understand them. The energies of the Ascension show us that the body is not left out of our relationship with the Father. What happens to our body is a symbol of the commitment of that love. The love of the Father that calls Christ back to him in his body also calls us back in our body to the same glory that Christ shows.

In our contemplation here, we can experience in our body something of that glory. We know that matter is compressed energy. In resurrection, the matter of the body becomes liberated. In the Ascension, that liberated energy becomes a manifestation of love. As we pray this contemplation on the Ascension, we can pray to experience our bodies as energized into a love liberated for intimacy with the Father and for creative service in the world.

Questions for Prayer and Reflection

1. What were the significant moments of this contemplation for you? How did you experience them? Why were they significant?
2. What does this contemplation reveal to you about the Father's love for you?
3. How does it reveal you to yourself?
4. What does it reveal to you about what your body is capable of being? How does this change your self-image?
5. How do you find yourself leaning into the love that desires you?
6. When you reflect on the journey that is your life, what can you chart as the significant moments that made you more aware that you are loved and capable of loving?
7. What stops you from loving?
8. What do you need to transform those blocks into creativity? What happens when you pray out of that need?
9. In your conversations at the end of the prayer with the Father and with Jesus, what has been given to you?

7th Exercise: The Gift of the Spirit

(Acts 2)

Scripture verse

> The fruit of the Spirit is love, joy, peace, patience, kindness, goodness, faithfulness, gentleness, self-control.
>
> (Galatians 5:22-23)

From the Spiritual Exercises

> We call Spiritual Exercises every way of preparing and disposing the soul to rid itself of all inordinate attachments, and, after their removal, of seeking and finding the will of God in the disposition of our life for the salvation of our soul.
>
> (Sp. Ex. #1)

Grace to be prayed for

> Here it will be to ask for the grace to be glad and rejoice intensely because of the great joy and the glory of Christ Our Lord. (Sp. Ex. #221)

Finding Who We Are

Living fully and willingly in the world, without being seduced by its illusions, carries us farther along our spiritual journey to intimacy. We are not invited to flee from that world because of its brokenness. We are not to deny this life and this path in favour of some other-worldly paradise, or stoically defy death by pursuing pleasure. Rather, we are to live, fully, with all our pains and problems, and within the continuing wretched situation of the world. This is possible when we live rooted in our relationship with the Father, and share the gift of the intimacy between Father and Son.

That intimacy reaches another stage of its fulfillment in the Ascension of the risen Jesus back to his Father. Then there is an explosion of love – a "Big Bang" of spiritual intimacy – that results in the second manifestation of the new creation. The fruit of that coming together for us is Pentecost. The intimate union of the risen human Christ with the Father results in their united Spirit given to us. We may think of this as a wedding in which we are invited guests sharing in the joy of the union. In sharing this joy, we become part of that union while living in this world. This joy transforms the world and gives us the energy, courage, vision, and love, to be personal embodiments of God's Spirit in the world. This is what happened to the disciples in the upper room in Jerusalem after the Ascension.

They were gathered together there when "suddenly a sound came from heaven like the rush of a mighty wind and it filled all the house where they were sitting. And there appeared to them tongues as of fire, distributed and resting on each one of them. And they were all filled with the Holy Spirit and began to speak in other tongues as the Spirit gave utterance" (Acts 2:3-4).

We need to know that the word for "wind" and the word for "spirit" are the same in Hebrew. We also need to see that the giving of the Spirit in tongues "as of fire" manifests itself in the speaking in "tongues," which enflames the spirits of those who hear them and leads them to become disciples (Acts 2:41-42). At Pentecost, that first year in Jerusalem, God's very own Spirit is given to Jesus' companions, who share it with the world. It is the nature of love not to be withheld. In that sharing of intimacy, love becomes more and more present in the world and community is created.

Receiving the Gift

When we enter this contemplation, we ask to be given God's Spirit. We enter the scene as one of Christ's chosen gathered in prayer, and we open ourselves to receiving that Spirit. We allow that gift to descend through our bodies, feeling the Spirit's descent into every aspect of ourselves so that we are intimately connected to both heaven and earth. We feel the rootedness that grounds us, body and soul, arise until, in that descent and arising, we know we are the presence of love in the world. We remain in this state of consolation, calmly breathing in love to our depths and breathing out love to the world. We stay in this state as long as possible, and return to it during all the repetitions of this contemplation.

What we are given in this state of intimacy allows our vocation, whatever it is, to become manifest in the world. The word "vocation" and the word "voice" have the same Indo-European root – *uek(s)*, "to speak." When we find our vocation, we find our voice. Finding our vocation means expressing our deepest desire in our life and with our life. The "tongue of flame," given to each of those in the upper room in Jerusalem after Jesus' ascension, is given to us. Our daily lives manifest a life that is the spirit in the world. A vocation is an expression of life that gives life, shares life, and celebrates life. A vocation to priesthood or religious life is only one of countless forms of vocation. What the disciples received at Pentecost was such a vocation. Through it they finally found their voice. Their life, difficult though it would be, becomes a celebration of intimacy.

Sharing the Gift

After the gift of the Spirit in tongues of fire, the disciples spoke in tongues so that all who heard them, even though they were of different nationalities and spoke different languages, understood. This gift allowed them to enter into other people's worlds, to touch their lives and transform them. We have contemplated this pattern of God's mercy before. In the Incarnation, God became a vulnerable human and was born a baby in Bethlehem. In the passion and death of Christ, that same God entered into the world's pain and suffering. Through his death, he entered the hellish confines of human existence where whatever is good, but alienated from the larger community of the good, is offered freedom and life-giving relationships.

Now, at Pentecost, we see that mercy fearlessly and compassionately entering the lives of those who had not experienced God's compassion. We experienced this in the first three Weeks of the Exercises. In the First Week, we encountered that love coming to us to heal and liberate us from sin. In the Second Week, we walked intimately with Christ into our own poverty and the world's to bring that mercy to others. In the Third Week, as companions of Christ, we journeyed with him into the depths of evil as he reveals in that evil a path to the transforming mercy of the Father. Now, in the Fourth Week, we are offered the same Spirit that was given at Pentecost, so that we can live in the world creatively, joyfully, and fully alive. Because of the gift of intimacy we have received, we, too, can find a path through the evils of our day to the ever-present mercy of God. Our lives become a witness to that gift and to that path.

The creativity and joy we pray to receive in this contemplation is not just for ourselves but for others. This joy desires to be shared with anyone who has experienced that profound and ceaseless yearning, common to all, for life, love, freedom, joy, and for a community where we feel always and deeply at home. There everyone speaks and understands the language of the heart.

Questions for Prayer and Reflection

1. What happened of significance when you prayed for the gift of the Spirit? How did you feel? In what ways were you energized?
2. What struck you most deeply as you entered the contemplation as one of Christ's disciples?
3. Where else in your life do you feel creative and alive? How do you express this?
4. Where do you see the need for creativity and a fuller sense of life? Is there a link between your creativity and the areas of need in the world?
5. Do you have, or feel connected to, a community of creative people? How do you celebrate life together?
6. Who has helped you on your journey to being creative, free, and loving?
7. Whom are you helping to live life more joyfully, creatively, simply, hopefully? What is your relationship with that person or group?
8. What happens when you explore your spirit links with significant people in your life – living or dead, near or far, throughout the ages or in different religious traditions? How have these people made you who you are? How do they encourage you or confirm you in your spiritual journey?
9. Where is the Spirit leading you now?
10. In your conversation at the end of the prayer with the Father, with Jesus or with one of your spiritual mentors, what comes to you that is significant?
11. When you prayed through the above reflection, what aspects struck you the most? What happened when you used those as an entry into prayer?

8th Exercise: Contemplation to Advance in Love (I)

Scripture verse

> Therefore I tell you, do not be anxious about your life, what you shall eat or what you shall drink, nor about your body, what you shall put on. Is not life more than food, and the body more than clothing? Look at the birds of the air; they neither sow nor reap nor gather into barns, and yet your heavenly Father feeds them. Are you not of more value than they?
> (Matthew 6:25-27)

From the Spiritual Exercises

> Consider all gifts and blessings as descending from above.
> (Sp. Ex. #237)

Grace to be prayed for

> This is to ask for what I desire. Here it will be to ask for an intimate knowledge of the many blessings received, that filled with gratitude for all, I may in all things love and serve the Divine Majesty. (Sp. Ex. #233)

The Spiritual Journey

Our spiritual journey is like a spiral – we seem to return to the places, situations, or projects we left behind. We re-enter that world not as prisoners, trapped by its seductions, its illusions, and its temporary stays of relief, but as freed spirits. We see it in all its incompleteness and brokenness. In joy we realize that we are invited to work towards bringing it to a right relationship with God, so that it is part of the community of all creation and an ongoing manifestation of God's endless creativity.

We are inspired – by the love that calls us to life and then to more life – to share that life with those who reach out for love. We also gratefully accept the love offered to us by those who travel on the same path to the fullness of life. We give and we receive in love.

In this contemplation, St. Ignatius offers some insightful observations about the nature of love, knowing full well that it is one of the most misused and misunderstood words in any language. He says first that "love ought to manifest itself in deeds rather than in words" (#230). What we do reveals who we are. Who we are is revealed by what we value. We experienced this when we contemplated God's relationship to creation. God values us. We are the beloved. That love is shown in a mercy that forgives us our alienations and offers us an almost unimaginable intimacy with the Trinity and with all of creation. This is not theological theory or romantic piety. It is what God does because, for us, that is who God is. In these contemplations, we experience a God totally involved in creation, one who never stops producing, maintaining, and transforming it and us.

Here we encounter a God who enters a self-distorting creation to heal and redeem it from the perversions evil has inflicted on it. We encounter a God willing to transform evil into good by embracing the alienating forces of evil and death. That embrace allows the compassionate mercy of the Father to bring those forces into community. This is resurrection. We have met in our prayer a God who became human as we are human, who walked the path of being human in all of its joy and its terror, and who shows us the path that leads back to the one he calls, intimately and simply, "Abba." This is a God whose word is incarnate, whose relationship with us is found in what he has done for us. When we enter that relationship – as we have done in the contemplations in the Exercises – we discover a God who works with us and for us. It is a God who invites us to work with him, and with all those forces of creation who have committed themselves in him to love.

Creating Community

Such a love is communal and mutual. We do not love alone, or in a vacuum. Always – before us and behind us, above us and below us, surrounding us and embracing us – is the love of the Father and the Son. We experienced that love in the outpouring of the Spirit on us at Pentecost. That outpouring never ceases. In it we live and move and have our being. In prayer we come to deeper and more conscious realizations of that abiding presence, which is a pure, simple, unconditional gift. St. Ignatius says in setting up this contemplation that love consists in the mutual sharing of what is good. "For example, the lover gives and shares with the beloved what he possesses, or something of that which he has or is able to give; and vice versa, the beloved shares with the lover" (231). God shares Himself with us. In love, we are invited to offer ourselves to God. We receive and we give in intimacy. The giving and receiving is love.

Narcissism is the opposite of love. Narcissists demand love and see themselves as the sole object of love. Narcissists cannot return love. What they claim to offer as love usually benefits only themselves. Narcissism destroys community. Love, on the other hand, works to create community. Such a community is manifest in a mutual giving and receiving. It roots itself in the free generosity of God that extends itself everywhere and to everyone. Narcissism is closed by a selfishness that can be personal or ghetto-like, ethnic or racial, social or national. It is economic. It says, "If you love me, you will behave this way. You will love as I tell you to love; hate whom I hate. Your identity is found only in me." In this world, there is no other, just projections of the self.

Community is different. Community is the celebration of the gift of the other as other. Our intimacy with God does not make us God. Neither does that intimacy make God us. Intimacy makes us most truly ourselves, and makes us see God as always the Other, always open to us without devouring us. As creatures journeying into intimacy with God, we will never come to the end of that journey. God will always be Other, but we will become more and more loving as we enter into relationship with that Other-ness.

Community as relationship is open to this depth of intimacy. Integration into community does not mean being subsumed under a common ideology. It means maintaining the integrity of other-ness. At Pentecost, those hearing the apostles heard their own tongue. They did not hear an imposed national or ecclesial language. The gift of the Spirit creates intimacy. In intimacy we discover our identity.

The identity community offers is realized in the personal, the social, the national, and the cultural. These different levels of being human have common bonds. These in themselves cannot bring us all to the fullness of life. This is found only in the mystery we call God. In themselves, these are incomplete and transitory manifestations of the divine creativity in time. They are not ends in themselves. Who we are changes. Our societies are in flux. Our national identity is constantly being reinterpreted. Our culture evolves. These point beyond themselves to that creativity and to the fuller dimensions of community. We are always in transition. Even tradition is transitional. Evil emerges when these incomplete manifestations of creation hold themselves as fixed and whole and complete in themselves. Then they are not open to the continuing creativity of God.

The work of loving is first, to see everything and everyone as incomplete, and second, to realize that incompleteness is not a curse but a blessing that allows us to reach out, without illusions, for that fullness of life offered by the beloved, who is divine, to us and to all.

In that reaching out we share what has been given to us.

An All-Embracing Love

To experience this grace more fully, as we begin this prayer we bring to our awareness that we are always in the presence of God and the saints. We are always surrounded by the love of those who love us and by the forces of all that is good in creation. We acknowledge that all of these work for our good by protecting, interceding, encouraging, and celebrating our lives and our paths. The prayer reminds us we are never alone, and the energies of our lives are woven together in a community of love extending through time and space. This community works to heal our disorders, enlighten our ignorance, transform our alienations and unblock our creativity. As we become aware of this community, which is always present to us, even here and now, we can see it at work in our lives and in our prayer, which participates in this unceasing activity. Prayer and work, sleep and play, eating and voiding – all of these activities operate from the same stance of being one with God's spirit and God's energies in the world.

In this and the following contemplations, all of which are designed to make us more and more aware of this all-embracing love, St. Ignatius suggests that we ask for what we desire. "Here it will be to ask for an intimate knowledge of the many blessings received, that filled with gratitude for all, I may in all things love and serve the Divine Majesty" (#233). It is a grace to see our lives as they are. It is a great grace to see in all the aspects of our lives the abiding presence of love holding and transforming us even in the dark times. We will know we have received this grace when we discover that our prayer is filled with gratitude and when, out of that gratitude and that gratitude only, we are moved to enter into the work of building up the community of love that offers life to all.

Questions for Prayer and Reflection

1. In this contemplation, what moves you the most? Why?
2. How does this contemplation put your life in context?
3. What things in your life are, or have been, a blessing for you? What happens when you take time out to be grateful for them? How does that gratitude shape the way you feel about your life now?
4. How do you feel called to live a loving life now?
5. What areas in your world do you feel need transforming? What part can you play in transforming the world?
6. Make a list of the people, past and present, who form your community of love. What happens when you have a prayerful conversation with them as part of this contemplation?
7. In the course of these exercises, what has been given to you as pure gift?
8. What, in your loving, do you offer to your beloved? What do you offer to God?
9. How does your life reveal to you and to others what you really value?
10. In your conversations with the Father or with Jesus, what is given to you that is significant for your life?

9th Exercise: Contemplation to Advance in Love (2)

Scripture verse

> Blessed be the God and Father of Our Lord Jesus Christ, who has blessed us in Christ with every spiritual blessing in the heavenly places, even as he chose us in him before the foundation of the world, that we should be holy and blameless before him. He destined us in love to be his own through Jesus Christ. (Ephesians 1:3-5)

From the Spiritual Exercises

> I must be convinced that in Christ our Lord, the bridegroom, and in His spouse the Church, only one Spirit holds sway, which governs and rules for the salvation of souls.
> (Sp. Ex. #365)

Grace to be prayed for

> This is to ask for what I desire. Here it will be to ask for an intimate knowledge of the many blessings received, that filled with gratitude for all, I may in all things love and serve the Divine Majesty. (Sp. Ex. #233)

All Creation Is Charged with God's Energies

What have we received from God? Rather than thinking about it, let us allow the love that shapes us to reveal it. We are creatures, a part of God's constant creativity. We do not have the power of our existence within ourselves; in fact, should God remove his loving attention from us, we will simply cease to exist. The very basis of our existence is radical dependence upon God.

At our most material level, the elements that make up physical existence were formed at that first physical moment of creation. The very matter that was formed in the Big Bang billions of years ago, when energy became physical and exploded outwards – in the creation of universes and galaxies and solar systems that are still expanding into nebulae, burning up into supernova, and imploding into black holes – is the same matter that makes up our bodies. Our physical bodies contain the memory of the cosmos from its very beginning, and each of our bodies is a symbol of that cosmos. Our relationship to that cosmos is basic and eternal. We do not know all the properties of the matter of which we are made, but we do know that it makes us one with all of creation. Let us stay for a while in the mystery of our oneness with the elements of creation. In them and in us is the gift of God's indwelling.

Creation is made up of levels of existence. Biological life emerges from the swirl of proteins and carbon; we share that higher level of existence with the myriad plant forms that grace our planet. Grasses and seaweeds, giant trees and orchids, wheat and lichen are all related to our biological bodies. If we open our awareness to our ecological interconnectedness, we discover a mutuality in which we shape, and are shaped by, our relationships to plant life. We cultivate certain crops and modify the DNA of others. We depend on the pharmaceutical properties of some of these to maintain our lives or enhance our awareness of the mysteries that surround us. The mystery of God's indwelling is in them and in us. Let us ask for the grace to experience the wonder of that unity we share with the biosphere, and to experience God's indwelling there.

Beyond that level is our animal existence. We have heightened sensation and possess innate skills to gather food, reproduce, care for our young, create a clan structure, and explore our environment. Within our symbiotic relationship to the animal world are the totemic forces of our spiritual nature that are given animal energies, characteristics, and structures. Our human body is more than an animal body, to be sure, but our bodies belong firmly and irreducibly to the animal kingdom. In this prayer of thanksgiving, let us be aware of the gift of the body, the delight of the senses, our rootedness in the physical, which allows us to connect and communicate with others to form community and express intimacy. Let us allow ourselves to be open to the mystery and to the delight of God's indwelling in it.

Sacred Spaces

Encompassing all of these is Christ incarnate. In becoming human, Christ takes up into himself what makes us human – the material, the biological, the animal, the social. The humanity of Jesus finds its deepest expression as intimacy with the Father. The incarnate God shares with us the gifts of memory, understanding, will, imagination, creativity, and the freedom to choose and celebrate life. He shares with us as a member of the human family. He offers us the gifts that the Father has given to him: the gift of resurrection and the gift of union with the Father in the life of the Trinity. That gift allows us, even in our earthly pilgrimage, to become sacred spaces wherein the divine may dwell and embody the divine compassion on earth. When we open ourselves to that gift and experience it, we become the image and likeness of God on earth. Let us open ourselves to celebrating that gift of the fullness of life offered to us freely and joyfully now.

All of this enormous sweep of God's love – from the beginning of time through the cosmos, through evolutionary history and through the community of human history – leads up to the Incarnation and the resurrection of the Father's Son. It continues through the traditions of love that he offers to all. It comes, at this very moment, to our own life and loving. Let us take some time to enter into this history contemplatively. Let us allow the love that creates us and redeems us and loves us into journeying back to the Father to carry us to that intimacy of passionate union with him. There we may savour with our senses, physical and spiritual, the delight he has in us.

We have been given our own path, with our own blessed history, and our own personal encounter with salvation. We all have our own personal entry into God's particular love for us, and our own intimate sense of being the beloved of Jesus and of the Father. Let us enter into that blessed history revealed to us in this journey. Let us open and savour the gift that allows us to know deeply, intimately, and truly that we are the beloved and intimate of God.

In order to appreciate what we have been given, St. Ignatius, in the Exercises here, offers a prayer we can pray out of the deep affection we feel for God.

> Take, Lord, and receive all my liberty, my memory, my understanding, and my entire will, all I have and possess. You have given all to me. To you, O Lord, I return it. All is yours, dispose of it wholly according to your will. Give me Your love and Your grace, for this is sufficient for me. (#234)

In this context of love, the lover has given his life for the beloved. It is because of Christ's love for us that we have the path of intimacy, which leads to the fullness of love we desire. Here we offer our very identity to Christ, the lover. All we ask for is Christ's love and the gift of the spirit. It is enough, for that love creates, sustains, protects, and transforms us. That love lives out of the intimate knowledge that all is gift.

Questions for Prayer and Reflection

1. How do you relate to the community that is creation? How do you live out of those deep connections that extend through time and space and all of human history?
2. What are you grateful for? How do you show this gratitude?
3. What do you take for granted? How do you deal with those things?
4. How do you experience your rootedness in God and in creation? How does this manifest itself in your prayer and in your daily life?
5. What in this prayer moved you? What moved you the most?
6. How does this prayer shape your relationship with God?
7. If you were to write the "Take, Lord, receive" prayer of St. Ignatius in your own words, what would it look like?
8. What offering can you make out of love to the source of all loving? What occurs to you as you pray this question?
9. Where is the place of evil and human suffering in this dynamic of loving?
10. Where do you fit into it?

10th Exercise: Contemplation to Advance in Love (3)

Scripture verse

I give thanks to God always for you because of the grace of God which was given you in Christ Jesus, that in every way you were enriched in him with all speech and all knowledge – even as the testimony to Christ was confirmed among you – so that you are not lacking in any spiritual gift, as you wait for the revealing of our Lord Jesus Christ, who will sustain you to the end, guiltless in the day of our Lord Jesus Christ. God is faithful, by whom you were called into the fellowship of his Son, Jesus Christ our Lord. (1 Corinthians 1:4-9)

From the Spiritual Exercises

Soul of Christ, sanctify me
Body of Christ, save me
Blood of Christ, inebriate me
Water from the side of Christ, wash me
Passion of Christ, strengthen me
O Good Jesus, hear me
Within your wounds, hide me
Permit me not to be separated from You
From the wicked foe defend me
At the hour of my death call me
And bid me come to you
That with Your saints I may praise You
For ever and ever. Amen. (Prayer of St. Ignatius)

Grace to be prayed for

This is to ask for what I desire. Here it will be to ask for an intimate knowledge of the many blessings received, that filled with gratitude for all, I may in all things love and serve the Divine Majesty. (Sp. Ex. #233)

The Gift of Life

There are levels to revealing a gift. First the gift must be offered; then it must be received and accepted. Next it must be opened and used. Finally, it must be shared. Sharing is a celebration not only of the gift, but of the giver, the receiver, and the community that gift creates.

No matter who we are or what state we are in, we have all been given a gift: life. That gift goes beyond mere survival as wounded individuals. That gift of life asks us to see, know, and love ourselves the way God sees, knows, and loves us. Often our own pain, or the lies of the world, stop us from seeing that gift. Instead, we see life as harsh, nasty, and brutal, and a vicious struggle for survival. The very idea of life as a gift of love for love seems, at best, naive and sentimental and simply untrue. Many of us refuse to receive the gift. We see the gift-giver as demanding and judgmental, powerful and capricious, cruel and terrifying. We might say that since we did not ask to be born, we are condemned to live. Even if the gift has been thrust upon us, we do not accept it.

But we all have a dreadful hunger for love and truth, justice and community, beauty and joy, security and acceptance. Even if we do not accept the gift of life, the longing for such life never leaves us. It haunts our every waking moment, and all we say and do. It haunts our dreams and all our fumbling attempts at relationships.

Imagine one day saying to ourselves, "There must be more to life than what I have been enduring." We set out in our own quiet and secret way to see what that "more" could be. As we do, we start opening the gift of life. This is a difficult and a lifelong task, for we must become aware of the lies in our life. They give us the false image of ourselves as unlovable and unloving. They deceive us that we are alone and that God is a tyrant. Moreover, our lives are multi-layered. At every layer, lies and deceptions need to be unmasked and the work of restoring begun. As we enter this work, we continually discover the joy of living, and we discover the God who labours constantly to bring us to that joy.

Sharing Life

Indeed, in this contemplation to experience love, St. Ignatius asks us to "consider how God works and labours for me" (#236). As we labour to bring a fuller life into our world, we labour with a God whose delight is to bring that life into our world. In that labouring, we discover a God who has invited us to be co-creators of the community of love extending through time and space. We also discover our bonds with those others who also work at this one project of community. At this level we find out how interrelated we are with the saints and martyrs and mystics, the holy ones of every spiritual path and tradition. We learn that their works of love, as diverse as their identities, all share the one work of love – the work of a God whose compassionate care and mercy manifest themselves in that unceasing activity of creating.

When we join in this creating, we see and love the world as God does. We see its beauty and its brokenness, and join with the holy ones of all time in the sacred work of redemption. Then every simple act of kindness, every moment of humble service, every work of unnoticed devotion, every silent prayer, every quiet gesture of forgiveness, every act of celebration, is an expression of that sacred work. That shared life is the opening of the gift and the celebration of the gift.

Celebrating Life

All of this comes from deep within us and pours itself out in our daily lives. What we offer to all has first been offered to us. It is the gift of life. We humbly share it, knowing that when we act as the face and hands and heart of God in the world, we do so in lives we have handed back to God. We do so knowing that what passes through us into the world, though shaped and coloured by our unique personalities and times, is that unending, compassionate mercy of divine love. The sole delight of that love is that everyone and all things come to the fullness of life. There all evil will be transformed into creativity, all suffering will be healed into joy, all oppression will be rewoven into community, all death will be lifted up to resurrection. This is the journey to the fullness of life. It is reached through the gift of intimacy. It is a journey that never ends. We have before us the delight of celebrating life in ways beyond our present imaginings. Each moment opens to that delight. We enter it and are transformed. The furnaces of affliction become the flames of divine love.

When we enter the world with a heart transformed, the world is transformed no matter what we do.

Questions for Prayer and Reflection

1. Where are you on your journey of life as a gift?
2. What obstacles are you facing on that journey? How do you live with them?
3. What started you off on your journey? How has your life changed since you began it?
4. What image do you have of yourself? How does this shape what you do and how you do it?
5. What image do you have of God? How does this shape your relationship with him/her/the Trinity?
6. What sense do you have of the world and of your being in the world?
7. Where do you find others who openly share your values and your deepest desires? How do you support and encourage each other?
8. How do you celebrate life?
9. What is the next step on your journey?
10. What happens when you ask God and the community of God that question in prayer?
11. In this contemplation, and in your repetitions of it, what moves your spirit most to a deeper intimacy with God?
12. In your conversation with God, or the community of the holy, at the end of your prayer, what emerges as important for you now?

Conclusion: The Gift of Spiritual Intimacy

The Journey Begun

What have you done through the Exercises of St. Ignatius? You have gone on a journey where you have allowed yourself to be found by God. You have entered into a union with God that manifests itself in our mutual labouring to transform creation into community.

The Exercises offer us a way of looking critically and lovingly at ourselves, and offer us choices of how we wish to be present to our world. The illusions we accept to be ourselves are taken away in the First Week. We find our true life in the Second Week. In the Third Week, this life stands the test of death. In the Fourth Week, we are liberated from the power of death for the service of the Divine Mystery. Our journey calls us always to be moving beyond ourselves and ever deeper into the love of God. In order to do this, we are constantly drawn from the worlds we have imagined and into the world as imagined by the mystery of the God we describe as Compassionate Mercy. This journey never ends. As we journey through the Fourth Week, we discover that we are not carried to a mythic paradise. We find ourselves once again in the First Week, when we must discover even more deeply how we are loved. There is no end to God's love, and no end to our journeying ever deeper into that love and into the community created by that love.

The Importance of Reflection

For St. Ignatius, the most important thing in a person's life is to find God. Everything else is secondary. Finding God means more than having encounters with God. It is about more than recognizing that we have had those encounters. It involves discovering what those experiences mean and what direction they have given to our lives. That direction shows itself in what we do with our lives, in the friends we choose, and in the values we hold. For Ignatius, then, reflecting on our actions is essential; it is the only way of keeping hold of the gift of our lives.

In spiritual direction there is some confusion about this way of proceeding. Some people want the reflection to have the same sense of drama and involvement as the prayer experience. When this does not happen, the reflection process is dismissed or overlooked.

Ignatian prayer basically consists of three parts. First is the preparation for the prayer. Here we choose a suitable place and time for the prayer. We read over or consider what we will pray about. We ask for the grace we are seeking, and we ask the Spirit to enable our prayer. This disposes us to the state of praying. The second stage is the experience of the encounter with God. Anything can happen here. The third stage is the reflection on the experience. Did we receive the grace for which we prayed? How was it given? What were the moments of consolation and desolation in this experience? Why are those moments significant?

This book divides each exercise in this way. The first part disposes us to the prayer. The second part gives us the material of the prayer, while the third part presents a series of questions to help appropriate the prayer.

These three stages are all part of Ignatian prayer, but each has its own style and mode of operating. Each builds on the previous stage, and the final stage completes the prayer experience. Avoiding that stage causes God's communication with us to be incomplete.

In this concluding chapter, we take the opportunity to get an overview of the communication God has been having with us through these Spiritual Exercises. It deliberately uses a style and voice different from the rest of the book in order to create the necessary distance to allow you to see where you have gone and where you are going. We will pan back and out from the close-ups of the individual exercises and from the medium shots of the reviews of individual Weeks, arriving at an overview of what you have experienced since the moment you committed yourself to the journey of engaging with this book. This overview is a necessary part of the prayer experience, your encounter and communication with God.

If you abandon this stage or try to make it similar to the contemplative moment of prayer, you lose the fruit of that contemplative moment. As a result, you will not know what the prayer means, or where God is in your life, or what direction your life is taking. You fall back into uncertainty and sometimes even question the validity of what you experienced, especially when you encounter hard or painful passages.

We are not doomed to live our lives in uncertainty. Our journey shows us that we are rooted in love and are loved even when we may doubt ourselves or others or the path we walk. That love is present and communicates with us in our daily lives. When we reflect on what we have been and are given, we discover how God communicates with us. This is individual, personal, and intimate. No one else can teach us that language. It is the language of lovers.

It is one thing to love, but it is something else to know we are loved, and how we are loved. For some, that is more than enough. Still, there is always that excess, which is love's nature, to give more and still more of itself. Now it invites us to examine how we have journeyed into that love, and to see how we experienced each stage of that love as it manifested itself in our lives. The Ignatian tradition breaks this down into the experience of each Week. Now it seeks to show how that gift of intimacy was allowed to develop through the overall structure of the Exercises.

We look back to discover what happened to us and how God speaks to us now, taking unto ourselves more passionately and intimately the experience of the Exercises. Sometimes it is only years later that we come to understand what happened to us in a particular prayer period. It is only in the process of living and reflecting that we come to some understanding of what has been given.

Basic to the Exercises is the compassionate mercy of God. It runs through every Week, and every Week develops a deeper and more comprehensive awareness of how intimately that compassionate mercy is woven into our very lives on a unique and personal level. That mercy comes to us in the First Week to liberate us when we are trapped in sin. That mercy, in human form, invites us to walk a very human journey with him in the Second Week as we both return to the mystery he calls "Abba." That mercy enters into death to conquer the forces of death in the Third Week, and we are asked to endure with him. Finally, that mercy shares with us the Spirit of the resurrection and union in the Father in the Fourth Week. This mercy manifests itself in the gift of intimacy. Each prayer period carries us deeper and deeper into a spiritual intimacy. Spiritual intimacy does not take us away from the world. It allows us to be in the world as a sacred space where the world can encounter the mercy of God.

Our Personal Worlds

That mercy not only enters our human world, it enters each of our unique and personal worlds. We each live in a world that is shaped by our personal experiences. No two persons' experiences are alike. This is not to say that each of us is trapped in our own little world, though sometimes it may feel that way. We can communicate with one another, in spite of the many differences of culture, gender, race, age, and temperament, because we share at a most basic level the same human spirit. But the world that each of us is intimate with is a unique world of feeling and value. That world, personal and real for us, is a construct of our imagination. We live in imagined worlds, and the imagined is real. We may share a communal imagination, but each of us has a private imagination that is a unique composite of the diverse elements of the communal world. The way that composite is structured and maintained is individual. From this unique perspective we read ourselves, others, what passes for the world, and God.

To say that we live in these imagined worlds is not to say that we live in imaginary worlds. It is just that the imagined is the real. What we imagine is maintained by the stories we live out of. The imagined is a constructed world of texts. These are narratives that range from the genetic codes that name us, through individual and family stories, to the cultural histories that situate us in the bigger world. Our understandings of ourselves are encoded by these texts. When we engage in an Ignatian retreat, the conversions we experience move us from one way of reading ourselves, others, God, and the world, to another way. This occurs through yet another text that we call the Spiritual Exercises. The Exercises enable us to examine the stories we tell ourselves and others in order to hold onto our imagined worlds, but they also help us see the lies and deceptions these stories embody. This does not leave us without any stories. We need stories to live. We are never without stories, or ever outside of a story.The Exercises offer us a way of restoring our lives in such a way that the new story we find frees us and our imaginations. That new story is one told by the Father through the Word made flesh. It is a story still being written. We are not just puppets in this drama. Good authors tell us that when they are writing, the characters come alive and take on a life of their own. They also shape the text. It is the same with us and God. Our lives are co-creations. They are constructed out of the found materials of our experience.

These constructed worlds we live in are real to us. They affect how our energies are manifested or repressed, are known or unknown. We accept as normal, first, the ways our families have formed us and, next, the ways of life our societies and cultures offer us. The way we understand our very being has been informed by these stories, and while these texts allow some expression of who we are, they repress or ignore, subvert or displace those other expressions that could contribute to how we see ourselves. When this happens, the "I" that I feel myself to be, the "I" that I act out of, is not really my identity. Who I think and feel and say I am is not who I really am. In fact, we do not know ourselves. Other people know us. God knows us. It is these who inform us about ourselves. The Exercises offer us a way of seeing, knowing, and loving ourselves the way God sees, knows, and loves us, a way of understanding ourselves that we rarely experience. Instead, our self-understanding comes from others.

So how we read ourselves, the world, and others, including God, is a constructed text that, being distorted, distorts our reading. We might consider that text to be real, but "realism" is not "reality." Furthermore, this "realism" contains theologies. We create a God and believe it to be truly God. Often these theologies are not written from a rootedness in God. Rather, they emerge from an unredeemed world. Then how we see God and ourselves is quite different from the way God sees God's own self and us. God sees us as lovable and capable of even the most self-sacrificing love. This is the story given to us in the sacred texts of human history. The sacred text Ignatius uses is the Bible.

In the dynamics of the Spiritual Exercises, these two stories meet. In the plot of the Exercises, the story changes as we journey through the Weeks. The lies that we have accepted as real and that have shaped our lives are uncovered, and their abusive power is broken. Now we can enter a new story in which we journey with Christ through his birth, life, death, resurrection, and return to the Father. In that journey we discover that our story is a contemporary manifestation of the gospel. Our personal story becomes symbolic of the larger story of salvation. To appreciate fully that almost unbelievable gift of salvation, we must see what has happened to us in our spiritual journey. We will do this by looking at the experience, the dynamics, and the way the graces we prayed for came to us during the Four Weeks of the Exercises.

The First Week: Discovering God

Understanding Ourselves

Ignatius asks us in the First Exercise of the First Week to meditate on a particular telling of creation history. We may not approve of the way the myth depicts creation history, but it does contain valuable insights into our self-understanding. The myth Ignatius uses moves from the first sin – that of the angels – to that of Adam and Eve "and the enormous corruption it brought to the human race" and, finally, to the effects of one radically significant sin in the life of someone just like us. The first insight this myth contains is that the stories that shape our particular being participate in that history of corruption, however it may be understood. The stories of our selves extend through time and space and spirit. Whether we like it or not, we are part of that larger story.

It is the nature of the ego to deny or ignore that larger history, of which we are just a tiny part, and to seek to establish itself as the centre of the cosmos. In the first exercise, the presentation of that history, in mythic form, casts our usual view of ourselves into a more realistic mode. Even before we were born, the creation we will enter has been corrupted, and to such an extent that often and unwittingly we participate in that corruption. In the presentation of the Exercises, the question arises whether it is "useful" to give this meditation in its literal state. Some claim that the language of the "sin of the angels" and that of "Adam and Eve" is not relevant to contemporary culture. However pertinent that may be, a deeper resistance must be overcome in seeing that our very selves, and our very self-understanding, is caught up in the denial of that larger context. The quest for relevance often subverts the more difficult question of transcendence.

Exploring Our Blindness

Only when we see how we are trapped by forces larger than ourselves and beyond our control can we begin to realize why we have not been destroyed by those malignant agencies in creation. We have been protected by a love even larger than cosmic and human evil. The larger context of disorder is contained within the absolute context of the "Infinite Goodness" of God. When we ignore either of these contexts, or both, we operate out of a false notion of ourselves. This false perspective distorts everything we see and do. Even our understanding of God then becomes falsified, and our theology becomes a form of self-justifying ideology. We misread everything not only from our own personal bias but also from the deeper social and cultic narratives that give us the communal systems of understanding ourselves. The first exercise exposes our blindness. First, it presents the reality of our lives in a mythic form; and second, it presents in prayer our lived reality held in the love of God. That love allows us to see our lives as they are. It is the first stage in the path of intimacy.

The knowledge we gain from the first exercise helps us see our own sins. This happens in the second exercise. There we look at the ways in which we have personally been seduced and trapped by evil, and have even participated in doing evil. We cannot simply blame heredity, or the social context, for our sinning. We ourselves are also culpable.

Against this growing self-awareness comes the deeper awareness that we are held by God. Ignatius facilitates the journey from the first to the second through questioning (#53) and comparison. "What am I compared with all of humanity? ... What are they when compared with all the angels and saints in paradise? ... What is all of creation when compared to God?" (#58). The movement in those questions is from the self to God. In this intense, prayerful questioning, our image of ourselves as the centre of our universe breaks down. This does not happen in a vacuum. It occurs within the mercy of a God who desires that we know ourselves truly as being loved even though we are sinners. Ignatius asks those making the Exercises to have a conversation then with Christ on the cross, before whom they place themselves (#53).

For Ignatius, Christ on the cross represents a God who is willing to endure even a painful and humiliating death so that nothing and no one will be lost. It is a manifestation of love that goes beyond the limits of the human imagination. In our prayer we dispose ourselves to being loved in an intimacy that reveals our sin without destroying us. What is destroyed are the illusions that constitute a false self. In this encounter with such a love, the bonds that limit the human imagination are broken. Energies of the self are liberated, integrated, or renewed. But this is not easy for those on this path. They endure the struggle of the false self to hold onto fixed and cherished ways of seeing and behaving that are second nature. Fear traps them. But intimacy overcomes fear. When this happens, they experience a liberation of energy and a sense of wonder. They are amazed as they discover that such a love exists and that such a love cares for each one of us so intimately and personally.

The energies that make up our spirit are not just an amorphous collection of power. That power has been trained to express and understand itself in ways that have been shaped by society and the significant units of society, such as family, education, and religion. Even our basic desires have been socialized. What we feel we truly desire is not what we really need. One of the gifts of the First Week is to discover what we truly need. We need a God who loves us. That love is shown in our personal lived experience of being saved. That love does not condemn or reject us. That love says to each of us: you are lovable. Our acceptance of being loved makes us able to understand just how deeply we are trapped in sin. We think that if God really knows us, God won't love us. But God tells us, "I really know you and I really love you." Yet it is a life-and-death struggle to accept that intimacy.

When we do accept it, we discover who we truly are. This discovery energizes us in much the same way prisoners or addicts might feel when they are set free from what holds them captive. Here, the liberation from the distortions we have accepted as ourselves is not anarchy but rather the response to being loved as we are. The wonder and surging emotion we experience in the First Week comes because our lives have changed. That change makes us understand our lives differently.

Rather than dwelling in the obsessive enclosures of narcissism, we discover that we are invited to live out of the open myth that incarnates God's mercy. We do not have to be trapped by a single and reductive understanding of ourselves. The liberation allows us to hold simultaneously the many different and diverse stories that make up each of our lives. We can admit that we are blind, and that we sin in our blindness, but we also discover that we are cared for even as we sin and live in sinful situations. The tunnel vision that has dominated our lives and our understanding of them opens up into a fuller context of accepting God's mercy. As a result, we open to wonder and to the surging emotion of other possibilities for our lives. We discover in our new stories ourselves as loved and as sinners.

Love Offered and Accepted

The dynamics of the First Week deconstruct the story of self and the illusions of that false self. Those illusions consist of the way we see ourselves, others, the world, creation, and God. The deconstructions work by bringing to light what has previously been ignored or taken for granted in the false story. They bring to light the larger story of God's love. It shows us a love that has always been present in creation's time and in our own personal histories.

The larger story of a fallen creation is shown to affect the narrow world of immediate needs out of which we often live. In the Ignatian Exercises, that larger story moves from the fall of angels, through Adam and Eve – one radically destructive act – to our own sins, and then to hell. Additional exercises may include "death and other punishments of sin, on judgement" (#71). We are enclosed in a reality that goes beyond the immediate borders of our everyday concerns. We find ourselves in a "controlled" setting in which God's creativity is not apparent. The effect is a sense of entrapment beyond our power to escape. The "escape" provided comes neither from the world, nor from creation, nor from the sense of self we seek to maintain. It comes from Christ on the cross – a figure of the wholly absurd to the worldly self. That manifestation of God's love makes no sense to any form of selfishness. To be prayerfully present to that self-sacrificing love draws out all the poisons that prevent us from recognizing our truest selves. What emerges from this encounter is a history of sin and of our involvement in sin.

This does not foster a complacency with the self and its constructed self-serving stories. The ego's self-assurance is undermined. Moreover, the graces of shame and confusion (#48), sorrow (#55), and abhorrence (#63) that we pray for in the First Week also work to erode the pride of the false self. I feel "shame" when "I" admit "I" am accountable for my sinful actions, and I experience confusion when the "order" of the ego is experienced as disorder. Sorrow emerges from an awareness that we have created chaos when we thought we were doing only good. We experience ourselves embroiled in a lack of order from which we are helpless to extract ourselves despite our best efforts.

Then we abhor the evil we have done and we abhor the nature of our world. This debases our humanity by encouraging and promoting those forms of disorder that trap us, sometimes using even our most noble desires.

But with the deflation of the ego in the First Week, we discover that we are not destroyed. Instead, we discover a God working to find us through creation and to sustain our humanity even as we sin. We discover a God there for us in our helplessness and deceptions. The focus of the First Week is not to humiliate or destroy us. The grace we are given is that we are loved with a love that seeks and knows us as we really are. That love does not turn aside from loving us even when we turn aside from who we really are. The awareness of being so loved opens us up and directs us to desire lives of greater integrity. The intimacy we experience in the First Week liberates our desire. It moves us to the path of the Second Week. There we desire to restore the world: the human contexts we live out of; our histories; our relationship with God; our story of who God is. But we know that even though we are loved, the dynamics of disorder still run through our lives. How are we to live and share the intimacy given us in the First Week in ways that are creative and genuine?

The love we have been offered and have accepted in the First Week of St. Ignatius's Spiritual Exercises is just the beginning of the journey to unpack the gift of intimacy. To live it, share it, and celebrate it in our daily lives carries us to the rest of the Exercises. By the end of the First Week, we have been given an entry into reality. We now need to learn how to live that reality without falling back into selfishness. We need to learn to love ourselves properly: to express our deepest desire, to incarnate what we truly value, and to manifest our true relationship with God.

The Second Week: Discovering Ourselves

Looking at the World God's Way

In the First Week, God enters our story. In the Second Week, we enter into God's story and into God's way of telling stories, which is always through humans. God tells his story through our stories. This interweaving of our story and God's is done through contemplation on gospel texts. When we contemplate, we bring our life energies into dialogue with the life energies of God, as expressed in the incidents of scripture. In this weaving together of our energies and the divine energies, we become gospel: living texts of God in our world. Then there occurs an incarnation that is personal and unique to each one of us.

In the First Week, we operated out of a limited context of fallen creation. But, in the Second Week, the story broadens. The movement is from the world perceived in worldly terms to that same world perceived from the perspective of God. The liberation achieved at the end of the First Week allows us to see human affairs from God's point of view. The work of the Second Week shifts us from the narcissistic projections of the ego to the humble service of one called to be an intimate companion of Christ.

In the Second Week, we are invited to look at the world with the eyes and heart of God. We enter our first contemplation from the perspective of the Trinity, above time looking into time. With this contemplation on the Incarnation, our imaginations enter the space and the concerns of the three Persons of God. If the secular postmodernism of the world today, with its emphasis on image and sign, holds that we become what we perceive, the Exercises offer us a spiritual postmodernism that carries us to become what we imagine, energized by God's love.

The Second Week dares us to imagine. It dares us to imagine that we can make the world a more human place. Our imaginations can do this because First Week graces erase the repressive structures and dynamics of an imagination distorted by sin. It allows for something new to emerge – a personal dialogue with God that transforms the world. Here we can co-operate in the ongoing formation of a new creation. It is hard to imagine, given the violence of the present world, how this is possible.

Following God More Closely

Yet, despite the present climate of atrocity, the unimaginable is at work. God cares. God cares enough to find a way to save us. Even harder to imagine is that we can become God-like in our caring and in our doing. That is the grace of the Second Week: "To follow and imitate more closely our Lord who has just become man for me" (#109).

The Ignation text defines for us – in story form – how God operates in the world. This is a God of humility, born "in extreme poverty, and … after many labours, after hunger, thirst, heat and cold, after insults and outrages, [that] He might die on the cross, and all this for me" (#116). When we enter God's story through Ignatian contemplation, we imitate God's way of being in the world. We start to become the continuing presence of Christ in the world. We give up the self-aggrandizement of our ego for a path of humble service, desiring only what God desires.

We do this because we desire to be one with the love that has liberated us, a love that manifests itself in the emptying out described in Philippians 2:1-11. Thus, in the Nativity contemplation, which follows the Exercise on the Incarnation, the Ignatian text suggests to the one making the Exercises, "I will make myself a poor, little, unworthy slave ... and serve ... with all possible homage and reverence" (#114) Joseph and Mary in their time of need." Here the abstraction of the first line of the Principle and Foundation – "Humans are created to praise, reverence, and serve God" (#23) – is picked up and made human. We serve God in whatever way is helpful.

Those who engage in the Ignatian Exercises find themselves in an intimacy with Christ. It overflows in a service of contemplative love where they are united with the beloved. They embody in their particular ways the creativity of a God labouring in the world. This human labouring is modelled by the scriptural life of Christ.

Choosing a Standard

In the Exercises, the scriptural contemplations on the infancy narratives and the private life of Jesus act as prefaces to the contemplations on the public life of Christ. The significant meditation on "Two Standards" links the two, showing how Satan and Christ operate in the world. But the focus of the Exercise is to discover how the dynamics of Satan and of Christ operate in the very lives of those engaged in the Exercises. Here it is not a matter of choosing between the two, but of refining the ways we examine our lives so we may better understand how we can be trapped, and how we may better follow Jesus. The exercise helps us to identify with Christ and with his way of living in our world today, and to become aware of the wiles and strategies of that enemy who seeks to stop us from living like Christ in our world. It raises the question of how we discern when we seek to live out, in our daily lives, our deepest desire: union with the divine. In this meditation, we learn how we are tempted and how we are called by God.

When we enter areas of personal vulnerability, we find ourselves swayed by conflicting feelings. Ignatius describes these as the Standard of Satan and the Standard of Christ. The Standard of Satan is to covet riches – by using our supposed strengths to overcome that vulnerable situation – so we may more easily attain the empty honours of this world, [and so] come to overweening pride (#142). This approach reinforces our narcissism. Then we use our gifts not for some greater good, but to enhance our self-esteem in the eyes of the world. The Standard of Christ, on the other hand, invites us to accept our poverty in the face of that vulnerability, knowing that such a position means rejecting – and being rejected by – the corrupt values of this world. From this approach springs humility (#146).

Here the Ignatian Exercises present us with a certain reading of the Christ story and a certain way of inserting ourselves into that story. Christ's story is one of evangelical service to the Father through humility. The mission of Christ is to offer to the world the compassionate mercy of the one he calls "Father." He does the Father's will in all things. This is the basis of the Ignatian dictum of "finding God in all things." When we do the Exercises, we are disposed to find God in all things, as Christ did.

The process of intimacy and identification with Christ continues with a contemplation of specific incidents in Christ's life. Indeed, the rest of the Second Week outlines this call to service. The previous contemplations, from Jesus' Nativity to his setting out to the Jordan, show a Christ who manifests a radical dependence on God and on God's existential mercy. In that growing relationship with the Father, he waits on God to reveal most clearly what he must do. Jesus waits – from his boyhood experience in the Temple to his baptism at age 30 – for the Father to show him what to do next. In this hidden life, Christ is not inactive. He learns to be patient and to be attentive. He learns to wait. He disposes himself to the Father's time and to the Father's will. That gift is given to him at his baptism in the river Jordan. That radical and focused attentiveness is named in the baptism by the Father as "my beloved Son." As we enter these contemplations, we also wait to be named, in our attentiveness, the Beloved of God.

Waiting on the Father defines Jesus' presence in the world. He waits in the Temptations in the Desert. He waits until the Father and Peter connect for a human to name him "the Son of the living God"

(Matthew 16:16). Then he can change his mission. Now he can talk about his coming passion and death, for now it is possible for humanity to realize who is doing what in this new Passover. When his friend is sick, and then dying, Jesus waits for the Father to send him to Lazarus. We know that Jesus can heal and bring people back from the dead. We know that Lazarus is his friend, and that he is not far from his friend's home. Yet he does nothing, even though this gives him grief and anguish. He waits for the Father (John 11). He waits on the Father in his agony in the garden. He waits on the Father on the cross. There we see the fruit of his waiting. There the Father brings him to resurrection.

As we journey with Jesus back to the Father, we enter into an intimacy with him where he reveals to us who he truly is for us personally. This is what lovers do for each other. What he reveals is his union with the Father. This identity was revealed to Peter, and allows Peter to see, momentarily, who Jesus really is. He shares with us that identity as beloved of the Father. In that sharing, we, too, learn to wait on the Father.

The sequence of contemplations on Christ's earthly ministry given in the Exercises promotes the growing intimacy with the Father through union with Christ. This culminates in the last contemplation of this Week. It is Christ's entry into Jerusalem as king, which Christians celebrate on Palm (Passion) Sunday. From this sequence we learn what it means to be God in the world – not triumphalism or the despotism of an ego demanding worship, but focused, humble service in bringing the compassionate mercy of God to the concrete situations of daily life.

The kingdom meditation that introduces the Second Week of the Exercises is reappropriated in Palm Sunday, where Christ the King enters Jerusalem: not as conqueror, but as one whose life is so focused on his love for God, he is willing to face the seeming failure of his earthly mission and a painful death on the cross. At this stage of their spiritual journey, those doing the Exercises are likewise disposed to a similar passionate love for God. Ignatius's choice of scripture texts promoting this identification are simply those of evangelical service. They are not texts of healings, exorcisms, or power, though one may experience any of these in a contemplation. They are texts that witness in a specific, incarnate way to the mercy of God present in the world.

We should also note the peculiar absence of Mark's gospel in the pre-passion contemplations of the Exercises. Ignatius's Christ is not the existential mystery of Mark. Rather, he manifests the identity of a humble servant intimate with, and waiting on, the Father. Those of us doing these Exercises are invited to walk a similar path. We are not mysteries. We are to be known as ones who become intimate with the Father by what we do in the world.

The Three Classes

This witness is reinforced by a self-awareness that emerges from the Two Standards, and is intensified by a reflection on the Three Classes of People and the Three Degrees of Humility. The latter two Exercises, which immediately follow the Exercise on the Two Standards, develop the stance of going against selfish desires. They promote a desire for poverty because Christ was poor and, from that identification with Christ, for a similar humble evangelical service in the world.

Ignatius sees those in the Second Week of the Exercises as being in the company of the creator and redeemed aspects of creation. For example, in the Three Classes of Persons, the setting of the meditation is "to imagine me in the presence of God and all his saints" (#151). This is not a privileged moment. We live in that state every second of our lives, even though most of the time we are not aware of it. There we are invited to labour to redeem a fallen world. How can we respond to this invitation? This meditation shows the three possibilities open to us. We can live heedless of God or of ourselves. We can live in the hope that God will approve of all that we choose to do. Or, we can live simply for God.

Ignatius places this Exercise before any contemplations of Christ's public life. Christ serves the Father. Ignatius expects us to make similar choices in the way we live. The pattern of Christ's life is one of waiting on the Father. He waits eighteen years after telling his parents that he must be about his Father's business. He waits after his baptism in the Jordan. He waits in the temptations in the desert to do his Father's will in how he uses his gifts, fulfills his mission, manifests his identity. He waits for that moment when the Father enlightens Peter, who then sees Jesus as the Father sees Jesus. For them both he is the Messiah. Jesus waits on the Father to tell him when to go to Lazarus, whom he knows is sick, then dying, then dead, then buried. He could have healed him at any time and from any distance. But he goes only when it is for the glory of the Father. He waits on the Father in his agony in the garden. He waits on the Father on the cross. He dies waiting on the Father. He waits on the Father to resurrect him. As we grow in intimacy with Christ, we also wait on the Father. It is the Ignatian stance in the world.

In Christ's public life, a significant shift occurs in his evangelical service when Peter acknowledges him to be the Son of God. After that, the prophesies of the passion emerge. Jesus says that Peter's awareness comes from the Father. Peter's resonance with the Father allows him to identify Christ as the Father's saviour, the Messiah. Our work in the Second Week is to come to such an intimate knowledge of Christ that we, too, are able to profess that the one we have met in our contemplations is that same Messiah. When we do this, we can then move with Jesus, as his intimates, towards the second half of his ministry: the passion. We can do this because we have started seeing as the Father sees.

Our own growing resonance with the Father makes us contemporary words of God. Our growing closeness to Christ allows our own entry into his passion. We follow him wherever he is. In placing ourselves this way, we declare ourselves for God even in the face of death. What seems like human folly is really the expression of intimacy. Jesus has revealed to us his love for the Father. He has revealed to us the Father's love for him and for us. Our trust in that love, which roots us and gives us our identity, shows itself in our willingness to walk the path of the passion with Jesus. This is the grace of the meditations on both the Three Classes of Persons and the Three Degrees of Humility. We discover that we are willing to become "fools for the sake of Christ" (Sp. Ex. #167) as he is willing to become a fool for the sake of the Father.

If a person enters into the Spiritual Exercises with the desire to make a concrete decision about something, that decision is made during this Second Week. The grace of the Second Week is a bonded intimacy with Christ that leads us to desire to be with him, whatever he does, and to share with him whatever the Father decrees. Any correct decision resonates with Christ's own stance of waiting on the Father. Both witness to a dependence on the Father in works of evangelical service. His, and our, active entry into that servant poverty, which scripture depicts as the passion of Christ, happens for us in the Third Week.

The Third Week: A Passionate Love

The Ignatian Magis

In the Third Week we contemplate the torture and death of the physical body of Christ as written in the gospels. Those texts, presented from the perspective of the resurrection, depict his passion and death by the powers of the world as his total abandonment of his self-identity to the mystery of his Father, for whom he is the Beloved. Inasmuch as we have identified with Christ in the Second Week, in our contemplations on his sufferings we now share, on a spiritual and imaginative level, his fate.

The imagined world we constructed with the Christ during the Second Week, whatever decisions we have made, and the sense of intimacy we sought and found with him, are all offered up to the all-consuming mystery of the Father in the Third Week. Then, we become vulnerable. Our world, our decision, and our relationship to Jesus and to the Father are attacked by the powers of evil, to which we are still prey. Evil moves to render meaningless the things and relationships we hold dear. We experience this abandonment in our prayer. Our prayer moves through the levels of grief and anguish to a sense of numbness and then to a felt sense of nothingness. Here we experience no more than Christ did, and no more than his disciples did when he died. We sink beyond the narrative structures that inform our life. We sink even beyond the feelings that spontaneously tell us what we value.

The meaning of Christ's life for his disciples had been destroyed by his death. The two disciples on the road to Emmaus admit, "We had hoped he was the one to redeem Israel" (Luke 24:21). Christ's death destroys the world that his intimates had constructed around him. But what remains is not nothing. In that emptied space it finally becomes possible to see the divine play of the Father. It is only through death that resurrection can happen. It is only through the destruction of the worldly, explicate order of things that the divine, implicate order is revealed. Matthew's gospel depicts this as the rending of the temple veil (27:51).

Inasmuch as we can enter into the action of the Third Week, our world – the imaginative system we live out of – is exposed to the same dynamics that Christ and his companions encountered. This is different from the destruction that is a necessary part of the liberating process of the First Week. There the systems of illusion and deception are unmasked and devalued. In the Third Week, the Word made Flesh, the highest possible good on the human level, is undone. In the Ignatian magis, the human best is displaced by the divine better. Thus scripture quotes Jesus in his agony saying to his Author, "Not my will but yours be done."

Our commitment to the Ignatian magis permits the transformation of human effort into modes of resurrection. Then, like Christ in his passion, we "surrender" self-love and personal will and interests to that of the Divine Creativity. Out of that death comes resurrection. But, because we are human, our egos never disappear. However, death radically questions the ego's meaning and its activities. Hence the question Ignatius offers for reflection to the person contemplating Christ's passion in the presence of the creative mystery of God's love: "What ought I to do?" (#197).

What are we to do? How are we to describe the response of the those in the Third Week? Think of what happens to you when you accompany a loved one who is dying. After a while there are no words, no story, even no feeling. Emotion does not necessarily have to express itself in feeling. Instead, we experience numbness, blankness, a growing sense of meaninglessness of what might be considered socially appropriate at that time. All forms of human comfort and connection are erased. We simply wait in mystery. What remains is a radical simplicity oriented to the one Jesus calls "Abba."

This simplicity is also manifest in the Ignatian texts of that Third Week. It is the only Week in which there are no meditations or contemplations constructed by Ignatius. For those praying through that Week, there is the simple division of the passion into sections, if those divisions are helpful, and some limited instruction. The self-understanding created by the constructs and dynamics of the self, as depicted in the Exercises and mediated by personal history, is reduced to its basic orientation: towards God. If the person made and offered up a decision for discernment, here it is tested. Can it be maintained without the support of that person's giftedness, or society's approval, or the impetus of narcissistic behaviour? Is it still viable without "riches," "honour," or "pride"? If the decision is a manifestation of these latter three, its impetus is destroyed in the entry into Christ's passion. The person holding that decision is unable to be with Christ in his passion.

In the Third Week, we come into some experience of the mystery that we are to ourselves. That mystery connects intimately with the mystery we call "Father." The correctness of any decision made is based on whether it facilitates or hinders the intimacy between these two mysteries.

The texts of scripture and the text of Ignatius mediate between these two mysteries. The scriptural texts contain a minimal narrative of what is happening inside Jesus and very little information of what is happening outside of him and around him. Similarly, the Ignatian text lacks much instruction or reflection. Both texts tend towards "emptiness." Both are characterized by huge gaps. For example, in Matthew's gospel (ch. 27, between verses 35 and 36) the act of crucifixion is not described. Moreover, in that paragraph (verses 32-44), five of its nine sentences begin with the metonymic conjunction "and." Metonomy indicates the fragmentation of perspective where moments are not joined by the unifying context of metaphor. People in trauma are not coherent. They babble. They do not priorize or evaluate in an integrated manner what they have experienced. Every fragment of their experience – from the most essential to the most unrelated – is given equal value. The scripture passage, even written years later, reveals the rhetoric of trauma. What has happened goes beyond the limits of the human imagination. We are left with a set of fragments of differing spiritual value linked together by "and." What holds each of the texts of the Scriptures, of the Exercises, and of the retreatant together is beyond earthly powers. This is not faith as intellectual accent. This is faith as relationship. It is the entry into a passionately lived intimacy with God that goes beyond the sensible. It establishes a rootedness in the Father that is the mission of Christ. Yet, it feels like "nothing" (Isaiah 49:4).

Shame and Confusion

A similar erasure of human meaning occurs through the graces to be prayed for at this time. Those involved in the Third Week are instructed to beg for "shame and confusion," which we experience when the self dissolves into mystery. This is not the shame and confusion that come in the First Week with a true awareness of ourselves as sinners. This is the shame and confusion that come when we move to a felt sense of loss of the self and the meaning we found in the Second Week. A sense of identity that fills us with life and purpose has been taken away. What was taken away from Jesus in his human suffering is also taken away from us as we remain with him.

How, then, are we to understand this shame and confusion that is the grace of that Third Week? It emerges from the sense of horror and the abjection of self we experience in the presence of the sublime. It is the sense of defilement (as when Moses takes off his shoes in the presence of the burning bush, because the place is holy) that we experience when we "intrude" on a sacred space and moment. The shame and confusion occur because we are breaking taboo. When Christ broke taboos, the social texts of belonging – by not washing, by desecrating the Sabbath, by consorting with the impure, by calling himself the Son of God, by cleansing the Temple – he did so in response to the higher value of his calling as the Beloved of the Father. But while this higher value radically relativizes the norms of the social and religious order, and displaces their claim to legislate the Absolute, the "lower" powers assert their authority in destroying him physically.

Similarly, when we break taboos within our own socialized ways of acceptable behaviour, both patriarchal and matriarchal, we, too, are destroyed. When we have interiorized these ways of being, we experience that destruction as emptiness. This is the experience of the "nothingness" we encounter in the Third Week. But when we break these taboos within lived awareness of God's mercy, we also open ourselves to being resurrected.

From Death to Life

The Third Week, then, is the passage through the death of self. In that passage, the worldly understanding of death is inverted. The implicate order of the divine plan becomes explicate. Death is revealed not as the end of life, but as a transition to that mystery beyond sin's power, absorbing and transforming the meaning of death. The meaning of sacrifice we encounter here is both "to kill by offering up" and "to make holy" at the same time. What, in the secular context, is confusion, in the faith context is mystery. Sacrifice changes the fragmentation by death of the closed and broken myths of life to the open myth of resurrection.

In sacrifice, what constructs and maintains the social world, the symbolic order of laws, institutions, customs, traditions, is rent. In Matthew's gospel, this is shown at Christ's death when the temple veil is split, and the dead rise and roam about the streets. The division between the two worlds – the secular and the sacred, the worldly and the otherwordly – is overcome. Worldly values are overturned or inverted. Thus, to the Jewish sensibility of Jesus' time, crucifixion was an abomination. It was the manifestation of a radical impurity incompatible with temple order and ritual. Their symbolic order could not countenance the order of "Abba" where a shameful death introduces the unimaginable Other into the world. But that is what happened. As Peter points out to the rulers of that symbolic order after the resurrection, "This is the stone which was rejected by you builders but which has become the cornerstone" (Acts 4:11). For the believer, the crucifixion is not an abomination but the highest manifestation of self-sacrificing love.

In God's merciful love for all of humanity, what has been laid waste by the powers of the world still continues transformed in that world, but beyond the imagination of that world. The wasted becomes the resurrected body, the food of life, the Body of Christ for the Christian community. The same mystery that feeds those enduring the annihilations present in the Third Week is the very same mystery to whom Christ turns in his first temptation in the desert. It is not food, but rather the relationship with God, which gives life. It is significant that Ignatius puts within the Third Week exercises the "Rules with Regard to Eating." There he emphasizes the control of the appetite and the disordered appetite by focusing on more spiritual things (#214, 215). Those spiritual things give value to the appetite. The physical finds its full meaning only in the spiritual.

In the Third Week, and at those times when social norms and constructs lose their authority, it is very easy to fall into the more primitive mode of basic gratifications. Ignatius prevents this return to those First Week temptations and to the sensual body as the basis of satisfactions by asking us to share, or at least bear witness to, what "Christ Our Lord suffers in his human nature" (#195). The Third Week asks, "What ought I to do and suffer for Him?" (#197). Within the mysterious freedom of God's mercy, for whom anything is possible, the Third Week indicates a process of salvation in which love is not a cure, or a return to some stable and established mode of existence, but rather a radical irruption of the divine into human suffering, carrying it to resurrection.

In that human passion we enter a love that risks death. The Son enters death in a passionate love for the mystery he calls Father. The Father, in his passionate love for his Son, the "Beloved," reaches into death and brings the Christ to resurrection. Resurrection belongs to a significantly different order of existence than rebirth, the cycle of nature, or a return from the dead, as happened to Lazarus and to Jairus's daughter. Resurrection creates an openness to the miraculous, to what is possible but beyond the powers of creation. It comes as pure gift from God. It is offered to us as a manifestation of the intimacy that those who follow Christ have with the Father.

The Fourth Week: Celebrating Life

A New Way of Being

We cannot journey to resurrection. It comes to us. We can choose the way we live, and thus create the way we approach death, but death defines the limits of human endeavour. Only the power of God transforms the meaning of death for us, and only the power of God controls what happens after death. So resurrection remains a mystery. All we can do is reflect prayerfully on the stories of resurrection given to us. In doing so, we open ourselves to the power those stories point to and describe. That power breaks into our world to transform the way we imagine ourselves, others, and God.

This new way of being is one of openness. In that space we submit to being re-created by the Father. It is he, not history, who defines us. This is apparent in the First Contemplation (#218) in the Fourth Week of Ignatius's Exercises, when Our Lord appears to Our Lady. This encounter is not mentioned in scripture, but as Ignatius says, "It must be considered as stated when Scripture says that He appeared to many others" (#299). When we are gifted with the graces of the Fourth Week, we become an open text, sacred scripture, written by the Father. Our brokenness does not disappear; it is given new meanings. We are still broken people in ways the world sees and understands, but that brokenness becomes the script with which God writes a new story. As St. Paul says in his understanding of this gift, "I will boast all the more gladly of my weakness, so that the power of Christ may dwell in me. Therefore I am content with weakness, insults, hardships, persecutions and calamities for the sake of Christ; for whenever I am weak, then I am strong" (2 Corinthians 12:9-10).

Sin, the powers of the world, and our personal bias all tend to limit the meaning of things. Sin tells us that we are unlovable and incapable of loving. The world defines who we are in terms of nationality, ethnicity, and gender. We choose how we will present ourselves to others, and control who we think we are. Resurrection breaks down the power of these limitations. We discover that we are loved radically and unconditionally. We discover the gift of intimacy. We discover that we can love others in a self-sacrificing way for their good. We discover that we can be human in ways that are not conscripted by borders. We start seeing ourselves as mystery, participating in the Mystery we so inadequately call "God." We are possessed by a sense of wonder and creativity as we behold our world. We discover that we can celebrate what is life-giving on our paths. The intimacy that has loved us into being and calls us to new life makes of us a new creation in the world. This intimacy further invites us to work with all the powers of good to transform our world into a community where all are loved into the fullness of life.

Then we start to see in our own lives the dynamics of salvation history. We come from God; the path we walk is of God; and we return to God. The pattern, described in scripture as being found, getting lost, and being found again, echoes not only our individual journeys, but the journey of the human race and all of creation. What has happened in our lives is first the intimate entry of the Incarnation in our own personal, self-enclosed worlds of closed and broken myths. When we are opened out because of that love, we are invited to a deeper intimacy of journeying with the one who loves us. In that journey, Jesus brings us to the Father, and there we become companions of the Christ. We share intimately Christ's passion, where he disposes himself totally to the very human desire in him that seeks to be reunited to the Father. That journey home to the source of his life continues in the resurrection and ascension. The union of the resurrected humanity with the divinity of the Father results in an explosion of love we experience as Pentecost. In this gift of the Spirit, we become intimately connected to the life of the Trinity and to the work they do in creation to transform all that is, was, and ever will be into a community of love. We are intimates of God in the midst of this unfinished business. We share the life and the work of the Trinity in whatever we do. We see ourselves as committed to a loving relationship with all of creation. We see our lives as symbols of that commitment.

This awareness of mutuality is present even in the texts of the Exercises themselves. Thus, the riches and honour that Satan uses to tempt humans (#142) in the Second Week are now gifts shared between lover and beloved (#231) in the Fourth Week. Similarly, creation is not seen as going to hell (#106), but, from this new perspective, is an instrument of the sanctifying process (#236) of a God who works and labours in all things for our salvation. This is a God who gave us the Christ. When we bond with that Christ in the Exercises, we journey with him back to the Father and receive the gift of their mutual Spirit. We become signs of the continuing presence of the resurrected Christ on earth. Here we witness for others to Jesus' resurrection, which creates the open access all now have to the Father. As resurrection symbols, we live beyond ourselves into the self that we will become. Hence, in the Fourth Week, we were invited to "ask for the grace to be glad and rejoice intensely because of the great joy and glory of Christ our Lord" (#221). That joy and glory are not our own. They occur because of what has happened to Christ and has been manifested through his body. That resurrected body shows what is possible for every body. It manifests the gift of the Father offered to each of us.

For those living in the graces of the Fourth Week, that commitment is manifest in what we do. Ignatius points out that "love ought to manifest itself in deeds rather than words" (#230). Christ's resurrected body does different things than he did before his death. The risen Christ does no healing; he does not fight worldly or religious authority; but the disciples do so after they receive his risen Spirit. As he promises them, with the Spirit, they do more than he did. Still, his appearing transforms the way those close to him see and act. Resurrection becomes a site of new meaning. Thus, for Mary Magdalene, the "gardener" becomes "Christ" (John 20:15); for the disciples in the upper room before Pentecost, "fear" becomes "gladness" (John 20:19-21); for the disciples who are catching no fish one early morning, a lack becomes abundance (John 21:3, 11). Jesus' scarred body manifests the divine love.

Renewing Creation

As we participate in the gifts of the Fourth Week by accepting the gift Christ shares with us, we become resurrection sites for others. We experience the power of God moving through our brokenness to create Incarnation in our lived world. This emptiness is the necessary condition for the power of resurrection to become manifest through us. Awareness of our emptiness never goes away. It shows us that the grace of the Fourth Week is a pure gift. It is a manifestation of God's mercy, not our intrinsic right. We remain broken, even in our joy, just as the Christ, in his resurrection, still bears the scars of his passion. Through our emptiness, God's mercy enters the world, and draws up and out the pain and misery of fallen creation. In that emptiness, the world's misery meets the Father's mercy. The Buddhist concept of *shunyata* depicts this. In human consciousness there is "emptiness/ the fullness of being" at the same time. In resurrection we experience *shunyata*: simultaneous emptiness and the fullness of Being.

We do not disappear in that emptiness. Our identity is not found in ourselves but in the relationship God has with us. Now we understand "self"-as-emptied to embody mystery. As such, it is not, in its freedom, limited by worldly norms of acting and self-understanding and presentation. It is flexible – it is all things to all people (1 Corinthians 9:22) – and it is indifferent, which allows it to be so passionate for the Father as to allow us to become "fools for Christ" (#167). Here we become signs of contradiction in the world and displace closed myths with mystery.

The destruction of the power of closed myths, especially death, produces the creative and joyful quality of the Fourth Week. Particular ideologies with single and restrictive readings of reality are devalued, and the diversity of what is given through God's abundance is celebrated:

> All things counter, original, spare, strange;
> Whatever is fickle, freckled (who knows how?)
> With swift, slow; sweet, sour; adazzle, dim;
> He fathers-forth whose beauty is past change.
>
> (Gerard Manley Hopkins, "Pied Beauty")

In the same way, we are accessible multiple readings, so that we become, like St. Paul, "all things to all people" (1 Corithians 9:22). This delight in difference is the manifestation of joy, which is a grace of the Fourth Week. As a eucharistic preface for Easter tells us, "the joy of the resurrection renews the whole world."

The entry into joy is not for spiritual self-gratification but for the renewal of creation, where we labour with the Beloved, as together we do the Father's will. Ignatius does not impose what we must do. He leaves it up to each of us to discern what we can do lovingly. He merely points out in the contemplation "Leaning into Love" that after considering what God does for each of us, and shares with each of us, "I will reflect upon myself, and consider ... what I ought to offer the Divine Majesty, that is, all I possess and myself with it" (#234). How we do this depends on our situation and abilities. As we share in the life and the gifts of the divine, we also share in a care for creation. All this arises from our loving response to the mercy of God. As we take up this care, we discover we are interconnected with all levels of creation and connected with the Creator. We live our lives only in the context of this connectedness, and not from some intrinsic nature, since at this level of commitment, the self is "empty," or at best a trace or gesture of the Divine Mercy to the world.

This work we do in the spirit of gratitude and joyful service, and our dialogue with the world become possible from this perspective. As the Spiritual Exercises of St. Ignatius show, when we accept and live out the orientation to love – our basic desire – this creates open spaces, possibilities, and transformations through which the Word becomes flesh in our time and in our bodies.

The path of intimacy that we followed here has brought us from alienation to community. We discovered the spiritual intimacy of a God who enters into the unloved areas of our life and shows us that they can be converted when we accept them to be held by God. This liberation into love carries us to journeying with Jesus as his companions in his mission to bring the Father's compassionate mercy to a broken world. Companionship with Jesus allows us to discover our own rootedness in the Father, similar to Jesus' human relationship to the source of all life. As his companions, we journey with him into a death that strips us of the defining power of the world. Here we discover our radical emptiness as the intimate experience of our identity in the Father. Out of that emptiness come the gifts of resurrection. Here we are invited to discover our humanity as signs of the new creation that journeys back to the Father in a celebration of life. The spirit the resurrected humanity of Christ shares by becoming united with the Father is given to us in our entry into our Pentecost. This gift allows us to be the Acts of the Apostles in our world. We become living words of the Father in the circumstances of our lives. We share what has been given to us and we are shared by what is daily given. There, we discover ourselves as community. The path of intimacy allows us to touch and be touched by all of creation held in the love of the constantly creating Trinity. We journey into that love of which there is no end. We acknowledge all in delight and gratitude as companions on that journey. Blessings always.

Appendix: Adapting the Exercises for Shorter Periods of Time

The path to intimacy is walked one step at a time. While this book presents a way of walking that path over an extended period of time, some readers may wish to use some of the material in a shorter period of time. There are many ways to do so. One way is to review the table of contents and see what appeals at the moment. This is not just chance. The Spirit speaks through our desires. Another way is to follow the suggestions given below. Some are offered as a retreat format, while others are by theme.

1: A Day of Recollection – Becoming Aware that We Are Loved

The Second Week: 18th Exercise
The Fourth Week: 1st Exercise

2: A Weekend Retreat

The First Week: 2nd Exercise
The First Week: 8th Exercise
The First Week: 6th Exercise

3: A Five-day Retreat

The Fourth Week: 6th Exercise
The First Week: 3rd Exercise
The Second Week: 9th Exercise
The Second Week: 5th Exercise
The Fourth Week: 7th Exercise

4: An Eight-day Retreat

The First Week: 7th Exercise
The Second Week: 7th Exercise
The Second Week: 14th Exercise
The Third Week: 2nd Exercise
The Third Week: 9th Exercise
The Fourth Week: 8th Exercise
The Fourth Week: 10th Exercise

5: A Healing Retreat

The First Week: 3rd Exercise
The Second Week: 8th Exercise
The Third Week: 4th Exercise
The Fourth Week: 3rd Exercise

6: Affirming Our True Self

The First Week: 1st Exercise
The Second Week: 1st Exercise
The Second Week: 13th Exercise
The Third Week: 1st Exercise
The Fourth Week: 4th Exercise

7: Making a Discernment

The First Week: 9th Exercise
The Second Week: 3rd Exercise
The Second Week: 12th Exercise
The Third Week: 8th Exercise
The Fourth Week: 6th Exercise

8: The Passion of the World

The First Week: 1st Exercise
The Second Week: 10th Exercise
The Third Week: 5th Exercise
The Third Week: 3rd Exercise
The Third Week: 10th Exercise
The Fourth Week: 2nd Exercise

9: A Light in the Darkness – Living Through Hard Times

The Second Week: 6th Exercise
The Second Week: 15th Exercise
The Third Week: 4th Exercise
The Third Week: 7th Exercise
The Fourth Week: 5th Exercise

10: The Beatitudes – Becoming One with God

The First Week: 3rd Exercise